NO FREE LUNCH

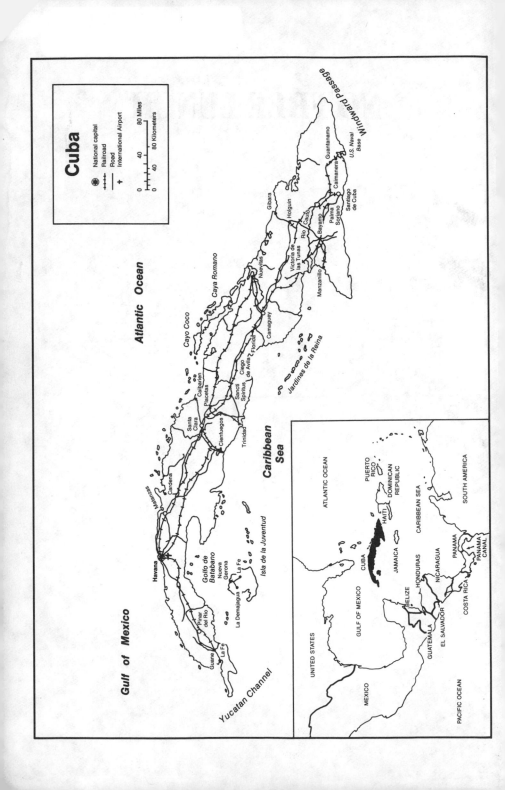

NO FREE LUNCH

Food & Revolution
in Cuba Today

by Medea Benjamin,
Joseph Collins and Michael Scott

A Food First Book
Grove Press, Inc., New York

First published in 1984 by
Institute for Food and Development Policy
San Francisco

First Evergreen Edition 1986
First Printing 1986
ISBN: 0-394-62233-2
Library of Congress Catalog Card Number: 86-216

Library of Congress Cataloging-in-Publication Data
Benjamin, Medea, 1952–
  No free lunch.
  Bibliography: p.
  Includes index.
  1. Food supply—Cuba. I. Collins, Joseph, 1945–   . II. Scott, Michael,
1945–   . III. Title.
HD9014.C92B46   1986   338.1'9'7291   86-216
ISBN 0-394-62233-2

ABOUT FOOD FIRST

Since its founding in 1975, FOOD FIRST, a non-profit research and education
center, has been dedicated to identifying the root causes of hunger in the
United States and around the world. Financed by thousands of members, with
modest support from foundations and churches, FOOD FIRST speaks with a
strong, independent voice, free of ideological formulas and vested interests.

In over 60 countries and in 20 languages, FOOD FIRST provides a wise array of
educational tools—books, articles, slide shows, films, and curricula for grade
schools and high schools—to lay the groundwork for a more democratically
controlled food system that will meet the needs of all.

For more information write to:

FOOD FIRST
The Institute for Food and Development Policy
1885 Mission Street
San Francisco, CA 94103
USA

Book Designed by Cecilia Brunazzi
Photos (unless otherwise specified) by Michael Scott

Printed in the United States of America
A Food First Book / Published by GROVE PRESS, INC.,
196 West Houston Street, New York, N.Y. 10014

TABLE OF CONTENTS

ACKNOWLEDGMENTS

We have acquired more intellectual, moral, and practical debts researching and writing this book than there is space to acknowledge. We are grateful to all who helped us along the path. It was complicated and frustrating, but always challenging.

The biggest debt has come in the final stretch: to Larry Rosenthal and Nick Allen, who took on the task of editing seemingly endless versions and transforming our excesses into more readable prose.

We are grateful to the several outstanding research assistants who worked with us over the past four years: Charles Bauer, Joel Charny, Luis Colero S.J., Michael Goldman, Irma Gonzales, Michael Morrissey, Philip Russell, and Lisa Shepperd. And to John Lear for careful indexing.

We are indebted to a number of Cuban institutions that helped us with our research, particularly the Offices of the Presidency and the Vice Presidency, and ICAP (Cuban Institute for Friendship with the People). Our thanks also go to many friends and acquaintances in the land of Jose Marti: small farmers and cooperative members, workers and managers of restaurants and markets, and foreigners living in Cuba whose thoughts, enthusiasm, experience, disappointments, and hopes helped shape this book. A special thanks to Lionel Martin who generously made years' worth of files and clippings on Cuba available to us.

We have benefited greatly from the inspiration, encouragement, and comments of colleagues around the world: Jim Austin, Solon Barraclough, David Baytleman, Edward Boorstein, Laura Brainin-Rodriguez, Claes Brundenius, Guy Chapond, Jacques Chonchol, Carmen Diana Deere, Arthur Domike, Eugene Donefer, Gustavo Esteva, Peggy Fenn, Cornelia Flora, Jan Flora, Carlos Florido, Nancy Forester, Howard Handleman, Cynthia Hewitt, Laura Kullenberg, William LeoGrande, Arthur MacEwan, Harry Magdoff, Gail McGarrity, Frances Moore Lappé, Ann Seidman, Bob Snow, Paul Sweezy, Nelson Valdes, Karen Wald, John Womack, Jr., and Andrew Zimbalist.

We also wish to thank Sandra Levinson and Jerome Nickel of the Center for Cuban Studies, Carmelo Mesa-Lago of the Center for Latin American Studies at the University of Pennsylvania, and

Alain Vidal-Naquet of the World Food Council. Many thanks to our colleagues at the Institute for Food and Development Policy and Oxfam America for the supportive environment so necessary to complete this work.

Nothing is done without money. For financial contributions critical to this venture we particularly thank Maryanne Mott and Herman Warsh; Lance Lindblom and the MacArthur Foundation (whose grant underwrote publication costs); and the many individual and group supporters of the work of the Institute for Food and Development Policy.

Finally, special thanks to special people. To Keith Wood who made our computers work, and to David Fitzgerald for putting up with a house taken over by the work on this book. To Joshua and Jonah for giving up computer time which will be returned with special interest, and to Vicki who held things together during Michael's absences. To Medea's parents, who put up with their roving daughter, and Kevin Donaher for his love and support. And to Arlen Siu, may her dual citizenship one day be an asset and not a liability.

We are not ignorant of the controversy this modest book may occasion, and while we are indebted to many, only we the authors can accept responsibility for what it says.

The Cubans themselves have learned that socialism is built with clenched teeth and that revolution is no evening stroll. But, after all, if the future came on a platter, it would not be of this world.

EDUARDO GALEANO, *OPEN VEINS OF LATIN AMERICA*

THE FOOD WINDOW

In 1492, Christopher Columbus declared Cuba "the most beautiful country human eyes have ever seen." An American scholar, traveling throughout rural Cuba in the mid-1940s, called it "one of the most favorable spots for human existence on the earth's surface."[1] Yet since the Cuban revolution began over twenty-five years ago, the country's beauty seems to be in the eyes of the beholder. For some, the revolution has made Cuba paradise on earth and its leader, Fidel Castro, an heroic symbol of hope. For others, Cuba has become hell on earth, its leader a ruthless dictator.

Indeed it is difficult to read anything about Cuba that is not polemical. Either the facts seem irrelevant or they are interpreted in diametrically opposite ways depending on the ideological bent of the interpreter. Take, for example, Cuba's food rationing system. Some see rationing as proof that Cuba is a just society; others see it as proof that Cuba is an economic "basket case." Even something so seemingly straightforward as how to refer to Cuba's president has become politically charged. With his enthusiasts calling him Fidel and his detractors Castro, what should writers striving for impartiality call him? (As you will see, the only solution we came up with was to use several of his names interchangeably: Fidel, Castro, Fidel Castro, President Castro.)

The Focus on Food

The subject of this book, Cuba's food situation today, is hotly debated. Cubans who have come to the United States during the various waves of emigration since the revolution often cite food shortages, even hunger, as a reason for leaving. We told a Cuban-American at the Miami airport that we were going to Cuba to write about the food situation. "Food in Cuba?" he laughed. "Is there any left?" Yet Cuban government publications maintain there are no food shortages and that food is available in greater abundance all the time.[2]

Our purpose in writing this book was to get beyond polemics and to investigate firsthand the food realities in Cuba today. We wanted to study the achievements, problems, and issues raised by Cuba's agricultural and food experience. Observers of virtually every political stripe agree that there have been dramatic changes in the ways food is produced and distributed in Cuba. Many speak of the "Cuban model" of development, some with admiration, others with horror. We believe that the debate about the Cuban revolution's successes and failures—and the lessons to be learned about eradicating hunger and promoting development—can be more fruitful when grounded in fresh and substantive data and analysis.

In a world where as many as one billion people go hungry, food justice is the primary issue for most third world people. As the Institute for Food and Development Policy's book *Food First* asserts, "Whether or not people are hungry appears to us as the primary test of a just and effective social and economic system."[3] A society's food system (from production through consumption) is so fundamental to its functioning that food serves as a "window" through which we can observe a great deal of any society's makeup. The food window can also make a country more understandable to a broad range of people since everyone seems to take some interest in food.

In the case of Cuba, there are several additional reasons for focusing on food. One, the U.S. government has sought to starve Cuba into submission through an embargo on trade. A second reason is that surprisingly little has been written about food or farming realities in postrevolution Cuba. No comprehensive work based on firsthand research had been published since the late 1960s—and there have been important developments in food and agriculture since then.

Finally, food issues are what we know best. They have been at the heart of the work of each of us for many years: Michael Scott as researcher on agrarian reform and director of overseas programs for Oxfam America, the private development agency; Joseph Collins as the cofounder of the Institute for Food and Development Policy and author of a number of books on food policy and rural development; and Medea Benjamin as a nutritionist with the United Nations Food and Agriculture Organization and the Swedish International Development Agency in several third world countries.

How the Work Was Carried Out

The project was initiated in 1978 with a proposal from the Institute for Food and Development Policy to the government of Cuba. We proposed an independent research project, financed through the Institute, to include field visits to Cuba and to be carried out with the cooperation of relevant ministries, government institutes such as the Institute for Research on Consumer Demand, and organizations such as the small farmers' association (ANAP). The project would culminate in a popular but well-documented book, over which the Cuban government would have no editorial influence. After long waits, as well as two visits to Havana to discuss the project, the proposal was officially approved in the summer of 1980.

We wanted to learn the answers to a host of questions. How has the nutritional well-being of Cubans fared since the revolution? Is hunger really no longer a problem in Cuba? What are the main complaints Cubans have about their diet? Why is there food rationing in Cuba today? Is rationing effective and what is its future? What are Cuba's agricultural priorities? Has the importance and role of sugar changed with the revolution? Does Cuba aim to produce its own food and does it succeed? Are private farmers free to grow what they please and sell to whomever they wish? Or may they operate only under government contract? Which are more productive, private or state farms? What progress has been made in organizing cooperatives?

Our research consisted of extensive library work and three field trips to Cuba from 1980 to 1983. Field trips lasted from two to six weeks and included as many as sixty interviews, some set up with assistance of the Cuban government's foreign liaison bureau (ICAP), others lined up on our own.

Within the government we were fortunate to make high-level contacts, commonly at the vice-ministerial level. After formalities and initial defensiveness, many government functionaries seemed comfortable and shared with us critical and up-to-date information. Vice President Carlos Rafael Rodriguez granted us three extensive interviews. Based on his years in the highest posts of the revolution, including the directorship of the agriculture and agrarian reform institute in the early years, he gave us valuable insights into food and development issues at different stages of the revolution.

We visited government ministries, state farms, cooperatives, private farms, stores, markets, schools, and research institutes. Independent of officialdom, we made numerous visits to individuals and groups in Havana, the rural area around the capital, and eight other provinces stretching the length of the island. Sometimes we followed up friendship networks in finding new contacts. Other times we struck out on our own, knocking on doors virtually at random, interviewing workers and farmers in field and factory. These independent forays were our reality check, letting us take the pulse of everyday people and providing us with further questions for subsequent official encounters.

Wherever we went we were well received. Few rural people ever guessed that we were from the United States, so infrequent has the U.S. embargo made personal contact with neighbors only ninety miles to the north. Generally we were first taken to be Bulgarians, then Soviets, Czechs, Germans, Argentines, and—as a last resort—Canadians. Once it was discovered that we were Americans, we were often even more warmly welcomed.

Medea Benjamin had the advantage of having lived in Cuba from 1979 through 1982. She worked in several Cuban workplaces, ate from the ration book, shopped in Cuban stores, gave birth in a Cuban hospital, and took part in the activities that constitute Cuban life today: public rallies, health campaigns, agricultural work brigades, meetings of the block committee, the women's committee, and union meetings.

Obstacles

No one should underestimate the difficulties of doing research on and in Cuba. There have been times over the years (especially in the final fact-checking stage) that we have been driven to grief about how the U.S. blockade has stifled everyday communications to and from Cuba. A letter takes six weeks or more; telephoning is practically out of the question; airplane flights are inordinately expensive and infrequent. Little information about Cuba—let alone reliable information—can be found today even in major U.S. university libraries. (While we were midstream in our project, the Reagan Administration sought to isolate the

United States even more by blocking the receipt of periodicals and books from Cuba by libraries and citizens; fortunately, first amendment advocacy deterred the Administration.)

A more subtle difficulty on the U.S. side is that most of the scholarly writing on Cuba is by children of emigrés whose passions threaten to interfere with their impartiality. Finally, only the naive could do a research project on Cuba without being aware that their names might be added to the files maintained by the Big Brother agencies of the U.S. government.

On the Cuban side, a siege mentality, probably inevitable in the face of twenty-five years of efforts by the world's most powerful government to destabilize the island nation, makes for a defensive, closed society. Visas are selectively issued. While statistical compendia get thicker each year, the knack for appearing forthcoming with data while withholding the heart of the matter remains. Statistical materials are filled with gross errors, contradictions, and critical omissions. Information on income distribution is difficult to obtain. We were politely told that line-by-line clearance from the vice president of the republic was needed to see it. Our request for clearance was never answered.

In Cuba, there are no counterparts to ourselves, independent investigators describing, analyzing, reflecting. Our firsthand sources were officials and everyday Cubans—farmers, farmworkers, consumers. Transportation is limited, and a car with driver, essential for independent visits to the countryside, can run up to $200 a day. For researchers who can only faintly recall life before Xerox, photocopiers are not to be found in Havana for love or money. And leaving Cuba on one trip, we lost thirty rolls of exposed film to the powerful East German X-ray equipment used in the Havana airport to screen luggage for explosives.

In *No Free Lunch*, we look at the food and farming policies and realities in a revolution that is now over a quarter of a century old. We discuss and analyze the many lessons to be learned, positive and negative, about Cuba's attempts to end hunger, to establish greater equity, opportunity, and security for all, and to develop its agricultural resources. We ask our readers to take up this book in the spirit we have tried to write it: the spirit of an open mind.

NO FREE LUNCH

CHAPTER 1

I,
black Simón Caraballo,
and I have nothing to eat today.
My wife died in childbirth,
My house was taken away.

I,
black Simón Caraballo,
now sleep in a vestibule;
I have a brick for a pillow,
my bed is on the ground.
I don't know what to do with my arms,
but I will find something to do:

I,
black Simón Caraballo
have my fists clenched,
have my fists clenched,
and I need to eat!

NICOLÁS GUILLÉN, *"The Ballad of Simón Caraballo"*

On the Eve
of Revolution

 Observers around the world were surprised in 1959, when, after only two years of fighting, a ragtag revolutionary army of fewer than two thousand managed to defeat a well-equipped army of thirty thousand. But a look at social, economic, and political life in prerevolution Cuba will help explain why the vast majority of Cubans from all classes supported the war against the Batista dictatorship, even if only a handful of them actually took up arms.

Detractors of the Cuban revolution commonly assert that Cuba was already fairly developed before the revolution. The academically inclined are wont to refer to United Nations statistics to "prove" their point. Cuba's per capita income in the 1950s—about $500 per person—was higher than that of any other Latin American country except oil-exporting Venezuela and industrialized Argentina. Cuba's "food availability" was outdone by few other third world countries. Even for "meat availability"—the ultimate benchmark in the West of prosperity on the food front—the island nation could boast of seventy pounds per person annually, about twice as much as Peru.[1]

But for Simón Caraballo and the 1.5 million other landless farmworkers, marginal farmers, and jobless Cubans, such per capita figures would have seemed a cruel taunt.[2] Half of rural families tried to get by on incomes of forty-five pesos per month.[3]

1

And while 70 pounds of meat were theoretically "available" annually for every Cuban, in fact only 4 percent of farmworker families ate meat regularly, according to a 1956–57 Catholic University Association survey. Only 2 percent of the families consumed eggs on a regular basis. (Many rural families with chickens had to sell the eggs to buy more filling staples.) Only 11 percent regularly drank milk.

"The reality is more indicting than the numbers indicate," the survey's authors commented. "The statistics are incapable of expressing the anguish of a family sitting down day after day at the dinner table—or what serves as a table—to eat the same thing with only slight variations: rice, beans, and *viandas* [cooking bananas and starchy root crops such as cassava, taro, and sweet potato]." Even with such a diet, poor families were forced to spend over two-thirds of their income on food.[4]

Sociologist Lowry Nelson wrote in 1950 of rural Cuba's "unsightly and unpleasant human landscape" and of the "naked children, their swollen stomachs testifying to an unbalanced diet and infection from parasitic worms."[5] Chicken with rice was the favorite dish, he noted, but "needless to say, it is not within the reach of large numbers of the rural population—or the urban, for that matter."[6] Poor folks' subsistence, according to Nitza Villapoll, a longtime student of Cuban food habits, was *sopa de gallo*. Perhaps the name ("rooster soup") made it sound palatable, but it was nothing to crow about, just a mix of water and brown sugar.[7]

"Rooster soup" was especially important during the eight- to nine-month "dead season" between sugar harvests. The harvest season cranked up in the dry month of January and wound down three or four months later, before the onset of the May rains. This enervating annual cycle of lean and fat months set the rhythm of life for most Cubans, especially for the poor majority in the countryside. An American observer commenting on the effects of the dead season spoke of "tens of thousands of families sliding down the dietary scale into undernourishment on a handful of beans and a bit of cassava or taro."[8]

In prerevolution Cuba, as in most parts of the world today, diet depended on income. If you had money, you could eat as well as anyone in the United States or Western Europe. But in prerevolution Cuba, there was tremendous inequality in income distribution.

The inequalities reflected differences between owners and nonowners of land and capital resources; differences between the steadily employed, the seasonally employed and the unemployed; differences between unionized and unorganized workers; and differences between urban and rural residents.While there were no official figures for income distribution before the revolution, two researchers' separate estimates indicated that the poorest 20 percent of Cubans received only between 2 and 6 percent of total national income, while the richest 20 percent received more than 55 percent.[9] Vice President Carlos Rafael Rodriguez, a distinguished economist, estimates that the wealthiest 15 percent of families captured 43 percent of income.[10]

See p. 203
- for name

Since most Cubans lived in the countryside and tried to make a living from agriculture, control over land was a key factor in income distribution. At the top of the economic ladder were the owners of the huge sugar plantations and cattle ranches which sprawled across the countryside. On the eve of the revolution, the largest 9 percent of all farmowners possessed 62 percent of the land, while 66 percent had only 7 percent.[11] At the bottom were some one hundred thousand tenants, sharecroppers, and squatters who owned no land at all. Of all farms, 70 percent were operated by nonowners who were often forced to pay land rents far in excess of the legal limits. Some coffee farmers, for example, paid rents up to 40 percent of the value of their crops.[12]

Preventing landless people from "squatting" on land so they could grow their own food and make themselves less dependent on seasonal wages was a "major concern" of the large landowners, according to a U.S. government report.[13] In some areas, notably the Sierra Maestra where Castro set up camp during the war against Batista, squatters were driven off the land by armed agents of the landowners or even by the army itself.

At the very bottom of the ladder were the five hundred and seventy thousand landless farmworkers and their families. Prerevolution Cuba was unlike most other countries in Latin America: landless farm workers rather than small farmers made up the majority of the population in the countryside. They and their families constituted slightly more than a third of the country's 7 million people in the mid-1950s, yet they received somewhere between 5 and 10 percent of the national income.[14]

Fewer than 10 percent of farmworkers were permanently employed in the sugar mills. The rest were migrant field hands who, look for work as they might, found an average of only 123 days of work each year. It was a rare rural family in which the adult men were *steadily* employed.[15]

For both rural and city dwellers, employment was critical. Some seven hundred thousand Cubans—one-third of the working population—were unemployed for most of the year.[16] In addition to the landless farmworkers, the poorest people included the unemployed in the shantytowns of Havana, Santiago, and other cities. For them, life was a struggle for survival, living hand-to-mouth, doing odd jobs, washing cars, selling lottery tickets, stealing, or begging. In Havana alone there were at least five thousand beggars.[17] Also in the cities were an estimated two hundred and fifty thousand Cubans who lived off "the luxury life styles of the local rich and the tourists," as one author put it.[18] They were street vendors, shoeshine boys, prostitutes, pimps, and entertainers.

Blacks and mulattoes, who numbered at least one-third of the population, were among the poorest.[19] So were women, who made up only 9.8 percent of the total labor force in the early 1950s; the majority were domestic servants earning starvation wages of $8 to $25 a month.[20]

Women were often so impoverished they were forced to give up their children to Cuba's numerous orphanages. The Beneficencia Asylum was regarded as a tourist attraction by some in prerevolution Cuba. Sydney Clark, in his 1956 travel guide to Cuba, lists it under "Specialties that Fascinate." The door of the orphanage had "a revolving cradle or basket in which any mother may place her undesired infant, and close the door quickly so that no one save the imperturbable policeman on guard shall see her."[21] (Valdés is a common surname in Cuba because all the children in Beneficencia were given the name of its founder.) Begging mothers and their infant children were a common sight Sundays on church steps.[22]

Four hundred thousand urban workers had relatively secure incomes, averaging $1,600 a year—high by Latin American standards because of the strength of the unions.[23] However, there was a wide wage differential, ranging from a typical textile worker's $40 a month to an electrical worker's $500 a month.[24] Of employed Cubans, 11 percent worked for national or local government. With government's "important, if unstated, purpose"[25] being "personal enrichment," no small number of these officials had paper posts created as a form of political patronage or nepotism. In 1950, an astounding 80 percent of the national budget was spent on government salaries.[26]

There were also, of course, the rich, the tiny minority with the lion's share of the income. Historian Hugh Thomas estimates that there existed more millionaires, per capita, in Cuba than anywhere else in Latin America. More Cadillacs were sold in Havana than any other city in the world in 1954.[27]

The rich in the big cities lived in guarded residential areas, tropical versions of Chevy Chase or Beverly Hills such as the zone known as "El Country Club." "Society is to be found in the Yacht Club by day and the Casino by night," an American visitor wrote in 1946.

> The Yacht Club is a veritable palace by the sea. . . . On the beaches strong bronzed bodies display the smartest bathing togs and the best swimming and diving techniques. Children with Negro maids are beginning a social career that will take them to every such club in the world. . . . In the summer, society moves northward. Cubans know all the resorts from Maine to North Carolina and they pause on the way for shopping in New York."[28]

Cubans aspiring to move upward, as well as those already on top, aped U.S. lifestyles. ("Even our bad taste was imported," poet Pablo Armando Fernández noted.[29]) For these Cubans, Havana had to measure up not to other Latin American cities but to Miami. Air conditioners were status items—and the colder the home, office or restaurant, the higher the status. "Americans think we are silly to wear furs [given the tropical heat]," said a Cuban matron before the revolution. "But . . . the smartest New Year's party is outdoors at the Country Club—and of course we *need* furs."[30]

Some of Cuba's rich were concerned even with outfitting themselves for their afterlife: in Havana's Colon Cemetery, mausoleums were furnished with elevators, air conditioners, and telephones.[31]

The Poor Majority

In the countryside, two-thirds of the houses were palm-thatched huts[32] without toilets or even outhouses. Less than 3 percent of all rural houses had running water,[33] and only one in every fourteen families had electricity.[34] While Havana made Caribbean capitals such as Kingston and San Juan seem provincial, "the standard of living in the Cuban countryside lagged behind the levels in those islands," comments Thomas.[35]

In the cities, the poor lived as squatters in makeshift shacks or paid high rents for cramped tenements called *solares*. Recent arrivals to the cities lived in slums with such names as *Llega y Pon*, "come and squat."[36] Minimum sanitary facilities were often lacking. One-fifth of the families, with an average family size of five, lived in single rooms.[37] While electricity was commonplace, the rates were notoriously high and the U.S.-owned utilities company reportedly had the highest rate of profit of any utility company in the world.

Literacy and schooling reflected the same inequalities as living conditions. Cuba in the 1950s boasted four universities, although they were closed down in response to faculty and student protests during the final two years of the Batista dictatorship. But opened or closed, universities meant little to most Cubans. The World Bank's data showed that "while 180,370 children start the first grade, only 4,852 enter the eighth grade."[38] By 1958, approximately one-half of Cuban children of primary school age (6 to 14 years) were not attending school at all, compared to the Latin American average of 36 percent.[39]

Illiteracy was common: one out of four Cubans over ten years of age could not read and write. But this national average masked a significant rural/urban difference: illiteracy in the countryside was 42 percent, while it was 12 percent in urban areas.[40]

Health services followed the same patterns of inequality. While Cuba had the highest ratio of hospital beds to population in the Caribbean, 80 percent were in the city of Havana.[41] Havana province had 1 doctor for every 420 persons, but rural Oriente province had 1 for every 2,550.[42] Unsanitary housing and poor diets made curable diseases widespread. The World Bank reported in 1951 that between 80 and 90 percent of children in rural areas suffered from intestinal parasites.[43] In 1956, 13 percent of the rural population had a history of typhoid and 14 percent tuberculosis.[44]

These enormous inequalities meant that while the middle and upper classes lived well, the vast majority of Cubans needlessly suffered from hunger and poverty—despite the fact that Cuba was a nation of rich natural endowment.

Cuba's Untapped Potential

Cuba is as large as almost all the other island nations in the Caribbean put together; its principal island extends 700 miles and averages 62 miles in width. Cuba's total area exceeds that of Denmark, Belgium, and the Netherlands combined. Relative to its population, its agricultural resources are quite favorable. Nearly 60 percent of Cuba's farmland is tillable, an unusually high proportion.[45] Much of the land which cannot be plowed is suitable for grazing.

Situated on the northern fringes of the tropics, Cuba is blessed with a relatively uniform climate, favorable to production of most tropical and some temperate crops. The island's mountainous easternmost region lends itself to the cultivation of coffee, which requires tropical sun yet cool temperatures. The temperature averages 75 degrees, and Cuban farmers, unlike their counterparts in Florida, need never fear frost.

But the tropical climate is a mixed blessing. The heat and humidity create ideal breeding grounds for pests, and viral plant and animal diseases.[46] While Cuba's rainfall is generally adequate (but less than what one might expect for the tropics), there are occasional droughts as well as crop-devastating hurricanes. Since 1800, Cuba has been struck by 85 hurricanes, an average of about one every other year.[47]

Cuba's natural endowment also lacks the fossil-based sources of energy upon which modern agriculture has become dependent. No substantial oil or coal deposits have been found so far, and there are few minerals for chemical fertilizers. There are few rivers suitable for hydroelectric power and no inland water transport routes.

On balance, though, compared to most Caribbean island nations and other countries of the world, Cuba is favorably endowed for feeding its people. Yet in the late 1950s—on the "eve of the revolution"—Cuba's food and agricultural performance stood in stark contrast to its potential.

Two-thirds of Cuba's farmland went uncultivated. Almost half the total farm area was kept in pasture, most of it unimproved.[48] Vast Texas-style ranches often used good farmland to graze an average of only two head per five acres.[49]

While sugarcane was planted on more than half the total area under cultivation, yields on Cuba's sugar estates were notoriously low. Of the eighteen top sugar-producing nations, Cuba ranked seventeenth in yields in the 1950s.[50] In fact, yields were higher in the late 1800s than in the late 1950s.[51] In addition, every year about 20 percent of the planted sugarcane was left unharvested. When world markets were smallest, such as after the Korean War, as little as 57 percent was harvested.[52]

Sugarcane monoculture squandered Cuba's human resources, setting up the cycle of harvest and "dead season." During the harvest, the sugar industry demanded an extra labor force of four to five hundred thousand.[53] Most were needed for the grueling work of cutting the cane—all cane was hand cut—and taking it to the grinding mill. But miserable and miserably paid as the work was, during the long dead season there was virtually no work in the mills and there were only a few replanting jobs in the fields. Employment also plummeted in transportation, trade, and shipping. Some were lucky enough to find work in what remained of the tobacco and coffee harvests,[54] but half of all workers commonly could find no work during the dead season.[55]

Noncane agriculture was, with a few exceptions, similarly backward. Much was subsistence farming based upon corn and root crops. The low crop yields reflected the prospects of sharecroppers and squatters with little land security, little possibility of credit or technical assistance, and inadequate marketing outlets.

Almost a third of the food consumed in Cuba was imported, including staples that the island seemingly could have produced in abundance—rice, lard, vegetable oils, beans, potatoes, dairy products, eggs, vegetables and even canned fruits, fish, poultry, and pork.[56] In 1954, approximately $140 million was spent to import foodstuffs alone, more than one-quarter of total imports.[57]

The Sugar Cartel

Sugar monoculture was a direct result of the concentration of control over agricultural resources in the hands of a few wealthy Cubans and U.S. individuals and corporations. Sugar had dominated the Cuban economy since the early 1900s, when Cuba became the world's largest producer and exporter of sugar.

By the 1950s cane farms accounted for 42 percent of the value of all agricultural production.[58] Beyond that, much of the nation's industry, transportation, banking, and trade was inextricably tied to sugar. Manufacturing raw sugar from cane was by far the country's largest industry; the estates and mills were the railroads' principal customers and owners of two-thirds of the railroad trackage. Half of all bank loans went to the sugar industry. Raw sugar and its byproducts, alcohol and molasses, accounted for about 80 percent of the country's exports and paid for the bulk of imports.[59] When international sugar prices fell, the entire economy was pulled down. In fact, the wages of many nonsugar workers, as well as many ordinary prices, were tied by law to the international price of sugar.[60]

The cartel established by the major sugar mills and growers set up an internal quota system that virtually ensured underutilization of human and land resources. Since Cuba produced more than half of the sugar sold on the "free" world market, by the late 1930s major producers agreed to limit production to avoid a sugar glut which might bring prices down. The government set production quotas for all mills and growers.[61] But since these quotas could be changed during the season—depending on harvest prospects, U.S. sugar beet production, and market developments—growers set aside large "reserves" of land that otherwise could have been used to grow food or other crops. These reserve lands could be put into alternative production when world sugar demand was low, but in fact, much of the land was never utilized.

The internal quota system sealed producers off from competitive pressures. Inefficient, high-cost producers were protected. Efficient producers[62] had little incentive to raise yields by improving the skills or motivation of the work force, by updating cultivation practices (particularly weeding and the optimum use of fertilizers), or by introducing irrigation and new cane varieties. Little wonder that Cuba developed only one new cane variety in its hundred-year sugar history[63] or that most of the 160 mills in operation at the time of the revolution had been built in the previous century.[64] Agricultural research was minimal: while Cuba had over 6,500 lawyers, it had only 294 agricultural engineers.[65] Often what made sense from the standpoint of the individual rancher or sugar company, or even from the standpoint of the poor farmer, spelled waste and truncated development for the nation.

Dependence on the United States

Up to now we have only hinted at what was a major stumbling block for Cuba's development: its extreme dependency on the United States.

The Platt Amendment, forced into the Cuban Constitution in 1901 during U.S. military occupation, gave the United States the right to intervene whenever it decided a government was not "adequate." The United States landed troops in Cuba in 1906, 1912, and 1917. Even after the Platt Amendment was eliminated from the constitution in 1934, the U.S. government remained the dominant influence in internal Cuban politics. "Until the advent of Castro, the United States was so overwhelmingly influential [that] . . . the American Ambassador was the second most important man in Cuba, sometimes even more important than the president [Cuban dictator Batista]," former Ambassador Earl E. T. Smith later testified.[66]

Much of the Cuban economy was in the hands of U.S. companies and U.S. investments ran the gamut: manufacturing, commerce, petroleum refining, agriculture, mining, transportation, electricity, tourism. On the eve of the revolution, there were over one billion dollars in U.S. corporate holdings in Cuba[67]—or one-eighth of the total U.S. investment in Latin America, making Cuba second only to Venezuela.[68] U.S. firms directly employed about 160,000 workers in Cuba itself.[69]

Americans owned nine of Cuba's ten largest sugar mills in 1955, produced 40 percent of the island's sugar, and controlled 54 percent of the total grinding capacity.[70] Cuban branches of U.S. banks held almost a quarter of all bank deposits.[71] The telephone service was a monopoly of American Telephone and Telegraph.[72] The U.S.-owned Cuban Electric Company had a virtual monopoly on electric power—and charged rates even higher than those in the United States.[73]

Standard Oil, Shell, and Texaco refined imported crude oil. Procter and Gamble, Colgate-Palmolive, Firestone, Goodrich, Goodyear, Coca-Cola, Pepsi-Cola, Canada Dry, and Orange Crush all had subsidiaries in Cuba. U.S. citizens, often connected to the Mafia, also owned many of the island's hotels and ran the thriving gambling casinos and drug trade.

"A relatively small group of American businessmen have in their grasp vast economic power by the mere act of making business decisions," declared a study of U.S. investments in Cuba on the eve of the revolution.[74]

Every year the U.S. Congress made the single most important decision to the Cuban economy—the "quota" of Cuban sugar that could be imported into the U.S. market at the relatively high prices of U.S. domestic producers. Over a 35-year period, Cuba exported about 60 percent of its sugar production to the United States. Cuba's economy was not only dependent on a single crop but on a single customer.

Cuba's potential to produce consumer goods for its own people was undercut by the U.S. sugar quota. Cuba was granted preferred entry into the U.S. market for some of its sugar, its rum, and its leaf tobacco; in exchange, Cuba had to open its doors to U.S. goods. Duties were abolished for many U.S. goods and lowered on many more; internal taxes on goods of U.S. origin were lowered or lifted; and quantity restrictions on imports of U.S. goods were virtually eliminated. Restrictions on the conversion of pesos into dollars were prohibited so that profits made on the Cuban market could readily be taken "home" to the United States.[75]

Not only did an average of 80 percent of Cuba's imports come from a single trading "partner," but the Cuban economy also became totally dependent on imports.[76] "Every conceivable type of goods was imported," noted one U.S. economist, "from corn flakes to tomato paste; from nails and tacks to tractors, trucks, and automobiles; from thread to all types of clothing; from goods for Sears and other department stores to accessories for the home, fertilizers and insecticides for agriculture, and materials and equipment for industry and construction."[77]

A 1934 memorandum by U.S. Secretary of State Cordell Hull argued that U.S. policy should actively discourage Cuba's agricultural diversification in order to maintain it as a favorable market for U.S. foods and raw materials.[78] But the subsequent U.S. sugar quota system made "active" discouragement unnecessary for the realization of Hull's goal.

Enforced dependency on the United States gave rise to a number of the ironies of underdevelopment that marked pre-revolution Cuba. An exporter of raw sugar, Cuba imported candy.[79] Cuba exported tomatoes but imported virtually all its tomato paste. Cuba exported fresh fruit and imported canned fruit, exported rawhide but imported shoes. It produced vast quantities of tobacco but imported cigarettes. (So many American brands were imported that in 1959, nine of Cuba's twenty-four cigarette factories were not functioning.)[80]

To add insult to injury, even "Havana" cigars were increasingly manufactured in the United States: Cuba exported leaf tobacco as raw material for the U.S. cigar companies that shifted manufacturing operations from Cuba to Florida in part because of high U.S. tariffs on Cuban-manufactured cigars.[81]

Rather than develop its productive capabilities, Cuba shifted its investments to nonproductive areas like tourism, real estate, and import-export. Cuba became a market to be milked for all it was worth. Little was invested in its future: in fact, between 1952 and 1958 there was a net disinvestment of $370 million and the per capita gross national product declined.[82]

Under the U.S. quota system Cuba received a comparatively good price for its sugar (though for only a part of its total production). But there was little prospect that Cuba's share of the U.S. market would grow. Indeed, throughout the 1940s and 1950s, the amount of Cuban sugar purchased by the United States consistently declined. At the same time, the quota system undercut any movement toward food self-reliance. More important, the concentration of control over the nation's agricultural resources, as well as the economy as a whole, prevented the creation of jobs that could have meant food security for the hundreds of thousands of poor Cuban families.

In 1950, the World Bank sent a team of experts to study the stagnating Cuban economy and to recommend ways to pump life into it. Prominent Cuban doctors told the Bank team that more than 30 to 40 percent of the people in the cities and over 60 percent of those in rural areas were undernourished.[83] The Bank acknowledged that lack of money, caused by lack of year-round employment, was one of the chief reasons people could not get enough food or enough of the right foods.

But the Bank's three recommendations for eliminating hunger

were band-aid measures: Cuba should "carry out a vigorous campaign to educate the people in elementary principles of proper
diet and sanitation"; it should "support all appropriate measures
to ensure that all rice consumed in Cuba is enriched"; and finally,
the country should expand the work of the five Cuban charitable
institutions that "offer a three-month vacation in the country to
undernourished children."[84]

But was the problem of the hungry that they didn't know how
to eat? And why worry about enriched rice when the fundamental problem was that the undernourished didn't get enough to
eat; for them a lack of minerals and vitamins was of secondary
importance. And as for the "vacation center," what would happen to the children after their vacations when they returned to
families whose small plots could not feed them or in which no
one could find work for more than a few months a year?

As this group of foreign experts was recommending enriched
rice, Fidel Castro and his comrades were already planning a radically different menu for change. Given the gross inequalities in
Cuban society, the poverty and hunger, the disease and illiteracy,
and the astonishing waste of agricultural resources, it should
come as no surprise that thousands and thousands of Cubans
from every walk of life took to the streets to welcome Fidel's
band of revolutionaries on New Year's Day, 1959.

CHAPTER 2

Our duty is, I repeat, first of all, before anything else, to see to it that no one in Cuba goes without food.

CHE GUEVARA, then president of the National Bank, June 1960[1]

It's true that with this system of distribution, those in privileged positions will now be less privileged, but those who are hard up . . . will radically improve their situation.

FIDEL CASTRO[2]

How the Poor
Got More

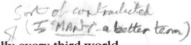

Sort of contradicted (I "MANY" a better term)

In the capital cities of virtually every third world country, many people go hungry, even starve, every day. Yet no one goes hungry because of a shortage of food. Usually, you can just go to the store—in some countries, to the U.S.-style supermarket—and buy as much as you want. *If* you have the money. The widespread hunger in Mexico City is not because food is scarce—Mexico is a major exporter of food—but because some people are too poor to buy as much as they need. Income, not food supply, is the major limiting factor.

The same, of course, is true in the United States. Our country is by no means free from hunger, but one look at our supermarkets and warehouses makes it clear that the problem is not a lack of food.

In most market-economy countries, food is sold at the highest price the market will bear. In other words, those with enough income can buy whatever they want, while those without sufficient income are left to go hungry.

But suppose all of a sudden many people, especially the poor majority, had more money. This was the situation in Cuba in the first several years of the revolution. The revolution's leadership viewed inadequate income as the reason why people were undernourished, so it set into motion policies designed to boost the earnings of the poorer half of society as well as to enlarge the

15

share of their earnings they could afford to spend on food.

But once people had more money to spend on food, it became clear that there was not enough food to go around. How could the government deal with the shortages? One simple solution would have been to let prices rise, thereby reducing the number of Cubans able to buy the food. That would have dealt with the shortages but not with people's hunger. As Prime Minister Castro recalled several years later, "A price policy to compensate for this imbalance [between supply and demand] . . . would have been nothing short of a ruthless sacrifice of that part of the population with the lowest income." Such a policy was acceptable for luxury and nonessential goods "but never for necessities," he added.[3]

Not only would high food prices have contradicted the egalitarian philosophy of the new government, but it would have been counterproductive to winning the broadest possible support for the revolution. "What should we do with what we have, which is more than we had before but still isn't enough? The answer is simple: we must distribute it better," Fidel proposed.[4] In an attempt to find a more equitable form of distribution—by *need* rather than income—the government opted for rationing.

Money in More Pockets

But let's take a closer look at the developments leading up to the decision to implement a rationing system, starting with efforts to increase the incomes of the poor.

Above all, the government sought to generate fuller employment. Job opportunities for farmworkers soared. With the large estates converted into "people's farms" by the first agrarian reform law, there were one hundred and fifty thousand year-round jobs on these lands by August 1962 compared to fewer than fifty thousand in 1959.[5] Sugar plantation workers, previously unemployed during the long "dead season," now found steady work on the construction projects that seemed to be springing up everywhere—roads, schools, clinics, government offices, housing, etc. Early on, the government raised the minimum wage in agriculture,[6] but then fought against further wage increases lest there be less money for job creation.[7]

These and other measures made their mark: more and more of

even the poorer farmworkers had higher incomes than before the revolution. While only 29 percent of rural workers earned more than 75 pesos a month as of April 1958, two years later 44 percent did.[8]

Thanks to the new government's policies, many poor farmers also found themselves with more money. By granting generous tracts of land to some one hundred thousand tenant farmers, sharecroppers and squatters, the first agrarian reform of 1959 freed farmers from the obligation to hand over to absentee landlords as much as 40 percent of the value of their crops.[9] Moreover, they could now obtain cheap credit from the government, as well as count on stable prices for their produce.[10]

In urban areas, many workers won substantial wage increases, thanks to the strength of their unions. No longer did workers' demands for a larger share of the wealth their labor produced run up against the violent repression of the Batista dictatorship.[11] Even the earnings of the poorest workers notched upward. By one estimate, the lowest 40 percent of income-earners enlarged their slice of the national income "pie" from 6.5 percent before the revolution to 17 percent by 1962.[12]

Gains for the urban unemployed came more slowly, but by 1962 expanding state payrolls and productive investments were sharply cutting unemployment. Of those workers who had found employment for less than six months a year before the revolution, 86 percent were finding work for ten or more months three years later, according to one survey.[13] Higher wages and reduced unemployment meant more money in the hands of poorer urban households, especially those with more than one wage earner.

The new government also sought to enable low-income households to spend more of their earnings on food. It made basic social services free for everyone. Included were not only schooling, medical care, medicines, and social security, but also water, burial services, sports facilities, even public phones. The government lowered the charges for electricity, gas, and public transport that had eaten up so much of working people's earnings. The numbers racket and other forms of gambling that preyed on the incomes of the poor were outlawed. In 1960 the government initiated its "urban reform" by decreeing bold rent reductions of up to 50 percent. A year and a half later, the maximum rent was set at 10 percent of the income of the head of the household.[14] Since many poor families lived in tenement housing notorious for exploitative rents, rent reforms in particular left appreciably more money for them to spend on other things.

The net effect of fuller employment and expanded free or highly subsidized services was an historically unprecedented redistribution of income—the transfer of 15 percent of the national income from property owners to wage earners in the first year alone.[15] In few other societies have the poor and middle classes so rapidly found themselves with "extra money" on their hands.

What did people do with so much extra money? Among the most pressing desires for the poor was to eat more and better. Rural families, freed from landlord obligations and money-lenders, could eat more of what they produced. Peasants who for years had raised pigs but could never afford to eat them, now could. Nationwide consumption of such coveted foods as pork and milk soared; beef consumption shot up by 50 percent in just two years.[16] Even the economically better off wound up consuming more locally produced goods since it was increasingly difficult to go on shopping sprees in Miami or buy luxury imports in Cuba.

Supply Lags Behind Demand

But supply failed to keep pace with the growing demand. Overall agricultural production was handicapped by the flight to the United States of administrative and technical personnel, an elite unwilling to adjust to the new changes. The consequent lack of organization and technical experience on the newly created people's farms and cooperatives lowered production. The Eisenhower administration's 1960 embargo on most exports to Cuba seriously disrupted the island's agriculture, which had become dependent on the United States for farm machinery, fertilizers, pesticides, seeds, and other inputs. In addition, the Central Intelligence Agency fostered acts of sabotage, including burning fields and slaughtering cattle. Such sabotage, as well as repeated military attacks culminating in the Bay of Pigs invasion in April 1961, forced Cuba to divert scarce human and material resources into defense, exacting a toll on production. As if all this were not enough, a severe drought in 1962 further aggravated food production problems. (See Chapter 9 for further discussion of production problems in the early years.)

In a reversal of the pre-1959 pattern, shortages became more chronic in the cities than in the countryside. Finding ever fewer consumer goods to buy, especially imports from the United States, tenants and sharecroppers had little need for cash and thus produced less for the market.[17] Consequently, there was less food in the cities. *Viandas* in particular began disappearing from city marketplaces. Plantains (cooking bananas) were no longer trucked in daily to Havana but consumed in the eastern provinces where they were grown.[18]

Shortages often triggered more shortages since the lack of one item meant greater demand for others. By mid-1961, when taro, a usually abundant root crop, became scarce, people bought out sweet potatoes, putting pressure on the supply of white potatoes, and so on.[19]

The disruption of normal imports further aggravated supply problems. As we discussed in Chapter 1, Cuba had become dependent on the import of large quantities of food—wheat, rice, beans, lard, poultry, dairy products, and eggs, even onions and garlic. With over 70 percent of these imports coming from the United States,[20] the abrupt embargo on U.S. trade with Cuba left the country in dire straits.

Take the case of pork lard. While such an example might seem odd, the fact is that Cuba consumed prodigious quantities of lard, importing about 85 percent of it from the United States.[21] In a desperate search for substitute suppliers, the Cuban government found to its dismay that not only were prices significantly higher elsewhere (partly due to steeper transport costs) but nowhere outside of the United States could enough lard be found on such short notice.[22]

The U.S. embargo created a myriad of additional import problems. Since Cuba was so close to the United States, its ports and warehouses had been designed for frequent short hauls by small ferryboats from Florida and New Orleans. Once those sources of supply were cut off, Cuba found itself ill-equipped for transoceanic trade.

Edward Boorstein, an American economist working with the Cuban government in the early years of the revolution, vividly recounts the daily headaches that resulted when food now had to be imported from faraway countries such as Japan and Egypt: one "small crisis" erupted when news came that a ship was about to arrive from Shanghai with 5,000 tons of soybean oil, an urgently needed substitute for lard. "Where should all this oil be put? Shipments of fats and oil had never arrived in such large amounts before," Boorstein wrote. "Several people had to chase around for a week trying to find out if some of the tanks at the petroleum refinery could be cleaned out and used to store the oil, or if some tanks ordinarily used to store molasses were free." Things went no better with a shipload of onions from Egypt: without a suitable warehouse, the onions began to sprout, leaving the government with no option but to figure out how to get rid of them at once, if need be by giving them away.[23]

Cuba depended not only on imports of U.S. food, but also on importing the materials needed to package the food, the machines needed to process the food, the trucks needed to transport the food, and so on. The U.S. trade embargo revealed the true depth of Cuba's food dependence. In the famous Cuban novel *Memorias del Subdesarrollo* (better known outside Cuba in its film version *Memories of Underdevelopment*), the protagonist complains: "For the past few weeks there hasn't been a soft drink to be had anywhere. I never thought that the manufacture of soft drinks could be paralyzed just because there was no cork for the caps. Never . . . could I have imagined how many insignificant things are necessary to keep a country running smoothly. Now you can see everything inside out, all the hidden entrails of the system."[24]

The irony of the mounting food crisis was apparent by the third year of the revolution. Prime Minister Fidel Castro, in a high-level national conference on production in 1961, responded to Western reports about Cuba's shortages: "The problem in Cuba is not one of hunger. That was the problem before, when three to four hundred thousand people didn't have a cent in their pockets. Our problem is precisely that now people have work and have money. . . . While production has gone up since the revolution, it hasn't caught up to the increase in purchasing power. . . . The only way to produce more is to put everyone to work, but by putting everyone to work, we find that the goods and production capacity which existed fall short of the demand created."[25]

Beyond the Free Market

Even in the revolution's first months, it was clear that the ground rules of the "free market" could have taken care of the shortage problem—with higher prices. Under that system, consumers with the highest incomes would pay whatever necessary to eat what they wanted, leaving the remainder to the next highest bidders and so on down the income ladder until nothing was left. There would never be "shortages" because under the ground rules of the free market, there is no shortage when all *effective* (money-backed) demand is being satisfied. Thus from the free-market viewpoint, there would not have been a "shortage" of food in Cuba even if it were priced way out of the reach of many poor Cubans.

Cuba's new government knew that under free-market rules, profiteers would quickly corner every scarce commodity to speculate on skyrocketing prices, at least until food supplies caught up with the increased amount of money in people's hands. Whatever early gains in their living standards rural and urban workers had made would just as quickly be wiped out. Such a development was so unacceptable that the government knew it could not wait for the hoped-for production increases. Instead it tried price controls.

Just three months into the revolution the new government set official prices for rice, milk, bread, and beef products. Two months later, in May 1959, the Ministry of Commerce added to the list butter, pork, cheese, potatoes, and other items, including consumer goods such as soap. At the same time the Ministry placed ceilings of 10 and 20 percent respectively on wholesale and retail profit margins. In the subsequent months, the prices of children's foods and virtually all other staples were frozen and added to the list of price-controlled goods.[26]

Still the situation was far from under control. Price controls are extremely difficult to enforce in a society with a multitude of small retailers and with the unwritten law that everyone looks out for him or herself. Speculation as well as hoarding were widespread enough for Fidel Castro to label speculators "the number one enemy of the revolution."[27]

In an attempt to stem speculation, the wholesale food business was nationalized and those retail stores accused of hoarding and profiteering were taken over by the government. By 1961, some eight thousand retail outlets had been taken over.[28] And in August 1961 a law was passed prohibiting the resale of certain basic goods.[29] At the same time, the government's agrarian reform agency set up *tiendas del pueblo* (people's stores) in the rural areas in an effort to improve the supply of basic consumer goods—at official prices. There were two thousand such stores spread throughout the countryside by 1961.[30] These stores extended credit generously, in contrast to the usury that had been so common.[31]

But try as the fledgling government might, speculators' prices reigned as supply problems multiplied; and it was poor Cubans who were getting the short end of the stick. What was amounting to rationing by income flew in the face of everything the revolutionary leadership stood for. The government might have opted simply to make certain basic staples available to the poor at low prices (and thus to create different diets for the rich and the poor), but they decided instead to institute a rationing system for *all* Cubans, covering the most important food items.

The first item rationed was lard. The neighborhood organizations, known as the Committees for the Defense of the Revolution, were instructed to conduct a "lard census." Based on the census and the total supply of lard, in mid-1961 the government set the maximum amount of lard that any person could buy at one pound per week. In March 1962, the National Board for the Distribution of Foodstuffs was created to ration rice, beans, cooking oil and lard on a nationwide basis; soap, detergent, and toothpaste in the 26 major cities; and beef, chicken, fish, eggs, milk, sweet potatoes, and other root crops in Havana only.[32] All these items were eventually rationed throughout the country, and others were added: sugar, salt, bread, cigars and cigarettes, shoes, clothing, cloth, and numerous household items.[33]

Rationing was initially expected to be temporary. At the first National Production Conference, held when only lard was rationed, optimistic officials gave short shrift to problems. Not only would beef shortages be overcome, they predicted, but within eight years Cuba would be exporting $300 million worth of beef annually.[34] With vast increases in pork, poultry, cattle, and dairy production, there would be "protein to spare" by 1963.[35] In his closing address to the conference, Fidel Castro promised an end to lard rationing by 1963, as well as a quick solution to shortages of chicken, beans, root crops, and fish.[36] In 1965, he predicted that food rationing would end the following year.[37]

Cuban leaders were not alone in their optimistic projections during the early 1960s. French agronomist Rene Dumont, an early adviser to the revolutionary government (and later a strong critic), stressed in September 1960 that "underproduction was such, before the Revolution, that Cuban agriculture cannot but advance, even if errors are still committed." He pointed out that if Cuba were only cultivated with the same intensity as southern China, the island would be able to feed 50 million people, then over seven times Cuba's population. Economist Charles Bettelheim, also a foreign adviser, wrote of Cuba's "absolutely exceptional agricultural possibilities" and noted that "studies made by specialists in agriculture and livestock showed that within a relatively few years (generally from ten to twelve) it will be possible to multiply the production of many commodities by a factor of three, four, five, or even more, without any great investment effort."[38] Such heady optimism emanating from these and other distinguished foreign advisers undoubtedly influenced the Cuban leadership in its conception of rationing as an interim measure.

But everyday reality proved to be far less generous. Rationing, as a way to equitably distribute scarce goods, continues to this day.

CHAPTER 3

The ration card is not only a testimony to scarcity. The Revolution has converted it . . . into a testimony to equality in difficulties.

ADOLFO GILLY, *INSIDE CUBA TODAY* [1]

The ration book—the Cuban consumer's hated little passport to survival.

CHRISTOPHER DICKEY, *WASHINGTON POST* [2]

Living on the *Libreta*

Food rationing is not exclusive to any political system. There are socialist countries without rationing (Hungary, Yugoslavia, East Germany, Bulgaria, and Czechoslovakia, for example) and capitalist countries with rationing. Rationing is found today in countries as different as China, Pakistan, Bangladesh, Burma, Mali, Egypt, Nicaragua, and Poland. There was food rationing in the United States and Europe during the world wars.

But there are vast differences in the various ration systems. One major difference is whom the system includes. Some systems are designed to serve particular groups or sectors. Rationing in Burma and Bangladesh, for example, favors government employees and the military. The Cuban system is the most comprehensive in that it includes everyone regardless of occupation, residence, or income.

Another major difference in ration systems is what is rationed. Most countries pick one or two items (usually the staple grains) to ration. To keep costs down, governments may choose the *least desirable* food so that the rich will "voluntarily eliminate themselves from the program." In fact, a U.S. Agency for International Development study of consumer food price subsidies recommends that governments select a "low-status food, one that is widely consumed by the poor but is not preferred by the relatively wealthy. If several qualities or grades of a food are available, the low quality should be selected."[3] Such programs, while helping to fill the bellies of the poor, reinforce class distinctions.

25

The Cuban system does not select one or two of the least desirable goods to put on the ration, but includes all foods considered essential for an adequate diet. Unlike many countries, it has refused to use rationing as a way of reinforcing distinctions between the diets of the rich and the poor. On the contrary, rationing has been used to close this gap.

How Does Cuba's Ration System Work?

Ration books (*libretas*) are distributed each year by household. Each household chooses the neighborhood store where it wants to shop and then registers with the National Rationing Board (OFICODA) to have its rations sent to that store. The household must continue to buy in the same place. If for some reason the members of a household want to change stores—another shop becomes more convenient, they dislike the grocer—they can go back to the rationing board and reregister elsewhere. A household must also reregister if it moves to another neighborhood, and it must advise the rationing board of any change in household size—through births, deaths, marriages, or whatever—so that its ration may be changed accordingly.

All stores are government-owned. The takeover of private businesses began just after the revolution when, as we mentioned, the government expropriated stores engaged in hoarding and speculation. It later nationalized all stores owned by Americans and those run by Cubans who had fled the country. The expropriation of the remaining 55,600 small private businesses—which accounted for about one-third of retail sales—came as a major part of the 1968 "revolutionary offensive."[4]

Prices for rationed foods remained frozen from the early 1960s, when rationing was introduced, until 1981, when they were modestly raised. But even the new prices are low. Prices are uniform throughout the nation, no matter the size of the store or the distance the goods were transported, so there is no point shopping around for a better deal.

Every member of the household is entitled to a fixed monthly "food basket" consisting mainly of rice, beans, oil, lard, sugar, salt, coffee, meat, and chicken (see Table 1, p. 35), plus a varying supply of fruits and vegetables, depending on availability. Certain groups are entitled to "extras" according to their special needs.

All children under 7, for instance, receive a liter of milk daily; children under 2 also receive twenty jars of strained fruit a month. Those over 65 may buy six cans of evaporated milk a month. Workers in particularly strenuous or hazardous jobs, such as miners, canecutters, and national athletes, are entitled to extra rations. During the harvest canecutters get about five thousand calories in rationed food items, more than twice the normal allotment. Then there are the many special rations (called *dietas*), provided with a doctor's prescription, that allow for the sale of extra food for pregnant women, underweight or lactose-intolerant children, and people suffering from such diseases as ulcers, diabetes, and anemia.

The amounts offered on the ration book have varied over the years, reflecting the country's economic situation. When the rift between Cuba and China led China to renege on rice sales in 1966, the rice ration dropped from six to four pounds per month. It went back up to six pounds in the early 1970s, and in 1976 was cut back to five pounds because of drought and rising import costs. The supply of fruits and vegetables depends on weather conditions: the heavy rainfall in 1983 led to severe flooding which wiped out most of the island's vegetables and cut rations significantly.

An uncritical look at the statistics on Cuban rationing over time can lead to the conclusion that the food situation has deteriorated. Carmelo Mesa-Lago of the University of Pittsburgh, author of a number of books on Cuba, compares 1962 ration figures with 1978–79, finding that in 1978–79, "quotas on fourteen goods were lower, two were the same and only three were higher." He concludes that "rationing in 1978–79 was tougher than in 1962."[5] Statements like this are misleading for two reasons. First, early ration figures were often inflated, since the amounts indicated on the ration were not always available. For a number of years now supplies have generally been sufficient. Second, Mesa-Lago's conclusion ignores the fact that many currently rationed goods are also available off the ration. The canned milk ration, for example, was cut in half, but there is now fresh milk available off the ration. So a decrease in the amount rationed might actually mean an increase in consumption.

Nowadays we must keep in mind that for the vast majority of Cubans the ration supplies only part of the basic diet. The remainder, purchased through nonrationed sources (see Chapter 4), has increased the variety and the quantity of the Cuban diet. A number of important sources of both protein and calories—eggs, spaghetti, fish, and butter—have been "liberated," that is, taken off the ration, and can now be bought in unlimited quantities, mostly at low prices.

A Closer Look

The Garcías are a typical Havana family of five: Jorge and Carmen; their two children, Pablo and Mariana, ages four and one; and Abuela (grandmother). Both Carmen and Jorge work outside the home, earning a combined monthly salary of 368 pesos. Abuela, a retired school teacher, gets a monthly pension of 75 pesos. Abuela takes care of the house and the baby; Pablo is in day care.

All five are on the same ration book. Aside from the basic ration, the children each get a liter of milk a day, the baby gets extra baby food, and Abuela, since she's over 65, is entitled to buy three extra cans of evaporated milk a month. Jorge has a special diet because of his ulcers, which entitles him to two extra chickens a month and a liter of milk every other day.

The Garcías buy their rationed goods in four places: the *bodega*, or grocery store, for the monthly "food basket"; the *carnicería*, or butcher shop, for meat and chicken; the *puesto*, or vegetable stand, for fruits and vegetables in season; and the *lechería*, or dairy store, for bottled milk.

Not only do they shop in four stores, but they often stand in line at each one. This was a serious problem during the 1960s and early 1970s, and women often gave up their jobs so they could queue for food.[6] The lines have shortened over the years, but households with an unemployed adult who has more time for shopping still tend to eat better than those without.

In the García family, Abuela does most of the shopping, especially for the daily items like eggs, milk, bread, fruit, and vegetables. Jorge and Carmen shop for the monthly items since they are the heaviest to carry.

It's now the beginning of May and time to get the new month's ration. If the Garcías have not yet run out of rice, sugar, or lard, which are usually the first to go, they prefer to wait until the second or third day of the month when the *bodega* is less crowded. There seem to be fewer lines, however, now that you can get an advance on your ration a few days before the month begins.

Shopping at the *bodega* would go faster for the Garcías if they were on "*Plan Jaba*" (Shopping Bag Plan). Then they would have a special stamp in their ration book certifying that all the adults in their household were employed and entitling them to stand in a line which is served faster than the normal line. (Three *Plan Jaba* customers are waited on for every one non-*Jaba*.) Since Abuela does not work outside the home, the Garcías do not qualify. *Plan Jaba* was introduced in 1971 to help the increasing number of married women entering the workforce. The original idea was that in families where all the adults worked outside the home, someone could drop off the shopping bag on the way to work and pick it up in the evening filled with the rationed goods. Many variations cropped up, and by the early 1980s the two-line version had become commonplace.

Before walking down the block to the *bodega*, Jorge and Carmen collect everything they need: the ration book, two big straw bags to carry the groceries, two empty bottles for cooking oil, last month's empty baby jars, and a container for lard. The outside of the *bodega* is made of metal sheets which roll up like garage doors, leaving both sides open. Inside, the goods are stacked up on shelves behind the long U-shaped counter. A big sign reading *Venta Libre*, unrestricted sale, separates the rationed from the nonrationed foods. A blackboard lists the items, the amount allocated per person (if rationed) and the price. The only advertisements are posters urging people to save water and electricity and to return all empty bottles lying around the house. There are no brand names and no fancy packaging to catch the eye. It is obvious that the sale of food is not a money-making venture, but a take-it-or-leave-it service.

When the Garcías get to the *bodega* there are six people ahead of them. But lines are not always what they appear to be, for you can mark your place, go away and come back later. As soon as they arrive, Jorge shouts *"el último?"* to find out who is the last person in line and then asks who is next to last in case *el último* disappears.

Lines have become part of the social fabric of Cuban society. They provide an opportunity to meet neighbors, gossip, and discuss local news. Contrary to the Western media's portrait of downtrodden masses stoically waiting for a handout, lines are a lively forum for voicing complaints about poor-quality consumer goods, bad service, and the lines themselves. Today is no exception. Jorge and Carmen walk into a heated debate on the quality of last month's lard. "I've never seen anything like it," grumbles the woman in front of them. "It got all foamy when you heated it and stunk to high heaven." "It was so thin it must have been watered down," contends another. The grocer, overhearing them, breaks in to assure them that this month's lard is fine. So they move on to rice. "I heard the rice is full of bugs. My neighbor said it took her a half hour to clean it." "But at least it's white. Last month's rice had this awful brown tint. I did everything to whiten it; I tried squeezing lemon on it and even washed it in detergent, but nothing worked."

Tomás, the grocer, has worked in the same store for years and knows all his customers well. When the Garcías' turn comes, he asks how the children and Abuela are doing, while mechanically flipping through their ration book to the right month. "The works?" he asks, for one can buy the monthly ration either all at once or bit by bit. "Might as well," replies Carmen, and Tomás begins to gather May's ration for five people and mark it down in their book.

The first item is rice, five pounds per person (the equivalent of ten cups). Tomás scoops twenty-five pounds into paper bags, neatly folding the bags so the rice won't spill. He does the same with the sugar, which is rationed at four pounds each, and the salt, rationed at a half pound each. Then come the beans. The ration calls for twenty ounces of legumes per person. These may turn out to be black beans, kidney beans, pinto beans, split peas, garbanzos, or lentils. You get two different kinds of legumes, depending on availability, with the black and kidney beans the most desired. Split peas are the least popular. This month's ration is half black beans, half split peas. "Hell," groans Jorge, "I've got split peas coming out of my ears. At work we get them every day for lunch." "Just give us the black beans," Carmen tells Tomás. "We still have plenty of split peas from last month, and if Abuela wants more she can always come and get them another time."

"How do you want the fat?" asks Tomás. When there's an ample supply of both lard and oil, you can usually get whatever proportion you want. Abuela prefers lard for frying, but Carmen likes to make potato and macaroni salads and uses the oil to make mayonnaise. "Half and half," they decide. The grocer fills the empty bottles with oil from a big barrel on the counter, then scoops the lard into a metal container.

The next item is canned milk. The children and Jorge, with his special diet, get to buy bottled milk from the *lechería*, so only Carmen and Abuela buy their milk at the *bodega*. Carmen gets the normal monthly ration of three cans, and Abuela gets six, the ration for older adults with their need for more calcium. The milk is neatly stacked on the shelves behind the counter, and Tomás pulls down nine cans. The ration is usually divided equally between evaporated and condensed milk, but for the last few months there's been only condensed milk. As Tomás explains to customers who ask, there's a shortage of evaporated and since that's the milk given to many infants with digestive problems, distribution to the general population must be curtailed.

The coffee ration is four ounces per person per month. Even though the Garcías get a ration for five people while only the three adults actually drink coffee, they still never have enough. They also complain about the quality. They used to get pure coffee but with the government's 1981 decision to increase coffee exports in order to earn more foreign exchange, a 70/30 coffee and chicory mix was substituted. At first, consumers were given a choice, either six ounces of the mixed product or four ounces of pure coffee, but later pure coffee was eliminated and the mixed coffee ration reduced to four ounces. Cubans, notorious coffee addicts, were obviously unhappy with the change, but their displeasure was mitigated by the fact that around the same time more coffee, albeit the mixed type, was made available off the ration, especially in snack bars and restaurants.

The next item is baby food, jars of pureed fruit. The Garcías exchange last month's empty jars for full ones. This month's flavors are guava and banana—ten jars each. The baby's not too keen on guava, but Carmen can usually trade them with the neighbors down the hall whose child hates banana.

Also on the ration are bath soap, laundry soap, detergent, cleaning rags, and toilet paper. Adults born before 1955 get three packs of cigarettes a month and adult males born before 1955 get four cigars. The born-before-1955 proviso was instituted in 1971 when the government decided to discourage smoking by ruling that only those who were over 16 years old at that time would be eligible for rationed cigarettes. Rationed cigarettes are a fifth the price of those sold off the ration.

As with baby foods, the cigarette allotment illustrates the fact that the ration does not cater to individual tastes or habits. One month you may get two packs of filtered cigarettes, one pack of nonfilters, and four cigars. But what if you only like nonfilters? Or what if you smoke only cigars? Or what if you don't smoke at all? Of course you're not obligated to buy any item on the ration. But most Cubans buy everything and then make complicated (often three and fourway) trades with their neighbors until everyone has what he or she wants. In fact, what is essentially a flaw in the system has evolved into an important basis for social interaction.

Next on the list is bread and Carmen selects a one-pound loaf. Officially each person is entitled to a half pound every day, but the Garcías could never eat two and a half pounds a day. With bread so readily available, Tomás does not even mark the bread ration in the book.

From time to time, there are extras on the ration—a jar of mayonnaise, a bottle of cooking wine, a bar of guava paste. And sometimes things are missing. "The tomato paste hasn't come in yet," explains the grocer. "Try next week."

Jorge asks Tomás when he expects to get in more soft drinks. "Don't remind me," he answers, shaking his head. "It's been sheer chaos with the soft drinks ever since they've been taken off the ration. It seems like people start lining up before the truck even gets here. The last shipment disappeared in two hours. Then when people got home from work and found the empties piled up, they were up in arms." "It's not fair," says Jorge. "Some people buy up four or five cases and others are left empty-handed. At least when they were on the ration everyone was guaranteed a case." "Bring it up at the next People's Power meeting," suggests Tomás. "You'll get plenty of support, that's for sure."

Carmen reminds Tomás that Pablo will be five years old next month. There is a special allotment of cakes, soft drinks, and beer (for the adults) on children's birthdays, *los quince* for girls (the equivalent of our "sweet sixteen," at fifteen) and weddings. "I hope we don't have trouble getting the soft drinks for Pablo's party," says Carmen. "Don't worry," assures Tomás. "Soda for *fiestas* gets top priority. I'll put in the order now so it'll be sure to come on time."

Tomás lines up all the items on the counter, jots down the prices on an empty paper bag and adds them up in his head: 25.20 pesos. Carmen pays, and they load the goods into their straw shopping bags and cart them home.

The *carnicería* is right across the street from the *bodega*. The butcher shop's only equipment consists of an old meat-grinder, a refrigerator, a cutting board, two knives, and a sharpening stone. The refrigerator dates back to the 1950s and is constantly on the blink, when sales are temporarily switched to the fish store down the block.

Abuela used to shop for the meat, until she got into a fight with the butcher for shortweighing her. So now Carmen goes. "If there's anyone you have to humor, it's the butcher," she laughs. "If you're on his bad side or he thinks he can rook you, he'll pawn off the worst cuts or clip off a few ounces here and there. So I bring him a sip of hot coffee now and then and we get along just fine," she winks.

Butchers are notorious for cheating their customers. By snipping an ounce of meat from each household's ration and selling it on the black market at 8 pesos a pound, a butcher could easily double his salary. Another trick is to trim second-class meat and sell it as first class, pocketing the extra 11 cents a pound, plus winding up with more first-class meat to sell on the black market. At People's Power meetings, many butchers have been accused of cheating and subsequently removed after investigation. Increased vigilance from both government inspectors and consumers has also helped keep them in line.

In Havana, meat is distributed every nine days. To reduce lines, customers are divided into two groups to buy on different days. But when the meat comes in late, as it did this week, both groups buy at the same time and long lines are inevitable. Carmen was at work when she heard the meat had come in and decided to use her lunch break to go pick it up.

She took her place at the end of the line and struck up a conversation with the woman in front of her. "This line doesn't move," the woman complained. "I've already been here fifteen minutes and only two people have been served. And then these women with *Plan Jaba* come in and push ahead of everyone. *Plan Jaba*'s supposed to be for families in which everyone works. And if they're really working, what are they doing in line in the middle of the day?" Carmen blushed. "I'm working, but I'm on my lunch break. Although I can see I'll never be back in time. Maybe I better go and come back later." "*¡Que va!*," exclaimed the woman. "Later, when everyone gets out of work, it'll be only worse. If you want, I'll save your place for you and you can come back in a half hour." When Carmen returned a half hour later, she still had to wait fifteen minutes before being served.

The meat ration in Havana is seven ounces of "first class" beef (which is usually thin steaks) and five ounces of "second class" (which can be chopped meat, stewing meat or sausage) every nine days. Chicken is often substituted for beef, in which case you get one pound. Occasionally there are other choices, such as smoked ham, ham hocks, liver, and canned meat. There is less variety in isolated rural areas, where often the only rationed meat is the unpopular canned meat.

Today there is beef, which Carmen prefers to chicken because "*rinde más*," it goes farther. Chicken is really only good for two meals, while you can get three meals out of the beef. Also, chicken is easier to get off the ration than beef is, although it's much more expensive that way. (Since 1980, you can often get live chicken on the nonrationed market, or you can always buy fried chicken for two pesos per portion from the restaurant chain *Pio-Pio* [Peep Peep], Colonel Sanders' Cuban cousin. Only since 1983 has fresh beef been sold off the ration and even then at high prices and only in a few stores. Thin steaks in restaurants cost at least 5 or 6 pesos.)

The butcher prepares the ration for five people—2 lbs. 3 oz. of first-class meat, 1 lb. 9 oz. of second class. "I'll give you some nice steaks," he tells Carmen, slicing the first-class meat into thin layers." "Make sure you don't give me any of that gristle," Carmen warns. "And cut the steaks thinner so we get more."

The "second class" meat is either chopped beef or stewing meat. Carmen chooses chopped meat because the children like it better. The butcher wraps the meats together in brown paper. Carmen pays, stuffs the package into her shopping bag, and rushes back to work.

TABLE 1 Monthly Ration for One Adult (1983)

ITEM	QUANTITY (one person)	PRICE/LB (pesos)	PRICE (pesos)
rice	5 lb.	0.24	1.20
beans	20 oz.	0.24	0.30
oil	8 oz.	0.40	0.20
lard	1 lb.	0.30	0.30
sugar (refined)[a]	4 lb.	0.14	0.56
milk[b]	3 cans	0.30/can	0.90
coffee	4 oz.	0.96	0.24
meat[cd]: beef	1 lb. 4 oz.	0.65	0.81
chicken	1 lb. 11 oz.	0.70	1.18
tomato sauce	1 can	0.25/can	.025
salt	8 oz.	0.03	0.02
bath soap	1 bar	0.25/bar	0.25
laundry soap	1 bar	0.20/bar	0.20
detergent	7 oz.	0.60	0.26
cigarettes	3 packs	0.30/pack	0.90
cigars	4 (per male adult)	0.15/ea.	0.60
bread	15 lb.	0.15	2.25
		Subtotal:	**10.42 pesos**

Other allocations

Fruits and vegetables (a typical sample)

potatoes	6 lb.	0.12	0.72
oranges	1 lb.	0.08	0.08
tomatoes	3 lb.	0.20	0.60
		Subtotal:	**1.40 pesos**
		TOTAL:	**11.82 pesos**

(a) In the central provinces, where fewer processed foods are available, an extra pound of sugar is distributed.

(b) Figures represent average adult ration; children under 7 years old get an additional liter of bottled milk/day at 25 centavos per liter. People over 65 get six cans/month.

(c) Distributed every nine days (either 12 oz. beef or 1 lb. chicken). Figures determined through following calculations: 1) Total annual number of meat rations is 40.5 (365/9); 2) There are twenty full rations each of beef and chicken annually assuming an equal division of the two (40.5/2); 3) Total annual beef ration is 240 oz./yr. (12 oz. ration × 20 rations/yr.); total annual chicken ration is 320 oz./yr. (16 oz. ration × 20 rations/yr.); 4) Monthly beef ration is 1 lb. 4 oz. (240 oz./12 mo.); monthly chicken ration is 1 lb. 11 oz. (320 oz./12 mo.).

(d) The meat ration in rural areas is slightly lower because there is more nonrationed meat available.

At the *puesto*, the fruits and vegetables for sale are stored in bins both in front of and behind the counter. Fresh produce is the most variable part of the ration. Some months there may be lots of tomatoes, potatoes, and peppers, and other months none. Like the *bodega*, the *puesto* sells both rationed and nonrationed goods, and there is a blackboard indicating the items available, the amount and price. The same item may be on the ration one day and off the next. Take potatoes. They may be delivered on Wednesday and put on the ration at two pounds per person. By Saturday, when everyone has had ample time to buy the rationed amount, the remaining potatoes are sold *por la libre*, that is, without restriction. Part of the reason is to get rid of the goods fast, for the *puestos* have no refrigeration facilities and produce not sold immediately often rots in the tropical climate.

Today Abuela finds there are bananas (one pound per person) and potatoes (two pounds per person) on the ration, and watercress, carrots, and beets *por la libre*. Since she had the baby with her, Abuela decided to shop in the late morning, when the lines are shortest. Lines at the *puesto* can be the worst of all, especially when scarce and very popular items like onions or garlic come in. But today only a handful of people are ahead of her.

The other people in line "ooh" and "aah" at Abuela's granddaughter, and the woman behind the counter, Clara, gives the baby a banana to eat. When Abuela's turn comes, she tells Clara to give her only big potatoes. "When you're done peeling those tiny ones, there's nothing left," she complains; she watches closely as Clara throws the potatoes onto the scale, picking off the little or rotten ones. When she reaches ten pounds, Clara tilts the scale so the potatoes go rolling into Abuela's straw bag. Then she goes for the bananas. "I'll find you a good bunch, Abuela," assures Clara, rummaging through the scrawny bananas until she comes across a decent-sized bunch. "I know how that little granddaughter of yours likes bananas." She carefully measures out the family's ration and, winking at Abuela, throws in a few extra for the baby.

For the Garcías, the basic ration costs 45.50 pesos a month, or 10 percent of their income. Adding the special rations they get for the children and Jorge's ulcer, they spend 67.25 pesos or 15 percent of their income on the ration.

The Garcías represent a mainstream Cuban household. But what about families at the bottom of the income ladder? A retired person living on a monthly pension of 65 pesos would spend 18 percent on the ration. For a family of five with only one wage earner making the minimum wage, the ration would eat up about 60 percent of its monthly income. This is indeed a hefty sum, especially considering that the ration must be supplemented by nonrationed food for an adequate diet. But this family would be below the Cuban poverty line of 25 pesos per person per month and would be eligible for social assistance. Given the low cost of other basic needs—housing, health care, education—virtually everyone can afford to buy the ration.

Generally the ration does not last the whole month. How long it lasts depends on the individual household, since the basic ration is the same for all. A two-day-old baby gets the same ration as a six-foot, twenty-five-year-old laborer. Of course, the infant's rice ration will not be put into storage until the baby grows up, but will be thrown into the family pot, so that the ration stretches further in households with small children. In households in which one or more members study or work away from home, the family continues to receive their rations. For these families, the ration is plentiful.

The ration is also sufficient for those who eat out often or rely heavily on alternative sources of food (see Chapter 4). But for families which depend on the ration for the bulk of their food supply, the last part of the month means slim pickings. "How can one person possibly live on just four pounds of sugar per month?" the wife of a small farmer asked us. "And if you had to make lunch and dinner for a whole month, how could you get by on the salt ration? And as for rice, we Cubans generally eat a quarter-pound each meal, so five pounds lasts only twenty days!"

How long the ration lasts also depends on how well meals are planned. Oscar Lewis, in his 1969 study of Cuban families, found that running out of food before the end of the month was a special problem for those Cubans who before the revolution only had enough money to shop a day at a time. For these families, lack of experience in food planning made it difficult to acquire shopping habits compatible with the rationing system.[7]

But as more and more food has been made available off the

ration, the *libreta* has begun to play a lesser role in the Cuban diet. In the following chapter we explore what additional sources of food Cubans have.

CHAPTER 4

*The dinner line forms early in the courtyard of the graceful
Spanish mansion that now houses La Verge, the most elegant
restaurant of Cienfuegos.... After one or two squabbles over who
arrives first, the doors open at 7 and dozens of workers from the
city docks, from the new cement and fertilizer factories, and from
government offices... are formally escorted by the tuxedoed
headwaiter to linen-draped tables. A three-piece combo tunes up
for dinner music.*

*Suddenly waiters burst from the kitchen with trays of huge, meaty
hamhocks, a delicacy known here as lacon natural. Just as quickly
from the patrons' pockets come plastic bags, and waiters help
parents, grandparents, and kids shovel the hamhocks off the white
East German china and into the bags. Within minutes, two-thirds
of the patrons have left.*

JONATHAN KWITNY, *WALL STREET JOURNAL*, December 21, 1983

Cuba à la Carte

During a couple of difficult periods in the first decade of the revolution, rations on the *libreta* represented virtually all the food available to Cubans. As one top Cuban planner said, "We're not ashamed to admit it: there were years when we had to live on the ration alone, and there was practically nothing in the cafeterias and restaurants. Those were years when we really went hungry."[1]

But the situation has changed radically since the 1970s. People can now obtain food off the ration in a variety of ways. One is by buying on the state-run "parallel market." Another is eating out at restaurants and snack bars, or cafeterias at school and work. And there are some alternatives which have been around since the toughest times in the 1960s: Cubans can purchase food directly from farmers (see Chapter 5), they can deal on the gray and black markets, or they can grow it themselves.

The Parallel Market

Since the late 1970s, there has been a substantial increase in the number of nonrationed foods.[2] The most important items "liberated" from the ration have been staples such as bread, eggs, fish, spaghetti, and butter. The supply of these staples has become sufficient to meet demand, and they are generally inexpensive. Seasonal fruits and vegetables can be purchased in unlimited quantities at relatively low prices as long as supplies last. Less desired vegetables, such as cucumbers, beets, carrots, and eggplants, are sold without restriction, often at such absurdly low prices as 1 or 2 centavos a pound. More desired ones, such as bell peppers, are rationed only before the season is in full swing and the market is flooded. Other goods may be on the ration one day, off the next.

Some foods are available at the same time on both the ration and the so-called parallel market. The critical difference between the two markets is price. A liter of milk, for example, costs 25 centavos on the ration and 80 centavos off the ration. Rationed vegetable oil sells for 40 centavos a liter; unrationed Spanish olive oil for 20 pesos a liter. The two-ounce package of coffee sold on the ration for 30 centavos goes for 3 pesos—ten times more—off the ration. In general, you can purchase all you want on the parallel market—if you can afford it.

There are some luxury foods which are never sold on the ration, but are available on the parallel market at high, sometimes exorbitant, prices. Some examples include canned peaches and apricot jam from Bulgaria, Spanish olives, and Cuban-made Camembert cheese. Cuban rum is also treated as a luxury and priced high to discourage local consumption and increase exports. (A quart of "Havana Club" export-quality rum was put on the domestic market in 1983 for the equivalent of five times the average daily wage.) During holiday seasons, however, lower quality rum is sold at a more affordable price. In short, while the ration furnishes staples, nonrationed foods often afford Cubans the "spice of life."

Where do Cubans buy nonrationed foods? In large measure, they are sold at the same stores as rationed goods. In following the García as they purchased their monthly rations, we saw that the grocery store, the milk store, and the vegetable stand all had sections labeled *venta libre*, unrestricted sale. Nonrationed goods are also sold in any of the few dozen formerly U.S.-owned supermarkets. Since the beginning of the revolution, new supermarkets have been built exclusively to sell nonrationed goods. Bakeries offer a variety of nonrationed breads and sweets. In addition, you can buy fresh fish off the ration at the fourteen hundred fish stores all over the island. Some fruits and vegetables can be purchased without restrictions and at fairly low prices at government produce markets called *ferias del agro*. But the quality is often poor. Private farmers' markets (see Chapter 5) were opened in 1980 in part to improve the quantity and quality of produce available off the ration. And starting in 1983, the government reopened Havana's old marketplace, the old Sears store, and smaller new stores (*mercaditos*) around the country to sell nonrationed foods.

There are also special stores for foreign diplomats and technicians. Visiting the grocery division of one such store, we found not only many imported items (including a full range of packaged and canned goods from the Cincinnati-based supermarket giant, Kroger's), but also vegetables, fresh and canned meats, and dairy products (including aged cheeses) produced in Cuba and rarely, if ever, sold elsewhere. These "*diplotiendas*" and "*tecnotiendas*" sell only to foreigners, and the imported goods are sold only for dollar-convertible currencies (thereby excluding most Soviets and Eastern Europeans.). Nonetheless, part of the food sold through these stores trickles down to some Cubans through friends and through resale on the black market.

Unlike rationed foods, the availability of which has been reliable for years, many nonrationed foods come and go. Spaghetti may be in the store one day but gone the next. Canned peaches may be available at one store or in one part of the country and not another. So keeping abreast of what is available, and where, has turned into something of a national pastime. Someone rushes into your workplace and announces that the store at the corner is selling packages of processed cheese for a peso; someone else volunteers to take orders, collect the money, and stand in line for everyone. Your neighbor comes home from work and the first thing she does is knock on your door to let you know that the supermarket down the block is selling chocolate cookies. You see someone walking down the street carrying boxes of saltines. Before you even get a chance to ask, he points down the street and says, "The store on Aguilar and Peñá Pobre."

When Bulgarian stuffed peppers first appeared in Havana in 1980, everyone rushed off to buy as many cans as he or she could afford. The shelves were emptied in a week. Relatives in the countryside sent urgent requests to forward cans of the peppers. When the dust settled, the national consensus was "they're OK but nothing great." Novelty over, in 1982 we found Bulgarian stuffed peppers stacked up in eight different places in the same Havana supermarket.

Growing Your Own

Another way to obtain food, of course, is to grow it yourself. But in Cuban cities, little food is grown. Urban Cubans seem to feel it is the government's job to provide food: to them, urban vegetable gardens smack of underdevelopment. "When I suggested to government planners of a new town that space between apartment buildings be set aside for vegetable gardens, they looked at me like I was a Martian," an American consultant to the Cuban construction ministry told us.

Hence, while flower gardens are common in Cuban cities, vegetable gardens are not. We have been told that, by law, flowers may be planted in front of a city dwelling, but nonornamental plants are permissible only in backyard patios away from public view. In the cities, fruit trees and, to a lesser extent, cages with small animals such as rabbits can be found, but only in the privacy of the backyard.

In the countryside, in contrast, much of the food eaten is home-produced. Since the early 1980s, state farms have set aside land for self-provisioning. These areas are farmed collectively as part of the ordinary work day. The produce is used in the workers' lunchroom and any surplus is sold to the workers, often at low prices. On one state root-crop farm we visited in November 1983, the self-provisioning area was producing everything from rice to garlic to chickens. By the end of 1983, half the state farms had such self-provisioning areas[3] and it had been decided to spread the practice to every state farm. A United Nations agronomist told us of his 1983 visit to a large state banana plantation where three thousand hogs were being raised for the consumption of the workers and their families. On several occasions pork was sold to the plantation's employees for only 40 centavos a pound, in sharp contrast to the 4.50 pesos a pound in the stores.

For more and more workers on state farms, as well as small farmers and cooperative members, the ration is often only a supplement to what they produce for themselves. Some rural families apparently buy their monthly rations, keep the cigarettes and refined sugar they cannot produce themselves, and sell the rest to the *acopio*, the government crop-purchasing agency, at a profit.

In other cases, we found members of rural families registering their names on the ration book of urban relatives with fewer food alternatives, rather than in their own households.[1] Similarly, there is a flow of goods to the city via weekend trips to country relatives or care packages sent by mail or messenger. In exchange, city folk send their rural relatives processed foods in short supply in the countryside, such as cookies and crackers, hard candy, and certain canned goods.

But it's not all in the family. Many city dwellers have cultivated "contacts" in the countryside, a practice of uncertain legality. One official assured us that it has always been perfectly legal to buy from private farmers, provided the sale is less than 25 pounds at a time and not for resale. But another official told us that as of 1982 all direct purchases from the farmer are prohibited. Before 1982, he continued, there was no blanket 25-pound maximum but purchase limit depended on the item: for example, 25 pounds for *viandas* but only 1 pound for garlic. No wonder the Cuban people themselves seem confused on this issue!

The Black–and Gray–Market

The black market and what we call the "gray market" are other important means of food distribution in Cuba. Trading goods obtained through the ration is a good example of the gray market in action. We saw that the Garcías traded baby-food rations with a neighbor because their child disliked that month's flavor. They also traded their excess milk for another neighbor's sugar. These kinds of trades go on everyday in Cuba and are really an unofficial way of adjusting for the fact that the ration allots a standard amount for everyone, regardless of individual tastes and needs.

Here is another example of a gray-market transaction. A retired man living on a small pension has a couple of mango trees in his backyard. The trees produce more mangoes than his family can consume. To make a little extra money, he peddles mangoes in the neighborhood. Gray-market transactions like this are technically illegal, but for a number of years they have not been prosecuted.

Black-market deals, on the other hand, often involve goods

stolen from government sources and then resold. Such sales are obviously illegal but are only sporadically prosecuted. We have already seen how butchers can shortweigh their customers and then sell the extra meat on the black market. Not surprisingly, black market prices are high. Chicken can fetch 3 pesos a pound and beef up to 8.[5] An administrator of a snack bar can snip a little cheese from the sandwiches and sell it on the side for about 4 pesos a pound.

Black-market transactions also include goods which are obtained legally by the seller but sold illegally. An important example is the private sale of coffee by coffee farmers. Since coffee is a valuable export crop and production is scant, it is illegal for producers to sell their "black gold" privately. But many Cubans contend that black-market coffee is a necessity for genuine caffeine addicts who could never reduce their consumption to the ounce-a-week ration. Rumors have it that during one crackdown in the mountainous coffee-growing region, police prowled about sniffing the air for the aroma of roasting coffee beans, a sure sign of black-market coffee since state-sold coffee comes roasted. Black marketeers reportedly concocted ingenious contraptions to snuff out the smell of roasting coffee, such as a pressure cooker with a rubber hose attached to divert the vapors into a covered jar. They also fabricated double-bottom containers to transport the coffee. Since 1983, when the state began selling coffee off the ration, the black market in coffee has been curtailed but not eliminated.

The difference between black market and gray market is not always clear. Take the example of trading rationed foods. Suppose that instead of trading them you resold them at a higher price? Or suppose that the retired man selling mangoes exhausted his own supply and started buying up fruit from others and reselling it? Or suppose a city dweller making trips to the countryside started buying larger quantities than his family required and sold the remainder to a few friends in his building? As you can see, there are many shades of gray.

And what about the buyers? Do Cubans know whether the goods they're buying are obtained through legal channels? Do they care? Let's look at Carmen and Jorge García again. Every week or so they receive a visit from an old woman who treks from door to door with a big shopping bag full of fruit. As soon as the children spot her, they run to tell their parents that the "guava lady" is coming. She knocks on the door and quickly slips into the house. They greet her as a friend and offer her a sip of coffee or a cold drink. She opens the shopping bag, takes off the towel concealing the fruit and shows what she has to offer today. Carmen and Jorge aren't sure where she gets the fruit. From her own garden? But it's an awfully big supply for one garden! They prefer not to ask. Her prices are high, but they buy from her anyway. Fruit is hard to get in the stores.

A few weeks ago Carmen was approached by another fruit seller. He was a young man standing on a street corner in the old part of town, whispering to passersby: "Guavas, five for a peso." She took a look out of curiosity, for it is not common to find someone selling on the street like that. He kept the guavas hidden in a doorway and ran to get a handful to show her. Unlike the "guava lady's" guavas, which were an assortment of different shapes, sizes and degrees of ripeness, these guavas were all uniform. They looked delicious, and she knew the kids would love them; but she was sure they were export quality and therefore stolen from the state. She refused to buy them.

Buying black-market goods is always a question of conscience. Many supporters of the revolution justify their black-market purchases by such arguments as "Everyone else does it," or "Even Ramón buys black market coffee, and he's in the Party." So you get ironic situations: the woman who participates in her street's Committee for the Defense of the Revolution, and spends her weekends practicing in the militia or volunteering to work in the countryside, but buys black-market chicken from the butcher, knowing that it comes from shortweighing her neighbors and probably her own family as well. The black-market forces Cubans to live by a double standard, and this is probably its most pernicious effect. The government's response since the late 1970s has been to make more nonrationed food available through legal channels, and this has effectively reduced the importance of black market foods.[6]

Eating Out: At Work and School

In 1982, over two million Cubans—one-fifth of the population— ate at least one hot meal a day in cafeterias at schools, work centers, and hospitals. (At hospitals, meals are served not only to the patients but to those accompanying them, such as the parents of hospitalized children.)[7]

Somewhat less than half of Cuba's workforce, or 1.3 million people, eat in *comedores obreros*, or workers' cafeterias. Midmorning and midafternoon *merienda* is served. This snack, particularly welcome in the morning in a land with a tradition of little or no breakfast, is usually something sweet—pastry, cake, or pie—and perhaps a soft drink or heavily sugared yogurt. Lunch is always a hot meal, the typical fare rice, split peas or beans, eggs or fish, a starchy vegetable, and dessert.

Food at the *comedores* was free until the mid-1970s, when a flat charge of 50 centavos a meal was introduced, considerably less than a comparable meal in a restaurant. Workers living far away without the choice of eating at home were exempted from the charge. In addition, individual workplaces often exempt those with very low incomes. Teachers in one school we visited told us how their union, after reviewing the situation of the poorest workers, unanimously agreed that five of them should not have to pay for meals. They presented the proposal to the school director who balked at first, but then gave in. Although a tight budget is important in today's Cuba, the "right to eat" ethic still wins out.

The quality of the food has been another bone of contention. Workers complain that their meals are tasteless and monotonous. Split peas, a lunchroom mainstay, are universally vilified. Government officials estimated in 1980 that one-third of the food served was left on the plates.[8] Even President Castro officially noted the need to improve the quality of food in the cafeterias.[9]

The waste problem used to be exacerbated by the system of selling meal cards on a monthly basis only. If you missed a meal one day, you ended up paying for it anyway. Beginning in 1982, a new system called the "optional plan" caught on fast. By late 1983, according to government figures, 86 percent of workplace meals (and even some in school cafeterias) were served under this plan. Each day the menu for the following day is displayed at the canteen, with all items listed a la carte. You purchase your ticket for the following day's meal, paying only for the items you select. This new method has cut down on waste, and every worker with whom we have spoken prefers it.

A more politically sensitive problem is that the *comedores* appear to have their share of corrupt administrators. One worker recalled how her cafeteria manager had once helped himself to most of the ham for the day's lunch before it got to the kitchen. The cook saved the day by proclaiming the day's meal to be soup, using the bare hambone for stock. The status of the work center also makes a difference. Centers connected with Communist Party committees, the military, and the police have a reputation for better food, more meat, better preparation, and more attractive dining rooms. State farms and cooperatives also appear to serve meals a cut above those at the typical urban *comedor*. This is not surprising given the new policy that every state farm produce more of its own food.

Comedores are also part of the school scene. Over one hundred thousand Cuban children between the ages of 45 days and five years attend day-care centers where they receive two hot meals a day plus two snacks.[10] The conviction that "there's nothing more important than a child" is evident in the food allocated to the day-care centers. When there's no fruit juice in the stores, you can bet the children will still be getting it; if there's a shortage of beans, the day-care centers have priority. The meals are adapted to the needs of the different age groups. A typical menu for children aged three to four would be fruit juice for morning and afternoon snacks; rice, chopped meat, crackers, vanilla custard and milk for lunch; and spaghetti, chicken, jello, crackers, milk, and water for dinner before going home. The charge for day-care meals is included in the minimal monthly fee. For day care from 7 a.m. to 7 p.m. Monday through Friday and every other Saturday, a family pays from three to forty pesos, depending on the combined income of the parents. The government calculates the true cost to be 70 pesos a month.

Over 518,000 boarding school students (mostly at junior high schools in the countryside) get all their meals free—Sunday evening through Friday—while their families continue to collect their rations, except for meat.[11] Most other students have half-day sessions and therefore get a morning or afternoon snack but no hot meals. In addition, junior high school students in the cities go to work in the countryside for 45 days a year, with all their meals and snacks provided by the government.

Eating Out: Restaurants

Aside from workplace and school cafeterias, Cubans can eat at
a wide variety of snack bars, cafeterias, and restaurants. Since
1968, all restaurants have been publicly owned and are operated
by municipal governments, and prices for the same dishes are
identical in the same category restaurant. Eating out in Cuba is
important because it not only supplements the ration and adds
variety to the diet, but also because it enhances people's sense of
well-being. The choices available today range from "fast food"
pizza and fried-chicken chains—excruciatingly slow by American standards—to deluxe dining with tuxedoed waiters, extensive wine lists, and prices to match.

But restaurant variety cannot compare with prerevolution
Cuba, which travel writer Sydney Clark called "a treat for epi-
cures."[12] Today, Cuba offers little variety. (Sample menu below.)
The only ethnic restaurants are several Chinese (with three or
four Chinese dishes), one Russian restaurant in Havana, one Bulgarian (with a menu more Cuban than Bulgarian), a few Italian
restaurants (rather like glorified pizzerias), and one Arab restaurant in the touristy Escaleras de Jaruco. The Little Rabbit spe-
cializes in rabbit, and the Little Pig in pork. But the restaurants
Cubans themselves seem to prefer are those serving traditional
Cuban food.

Cubans often go to restaurants to stock up on foods unavailable elsewhere. Three chicken dinners taken from a restaurant
may provide the basis for a week's worth of meals at home. Since
there is no official "take-out" service, Cubans engage in a ritu-
alized charade: while everyone knows the lone woman ordering
the three chicken dinners will be taking them home, the table is
set for her, complete with a glass of water, bread, and butter.
After the food is served and the waiter turns away, the woman
furtively scoops the food into plastic bags and stashes them in
her purse. The practice is so common that a "*nylon*" (plastic
bag) is a must in every Cuban woman's purse.

Service in Cuban restaurants is generally perfunctory and slow,
especially on weekends or the last days of the month when rationed foods are running out. Cubans seem to have more pa-
tience with the long wait for service once seated than they do
for the lines to get into restaurants. The lines can be particularly

LUNCH AND DINNER MENU

La Carreta, a "Category Two" restaurant in Havana (November 1983)

Cocktail: fish in mayonnaise .... 1.80 pesos
Sardines in oil 1.00

Fish soup 1.00
Bean soup (*potaje*) 1.00

Egg omelette, plain 1.00
Omelette, with sardines 2.00
Omelette, with onions 2.00
Omelette, with peas 2.00
Omelette, with fish 2.00
Omelette, with potatoes 2.00
Scrambled eggs 1.00
Scrambled eggs, with fish 2.00

Ham steak 5.00
Ground beef (*picadillo*) 4.00
Hamburger 4.00
Meatballs 3.50

Rice 0.80
Rice and beans (*moros y cristianos*) 1.20
Fried sweet potato 0.80

Caramel custard 0.60
Guava paste with cheese 0.60
Bread pudding 0.70
Flan 0.80

Coffee 0.20

Beer * 0.80

Bread and butter are extra.

---

*Plus a list of rum-based alcoholic drinks (such as "Tom Collins"), ranging from 1.50 to 3.00 pesos.

galling when you peer in the window and see that several tables are empty and some waiters are standing around with their arms folded.

For some years the government has been trying to combat poor service and management in restaurants. President Castro himself has made recommendations aimed at improving the "services, quality, hygiene, and treatment of the public" and called for specialized training for restaurant employees.[13] Cubans should pay only for what they get, Fidel advised. If the ham and cheese sandwich comes without cheese, something should be knocked off the price. In the late 1970s, restaurants were ordered to become self-financing, which meant that they had to do more business to get out of the red. Hotel restaurants, previously reserved for guests only, were opened to the general public. As in many other sectors, the government tried to boost worker productivity by linking salaries to a minimal output (a certain amount of gross receipts in the case of restaurants), with a system of bonuses for surpassing the minimum.

When the system was first introduced, the effects were perceptible. Some restaurants started trying to expand business by offering midmorning and midafternoon *merienda*, putting employees on the sidewalk to woo customers in for a snack. In Santiago one Saturday morning in January 1982, we even saw workers setting up stands to sell cookies in front of their restaurants. In subsequent visits to Cuba things seem to us to have settled back into the same slow groove. We observed, however, that many restaurants have begun to include on their menus a note to the customer inviting any criticisms to be written on the back of the bill and that menus are now more up-to-date on what is actually available in the kitchen.

Another serious problem plaguing restaurants and services in general is corruption. President Castro talked openly about corruption in a 1982 speech to small farmers.[14] He spoke of the administrator of a bar who, instead of giving 30 shots per bottle of rum, stretches it to 35; of the administrator of an ice-cream parlor who got 60 instead of 50 scoops out of every container, making three to four hundred extra pesos a day for himself.

"We can't allow anyone to steal ice cream from a child," said Castro, "or even a shot of liquor from a drunk. Why should they rob a poor drunk?" He put part of the blame on the government for having "put the church in the hands of the devil." By that he meant that work in hotels and restaurants was not considered high priority, so the Ministry of Labor would send the better workers elsewhere. Wages were low, and workers were often people who could not get a job elsewhere. Castro said an alarming percentage of them had criminal records and that the recruiting system had to be completely changed. He asked retired workers to come back to work and agreed to pay them their full pensions in addition to their wages. "We must find a way to recruit honest people for our hotels, restaurants, services and stores in general," he concluded.

And what about the traditional method of obtaining better service in a restaurant—tipping? Around the world it has been heard that the Cuban Revolution abolished tipping. A 1983 travel brochure written for North American tourists claimed that "tipping in Cuba is not allowed." We brought up the matter with workers in restaurants we visited. In one restaurant, the headwaiter informed us that he did not approve of tipping, for good service should come spontaneously without any hint of monetary motive. Later we shared what the headwaiter said with our waitress. "That's what *he* says!" was her instant response. Needless to say, we left a tip.

Who eats out? Let's take a look at the Garcías again. Before they had children, Carmen and Jorge used to eat at a nice restaurant about once a week. Living with in-laws, as most young couples do, they cherished evening meals out as moments of privacy. Besides, with two incomes and few expenses, they could afford to splurge on meals; in fact, they reserved Carmen's entire salary for that purpose. But now, with two children, they have less time for leisurely meals and less money to spend. Restaurant meals are reserved for special occasions, although they do go out for pizza or fried chicken once a week, especially towards the end of the month when the ration is running thin. On Sundays they take the children out for ice cream.

We got some notion of the "regulars" in restaurants by eating many times in the same Havana restaurants, such as "The Warsaw" (not a Polish item on the menu!), a second-class establishment on the ground floor of our modest hotel. (A full meal with a beer cost at least 8 pesos per person, just about the average day's wage.) Especially at midday, there are the "survivors." These are invariably white-haired ladies in flower-pattern dresses, wearing 1950s-style jewelry. They are surely among the highest-income Cubans, for they receive up to 500 pesos a month for life as compensation for property expropriated early in the revolution. With time to kill and little else to spend their pesos on, they eat out in table-clothed restaurants almost daily. These restaurants are also frequented by military officers, who earn relatively high salaries. In addition, Havana restaurants are favorite spots for families from the provinces—and here the social range can be quite great—who are taking their annual vacation in the big city.

Ice Cream

One of the favorite hangouts in every Cuban city is the ice-cream chain Coppelia. Before the revolution ice cream was imported from Florida, with Howard Johnson's 28 Flavors the prestige brand. Fidel Castro committed the revolution to outdo Howard Johnson's by churning out at least 29 flavors, ranging from vanilla to tropical fruits and even wheat. The ice cream is creamy rich and the flavorings, often imported, are generally of high quality. Cuban ice cream is one of the few commercially prepared and readily available food items which elicits raves from foreign visitors. Coppelia's flagship is an agreeable open-air location in the heart of modern Havana that can accommodate several hundred people at a time, and generally does, from its midmorning opening until its 1:45 a.m. closing. On weekends, the lines are long but fast-moving. In addition to its branches in every city, Coppelia's ice cream is found in restaurants and even in some rural areas. The hallmark of a truly prosperous farm cooperative is its own "Coppelita."

In addition to Coppelia, Cuba also has its version of Dairy Queen, selling soft ice cream called "*frozen*" (with a Cuban accent), as well as a Cuban "Good Humor" truck which sells ice cream by the pint rather than the stick (but devoured just as quickly). Ice cream is one of the few foods sold by street vendors, who are employed by the state.

Street Food

While Cuba is now a society of people on the run, eating still goes on at a snail's pace. There are no places to "grab a bite to eat." Eating out is time-consuming, except at odd hours. At home, it's hard to whip up a quick meal, since the traditional rice and beans take hours to make. Before the revolution Cuba, like most Latin American countries today, was full of street vendors selling quick meals and snacks. But the 1968 "revolutionary offensive" ban on all private selling took the vendors off the streets. Some people continued clandestinely making food at home for sale, but supplies were so limited that most of the ingredients had to be bought on the black market. This drove up the prices and made the activity illegal on two counts.

Food vendors began to blossom again in the late 1970s, when more goods became available off the ration and the entre-preneurial spirit seemed to be encouraged. In 1980, we met a woman on maternity leave who decided to use her "spare time" making ham and fish croquettes. The business took off, and soon she could hardly keep up with demand. She had started selling to people at the school across the street, and before long everyone was buying her croquettes instead of the ones made in the school cafeteria. ("A sawdust-like food looking and tasting like rope," is how a foreign journalist resident in Cuba described the cro-quettes sold in Cuban cafeterias.)

"My croquettes were twice as expensive, but no one cared because they were so much better," she told us. "I used real butter and good ham." When we asked her if what she was doing was legal, she just shrugged her shoulders and laughed. *"Quién sabe?"* (Who knows?) The irony is that this woman, before going on maternity leave, had worked as an assistant teacher in the same school, earning 135 pesos a month. Now she earned three times as much, made her own hours, and could stay home and take care of the baby at the same time.

It is precisely this irony which makes the government wary of such private activity. While it provides an essential service that the state has not been able to provide, it is so profitable that it encourages people to leave jobs which are seen as more socially productive. It also contradicts the socialist principle of "to each according to his or her work," for the profits to be made are far in excess of the work involved. When we visited this woman again a year later, the school had told her she could no longer sell there. She took this as a warning to stop before she got into trouble, so she abandoned the business and went back to her old teaching job.

Prices and the Public

Like food prices, restaurant prices remained stable for many years. Then in 1981, when food prices were raised, so were restaurant prices. The increases ranged from 11 to 30 percent, depending on the class of the restaurant. But at the same time, numerous restaurants were upgraded in class, which meant that in certain places prices shot up by 50 to 100 percent from one day to the next, with no change in the quality of the food or service. We were in Cuba at the time of the price hikes, and were startled to see a cheese sandwich in a snack bar jump from 60 centavos to 1.20 pesos, a meat dish go from 2.50 to 5 pesos, and a glass of soda from 10 to 25 centavos.

The response to the increases was "a groundswell of public uproar," as one foreign journalist described it.[15] Ten days later the government announced that "serious errors" had been committed. As a result, prices were completely rolled back. Moreover, two cabinet members, including the price commissar, were conspicuously absent from the new cabinet shortly thereafter appointed by President Castro. As of early 1984, restaurant prices remained unchanged.

We could not help but note the difference in public reaction to the increase in food prices versus the increase in restaurant prices. Many food prices also rose drastically—sugar and soft drinks by 100 percent, beans by 56 percent, beef by 61 percent—but they had been so low that the increases were seen as fair and not amounting to much in absolute terms. In contrast, restaurant prices were already fairly high, so that the increase was seen as abusive. In addition, the hike in food prices was preceded by a year of government efforts to prepare public opinion. These efforts stressed the growing subsidies behind the ration prices and the higher average incomes resulting from the wage reform.

Despite the growing number of ways and places to obtain food, demand for more and better quality foods has continued to outstrip supply. In 1980, the government attempted to further stimulate food production through the creation of farmers' markets. In the next chapter, we look at the introduction of free market enterprise into a nonmarket economy.

CHAPTER 5

Virtue must be nourished. But vice springs up spontaneously and grows of its own volition.

FIDEL CASTRO, April, 1982, speech to Young Communist League.

The Farmers' Market: A Dash of Capitalism

 First in line is a middle-aged woman lugging a straw sack bulging with cassava and plantains. She adds 3 pounds of taro, the starchy tuber most Cubans love. Altogether she has spent 9 pesos—a little more than the average daily wage—on *viandas* alone. "Sure they're expensive. But what's a meal without some kind of *vianda*?" she sighs. Behind her stands a young couple with an infant. They, too, order 3 pounds of taro, which Cubans consider the ideal weaning food. The man behind them says he has ulcers and can only eat bland food, so he comes to the market at least once a month to stock up on taro.

Over by the stalls selling live chickens, rabbits, ducks, and other animals, a well-dressed woman in her forties looks over the cuts of pork. It's her son's twentieth birthday this Saturday, and she promised to invite his girlfriend for dinner and make something special. She was thinking of buying just a few pounds, because at 3.50 pesos a pound for pork, you can't go overboard. But her eye is attracted to a larger piece. "40 pesos," says the farmer. "*Que va!*" she replies. "Way too expensive." But her mouth waters at the thought of all the fried pork skin (*chicharrones*). The fat would mean extra lard for the entire month and, of course, the bones would be great for black bean soup. "What the hell," she concludes. "I can get three good meals out of it.

And just one meal for the family in a restaurant would end up costing more. So it's not *that* bad."

"Hey, what do you think we are, bourgeois?" shouts a short, thin man in work clothes. "I make 138 pesos a month. You think I can afford to buy onions at 2 pesos a pound? Three lousy onions for 2 pesos. *Que va!*" All heads turn toward him, some voicing their agreement, others just nodding. The vendor remains imperturbable. "You don't have to buy them, you know. It's a free choice." The worker looks up at him in disgust. "You're all just a bunch of *bandidos*," he snorts. "And just look at those hands. You've never even been near the soil!" He stalks off without buying anything.

At the corner stall an elderly man stoops down to make room in his sack for 5 pounds of rice, 3 pounds of black beans, and 2 pounds of red beans. It's the second half of the month: The rice ration's running out, and the beans ran out a long time ago. "Sure, it all cost me 24 pesos," he said. "But the rice will tide us over till next month. And with 5 pounds of beans, together with what we get on the ration, we'll be set for the next two months."

Scenes like these became commonplace with the introduction in early 1980 of the private farmers' markets (*mercados libres campesinos*). While all private farmers were still required to sell their production quota to the government at fixed prices, the private markets would allow them to sell additional produce directly to consumers at whatever prices they could get. (For a discussion of private farmers and the revolution see Chapter 11.) The government's stated intention was to supplement its rationed and nonrationed marketing system by improving the variety and quality of foods available.

An Idea Whose Time Had Come

Allowing unregulated sales by farmers of their surplus production represented a major departure from past policy, which had severely restricted private food sales and offered private farmers little incentive to increase their production. In the early stages of the revolution, the government's main concern was to guarantee an adequate diet for the entire population. It saw its choice as controlling either food production or marketing. Since private farmers accounted for a considerable portion of the nation's food supply, the fledgling revolutionary government felt it could not afford to antagonize them by collectivizing production. Accordingly, it decided to control marketing by requiring farmers to sell the government virtually all crops not consumed on the farm.

But by the 1970s, with the government well in control of food marketing and the ration guaranteeing much of the basic diet at minimal prices, the idea of allowing farmers to sell their surplus at prices determined by supply and demand came under discussion at the highest levels of the Communist Party.[1] Proponents of these markets, such as Vice President Rodriguez, saw them as a way to provide dissatisfied consumers with greater variety (including more meat) and better quality (especially produce), while inducing farmers to produce above and beyond their government quotas. They also thought that allowing private producers to sell directly to the public would undermine the black market. But other party officials were concerned that farmers' markets would encourage many already well-off private farmers to seek individual gain rather than work for the common good. Critics also feared that legalized private sales would make individual farming too attractive at a moment when government policy favored pooling farms into producer cooperatives. (See Chapter 11.) With these objections, farmers' markets were shelved until 1980, when further pressures finally turned the tables in their favor.

Growing Consumer Pressures

By the late 1970s, the government had succeeded in fulfilling the "basic needs" of the Cuban population—a minimum diet, free universal education, free medical care, and, to a lesser extent, adequate housing. But raising the majority's standard of living made consumer aspirations soar. More Cubans than ever now wanted more than the basics—they wanted higher-quality goods and greater variety. Many people also had extra money to spend, since the basics were provided at minimal prices. In addition, since 1973, workers had been awarded individual productivity bonuses. But without desirable things to buy, such incentives were ineffective. Consumer goods (except on the exploding black market) had not kept pace with demand.

Consumer aspirations were heightened by the return visits of

Cubans who had left in the l960s. After the Cuban government granted emigrés permission to visit their families in 1979, they started returning at the rate of about a hundred thousand a year, bringing with them an array of goods not available in Cuba. This sudden direct exposure to the world's foremost consumer society—on top of the barrage of advertising Cubans received through Miami-based radio and television stations—made the Cuban lifestyle seem austere and drab by comparison. Certainly many of the over 120,000 Cubans who left their homeland in the 1980 boatlifts were seeking greater material comfort. Dissatisfaction with the limits of consumption in Cuba might well have been more widespread than most party officials had realized.[2]

The government responded with measures designed to improve both the availability and quality of nonrationed consumer goods. There was a visible increase in imports of canned and bottled goods from Eastern Europe. Sales to the general public of some products formerly reserved for export, such as citrus fruits and juices, were increased as well.

The government also relaxed restrictions on private sales which had been in effect since the 1968 "revolutionary offensive." A handicraft market was opened in Havana's Cathedral Square. The monthly magazine *Opina* began running page after page of classified ads for private sales and exchanges (e.g., "Family with one-bedroom apartment in the Vedado wants to trade for a two-bedroom apartment in Santo Suarez"). The government also allowed some private services (e.g., "Electrician fixes radios and TVs"). But the biggest innovation was the farmers' markets.

The 1980 decree establishing the markets set the following ground rules:

- Private individual farmers and producer cooperatives were authorized to sell. Also authorized was anyone who held any sort of land, including those with backyard plots and farmers who had leased their land to the government but had kept a few acres for home production. State farms were authorized to sell only the surplus from their self-provisioning land with the proceeds going to a common recreational and development fund for the farm's employees.

- Vendors were required to be producers; reselling was strictly prohibited.

- Prices were "free," that is, to be determined between buyer and seller with no government interference.

- The sale of beef, tobacco, sugar, coffee, and cocoa was prohibited—beef to avoid jeopardizing building up the national herd, and the others to preserve valuable foreign-exchange earners.

- Farmers were restricted to their local markets, unless they obtained written authorization to sell in markets elsewhere. This was to avoid a convergence upon Havana, where prices were apt to be higher.

- Farmers had to provide their own transportation.

- The markets were placed under the authority of People's Power, Cuba's elected governing apparatus, which would assign each market an administrative staff responsible for checking all documents, assigning space, and collecting a nominal daily seller's fee.

Problems in the Marketplace

Within months, farmers' markets blossomed throughout the island, with at least 1 in each of Cuba's 169 municipalities. From 1980 to 1982 we visited numerous farmers' markets throughout the island. Compared with the animated open-air markets of Asia, Africa, and Latin America, we found the Cuban markets small and subdued. The trading atmosphere varied with location (urban vs. rural), season, day of the week, and time of day. On a weekday in a sparsely populated rural area, the farmers' market had only a couple of vendors with meager offerings. On weekends in rural towns such as Guines and Cotorro we would find from twenty to seventy-five farmers selling their goods. Havana's two largest farmers' markets—Virgen del Camino and La Palma—always drew the greatest number of sellers and the largest variety of foods.

In a typical market we found ample stocks of common staples such as rice and beans. But shoppers told us that the great attraction of the markets was that they sold foods difficult to find in the government stores. "These are the things you used to be able to get only on the black market," a middle-aged woman whispered to one of us with a smile. "Now it's legal." Market favorites in-

cluded onions, garlic, rice, beans, plaintains, and the other standard *viandas*, as well as good-looking fresh produce and seasonal fruits, including huge avocados. There was Cuba's favorite
meat, pork (except right after holidays when farmers sold everything they could to take advantage of the especially high prices),
along with fresh cheese and a menagerie of live animals. The
animals' ruckus, especially when prospective buyers drew near,
lent a county fair atmosphere to the markets.

But all was not well. From our observations and conversations
with farmers and urban consumers, as well as from interviews
with government officials, we could see problems emerging with
this experiment in private food marketing.

*While more food did become available and at prices lower
than on the black market, farmers' market prices remained
inordinately—unexpectedly—high.*
In 1980 government officials told us they were well aware that
demand would initially outstrip supply, making it possible for the
sellers to get high prices. "But don't worry," they reassured us.
"On your next visit you will see that the farmers will have produced so much that prices will fall. It's the law of supply and
demand."

But prices stayed high. Rice and beans stabilized at somewhat
over six times the ration price. Some goods actually rose in price
by January 1982. Plantains, for example, initially sold for about
30 centavos each in Havana, and had climbed to 60 or 80 centavos, even 1 peso. The price of pork in the rural areas rose from
about 1.20 pesos per pound to 2.50 pesos, and in Havana it
jumped from about 2.00 pesos per pound to 3.50 to 4.00 pesos
and even more during holiday periods.

One reason prices remained high was that there was too much
money in circulation, perhaps more than the government had
anticipated. People thought that 1 peso for a head of garlic was
outrageous, but they wanted the garlic and had the money to
buy it.

Another reason prices stayed so buoyant is that the producers
proved themselves to be shrewd marketeers. (Indeed many
vendors were allegedly not producers at all, but middlemen—or
"middlepersons," as many were women.) These sellers aimed to
maximize profits through fat margins rather than by boosting the

total volume of sales. They would withhold an item from the market whenever it was in abundant supply through government marketing channels. One semiretired small farmer, who had sold off most of his land to the government in the late 1960s, proudly showed us the onions he had stored up for the farmers' market. While government farms produced only one variety of onion—and one that did not store well—he could easily plant several varieties and have a staggered harvest as well as set aside some varieties that store well. After the May 1981 harvest, government produce stores sold onions for 8 to 18 centavos a pound. By October, when the government had no onions to sell, you could find them in the farmers' markets in Havana for 2.40 to 3.00 pesos a pound.

The government had expected that participation by cooperative producers in the free markets would help lower prices—thanks to their more developed political consciousness and their larger scale of production. In practice, however, although the co-ops did in fact sell at consistently lower prices than private farmers, they did not sell frequently enough or in great enough quantities to have a permanent impact on prices. At the Guines market in a rural area not far from Havana, individual farmers were selling black beans at about 1.60 pesos per pound and red beans at 1.80 pesos, while the only production co-op at the market was selling both red and black beans at 1 peso per pound. But the market administrator showed us the books for September 1980, revealing that production cooperatives and state farms accounted for a mere 2 percent of sellers.

In some areas, the government itself tried to act as a competitive force, setting up nonrationed government produce markets (*ferias del agro*) alongside the farmers' markets. These markets sold at fixed prices that were higher than rationed prices but way below rates at the farmers' markets. In some places we visited, such as the market in Santa Clara in central Cuba, this worked quite effectively with fresh produce and root crops. But the state markets usually offered little variety and poor quality goods. In Santiago, the bustling farmers' market shared the same location with the government *feria del agro*, which seemed to have hardly any customers. Prominently displayed on the back wall of the stall was a blackboard with chalked-in prices for a wide variety of goods, all of which were remarkably lower than

those at the farmers' market just across the road. The only catch
was that the bins were empty, except for some lemons.

The markets made it possible to have more satisfying diets,
but only for those who could afford the price.
In the first quarter of l98l farmers' markets accounted for just 6.5
percent of *total* national food sales. But for certain nonstaple
items, the markets' influence was much greater. They had a virtual monopoly over garlic and fresh pork (excluding live hogs
bought directly off private farms). Other items the state does not
market at all—white cheese, peanuts, okra, green beans, and
tropical fruits like mamey (Cuba's favorite fruit), anon, chiri-
moya, and tamarindo—are available solely through private sales.
Certain foods, such as taro and plantains, are allocated through
rationing primarily to groups with special diets—small children,
the elderly, people with digestive problems, for example. Those
without such authorizations rely more heavily on the farmer's
market than the farmers' market share of total sales of these
products—15 percent for taro, 13 percent for plaintains—
would indicate. Even in the case of seasonal products which the
state does market, small producers' staggered planting gives
them a virtual monopoly on these products at certain times of
the year.

Some of these items, while unimportant from a national economic perspective, may make a world of difference to the individual—a phenomenon Vice President Rodriguez referred to as
"the importance of the unimportant." He explained to us the
classic case of onions and garlic. Even if the state were to fully
satisfy the demand for black beans, you can't prepare tasty black
bean soup without garlic and onions, and these two crops seem
to lend themselves to small-scale production by private farmers.

From a nutritional perspective, the availability of such "extras"
as condiments can determine whether or not a meal is even prepared. Cuban women often complain that they can't make bean
soup even when they can get the beans because "*no tengo nada
que echarle*" (I don't have anything to put in them). Thus the
nutritional significance of something like onions or garlic can be
far greater than their individual properties would suggest.

In addition to a better and more satisfying diet, the farmers'
markets also offered Cubans more social possibilities. Previously,

traditional hospitality was often stymied by lack of food; while the ration provides the basics for the family, it doesn't leave much for guests. With the farmers' markets, it became possible for many Cuban families to do more entertaining.

But all of this was mainly for those who had the money. With one chicken priced at about twice the average daily wage, not all families could afford to use the markets. There is no reliable information on the percentage of households that could afford to make *regular* purchases at the markets (by regular we mean at least once a month) since income distribution data in Cuba is a closely guarded government secret. When we pressed officials of the Institute for Research on Consumer Demand, they estimated that 50 to 80 percent of Cuban families bought at the markets at least once a month. High government officials estimated 50 percent, and the Havana representative of the U.N. Food and Agriculture Organization gave the lowest estimate, somewhere under 50 percent.

Those who did buy at the markets were further differentiated by what they were able to buy. For example, a low-income family might use the markets to buy extra rice and beans when its ration was running out and root crops to serve as "fillers." Those with a bit higher income might buy rice, beans, and root crops, along with garlic, onions, and some fresh produce like tomatoes, avocados, and the like. Those in the highest income group would be more likely to buy all of the above, as well as meat.

During two decades of revolution Cubans saw themselves as part of an egalitarian society in which the essentials were to be equitably shared. This increasing differentiation among people was a significant departure, resented by some.

While there was probably some increase in food production, increases were not all they appeared to be. Public resources intended for state farms apparently were often diverted for private gain.

Just how much additional food production can be attributed to the opening of the markets is hard to quantify, for official figures fail to account for goods that were previously channeled into the black market. But with the coming of the private markets there was a visible explosion of planting in the countryside, and innumerable patches of idle land, in both town and country, suddenly blossomed into gardens.

Apart from increased production, more food became available because farmers let less go to waste. In one of our visits to the countryside, for example, we came upon a tobacco farmer with a half dozen assorted fruit trees in his backyard. For years, he and his family would eat their fill, give some away to friends and relatives, and let the rest rot on the ground. However, with the advent of the farmers' market, he assured us, we'd no longer see such food going to waste. Other farmers also told us that they were giving less food away to neighbors and relatives, as well as consuming less themselves.

Increased production for the market did have its public costs. Theoretically, the government was not furnishing inputs for produce destined for private sale. But where else were producers to get pesticides, seeds, and fertilizers, since they were rarely sold on the open market? Many farmers complained to us that lack of inputs prevented them from producing more for the market. One small farmer near Santiago told us that if he could just buy a hose for watering the plot next to his house he could produce hundreds of pounds of bananas. Apparently, some farmers "diverted" the inputs they needed from government sources. One farmer told us that his "partner" in onion-growing was a tractor driver on a state farm who would plow the land with a government tractor. Others tapped the state aqueduct for irrigation. A cook at a veterinary institute was caught stealing large quantities of fertilized eggs, molasses, and feed to use in his private chicken-raising venture.[3]

In a few instances, the farmers' market cut into the government's capacity to deliver the full ration of certain items, something that many Cubans have come to consider sacrosanct. Many farmers were inclined to sell the least amount possible to the government in order to profit from the higher farmers' market prices. As one farmer asked us, "Why should I sell my onions to the state for 52 centavos a pound when I can get about five times as much on the private market?" For the Cuban favorite, black beans, the government was paying farmers 25 centavos a pound, but on the farmers' market they fetched five to nine times that amount.

While the market was officially presented as a means of strengthening the ties between Cuban workers and small farmers, in practice it increased tensions between them.
Food sold through government channels is heavily subsidized; prices, often much lower than production costs, have been raised only once since 1965. Cubans consequently have become accustomed to cheap food and many have come to consider it a *right.* So, unlike consumers in other countries who tend to be resigned to spiraling food prices, Cubans were outraged at the exorbitant prices in the private markets. While they may have been willing to go along with highway robbery on the black market, they had assumed that since farmers' markets were legal, their prices would be reasonable.

Some vendors, on the other hand, told us that their prices only seemed exorbitant because government food prices are inordinately low and subsidized. They also alleged that they worked harder and for longer hours than most urban workers and were therefore entitled to greater remuneration.

But many working people in the cities were palpably resentful when market vendors whipped out wads of bills and began flipping through them in search of "small change." In a single day a vendor could easily take in twice what a worker makes in a month. In 1981, the daily receipts of a vendor averaged 297 pesos, at a time when the average daily wage was slightly over 6 pesos.[4] One farmer we spoke with boasted that on a Saturday or Sunday he could rake in about 500 pesos; an article in the Communist Party newspaper, *Granma,* cited the example of a seller making 3,000 pesos in one day—a sum that would take the average worker a year and a half to earn.[5]

Antagonism between producers and consumers grew steadily. People dubbed the vendors "Los Bandidos del Rio Frio," after the popular Mexican novel and TV series. It was common to hear customers commiserating with one another at the market and venting their rage at the sellers. At one of the farmers' markets in Havana, we saw one customer turn livid when charged 3 pesos for scrawny bunch of bananas which, when available at a state store, would have cost about 20 centavos. He threw the bananas in the seller's face and shouted: *"¡Se acabó la alianza obrero-campesino!"* ("So much for the worker-peasant alliance!")

While the government thought the private market would do away with black market intermediaries, the opposite happened.

As we noted earlier, in establishing the farmers' markets, policymakers sought to curtail the black market and the operators involved in it. While succeeding in severely cutting into black-market territory (except in the case of prohibited items such as tobacco, beef, and coffee), the markets provided a field day for intermediaries. With an easing up of the restrictions on buying, selling, and transporting food, and with a lack of control in the marketplace, intermediaries were able to make a killing, especially in Havana.

Fidel Castro later alleged that 90 percent of those selling at the markets were go-betweens. He said they so skillfully manipulated the markets that "some of them would have been brilliant on the New York Stock Exchange."[6] They held back goods until supplies were scarce, illegally transported produce from the rural areas to the cities where they would fetch higher prices, and raised prices to extortionate levels when demand outstripped supply. For example, around the time of the New Year celebrations, pork, which is *the* fiesta food, soared to 4.50 or 5 pesos a pound in Havana—the equivalent of nearly an average day's wage.

The government stipulation that farmers sell their own goods themselves turned out to be difficult to enforce. How can farmers be busy tending their fields *and* selling at the market? A number of farmers insisted to us that they just didn't have the time to do both. While some farmers had family members to sell their produce, others did not. And how were farmers to transport their goods? It seems many of the market operators were truck owners who would buy from farmers, transport the goods to the city, and resell at enormous profits. During the 1982 congress of ANAP, the small farmers' association, several farmers took the floor to argue that farmers *need* intermediaries to sell their goods.

Perhaps licensing and regulating intermediaries would have been preferable to a blanket outlawing of nonproducer vendors. Deciding against licensing reflected the Cuban leadership's profound antipathy towards those who would profit by charging as much as the market could bear in selling what the work of others produced. But, illegal vendors, thriving in markets that were purportedly administered by the local People's Power organizations, cast doubts on the ability of People's Power to exercise effective control.

Sellers' extra income turned out to be a mixed blessing.

Producer cooperatives that sold at the markets were able to use the extra income on collective amenities ranging from additional beer at fiestas to a beach house for co-op members.

Many individuals who planted gardens to sell produce on the free markets were retired persons. For them, the free market represented a boon to their otherwise meager incomes and appreciably raised their standards of living. We met one such gardener, Manuel, a 65-year-old grandfather of eight, living alone on the outskirts of Batabanó, due south of Havana. In front of Manuel's modest house was a small garden completely planted with garlic and onions. Manuel had a bad leg and had to recruit help from a neighbor to hand water the garlic. But the effort was worth it, for the private market easily doubled his modest retirement pension.

But of all the producers, it was individual private farmers who gained the most from selling on the new markets. As some government officials had feared, the farmers' markets seemed to work against the government policy of encouraging more collective forms of production. Furthermore, only the smallest fraction of the monies brought in at the farmers' markets were funneled back to the state. Fidel Castro estimated that sellers at the markets earned about 200 million pesos in one year and paid a mere 40,000 pesos in fees. He argued that at least *half* their earnings should have gone to taxes and been used to benefit all the people in the form of new schools, hospitals, vacation programs, etc.[7]

Many private farmers—or their intermediaries—spent their profits on conspicuous consumption.[8] Some vendors recounted for us their new possessions—tape recorders, calculator watches, designer jeans, and other coveted imported items in short supply and available only through the black market or high-priced government outlets. "Lavishing it on liquor and women" was another common vendor's answer to our perhaps indiscreet questions about what they did with their profits. A bottle of export-quality rum is priced at the equivalent of the average urban weekly wage. One farmer is said to have moved his "head-quarters" into a suite in the Habana Libre Hotel, formerly the Hilton. Still others saved their money to buy cars and houses in the cities, paying exorbitant, skyrocketing prices totally beyond the reach not only of ordinary workers, but of professionals as well.

Thus the farmers' market threatened to increase the income gap that the government had spent so many years trying to close. "When a person sells chickens for 15 pesos, even if he raised them, that person is making more money in several weeks by selling a few chickens than a worker makes in a whole year," President Castro complained. "Now that worker keeps the transportation system going, produces textiles, builds housing, schools and hospitals, grows sugarcane, produces sugar, milk, eggs, and meat for the people. But he earns a modest salary. . . . This can never be reconciled with the concepts of socialism and communism."[9]

Too much money in the hands of a few also resulted in widespread corruption. So-called "free-market entrepreneurs" were able to shell out 10,000 pesos for 1950s-vintage Chevrolets (the equivalent of five years of work for the average Cuban); worse yet, they were illegally buying the few precious Ladas (Russian Fiats) which the government restricted for sale to exemplary workers. "They've corrupted vanguard workers and doctors," President Castro charged, "tempting them to make big money by selling their 4,500-peso cars for 20,000."[10]

The farmers' markets were corrupting even Party members, according to Castro. To illustrate the point, he described a Cuban who had cornered 50,000 plantains in the eastern province of Holguin that should have been sold to the government; the man had trucked them to Havana where he then convinced a member of the Party to store the plaintains in his home. Since a hurricane had destroyed much of the crop, the plaintains fetched the astonishing price of 80 centavos each. "Imagine, 50,000 plantains stored away, and in the warehouse of a Party member," Castro complained. "Corrupting our Party members . . . those are the kind that want to buy everything, even the Karl Marx Theater, and if they can't buy the theater then they try to buy the administrator."[11]

Confronting the Problems

More and more, people started to wonder why, after twenty or more years, the government-run food system was still unable to fully satisfy people's food desires. Also, after seeing what the farmers were able to produce in such a short time, as well as the quality of their produce, complaints about government-produced foods became more frequent.

Why was government produce so inferior to private produce? The conventional wisdom is that just as the small farmer cannot compete with the government in mass production, so the state farm is no match for the small farmer in terms of quality and freshness. The time and attention private farmers put into their work is unlikely to be matched by government farmworkers receiving a monthly salary.

Potatoes and tomatoes make the point. Government farms are able to grow vast quantities of potatoes under semimechanized conditions, and private farmers would never consider trying to compete. But it is in the fresh "quality" produce—such as tomatoes—where private farmers have the odds in their favor. Government tomatoes would be picked before they were ripe and stored in warehouses for who knows how long. Then they would be thrown into open trucks and exposed all day to the sweltering sun during delivery to retail stores. By the time they got to the consumer, they would often be tasteless, bruised, or rotten. The small farmer, on the other hand, would carefully tend each tomato plant in his garden and on market day would get up at daybreak to hand pick the ripe tomatoes. He'd carefully load them in the back of his car and then one by one place them on the counter at his stall in the market.

Another factor which exacerbated the differences between government and private produce is that the farmers tended to sell the poorest quality goods to the state and keep the pick of the crop for the private market.

The party leadership was obviously in a quandary. On the one hand, the markets were satisfying certain demands and many Cubans had come to depend on them as a regular supplement to their diet. On the other hand, the government and the country's highest political leadership could not continue to sanction the full-fledged corruption and price gouging that had invaded the markets, especially in Havana. ANAP, the national farmers' organization, undoubtedly aware of the slipping image of the small farmer in the minds of the public and the Communist Party, must have been concerned about potential backlash. Popular discontent mounted. On our visit to the farmers' market in the city of Santiago, one would-be buyer, a middle-aged black woman, cried out *"Misericordia!"* (Lord have mercy!) "Can you believe it? Three bananas for 1 peso! I don't know when Fidel's going to put a stop to all this."

A decision, undoubtedly at the highest level, was finally made. On February 28, 1982, the police swept down on all twelve markets in Havana (and apparently a few elsewhere on the island), arresting hundreds of vendors and confiscating tens of thousands of pesos worth of goods. Called Operation *"Pitirre en el Alambre"* (bird on the wire), after the code used by sellers to spread the word that police or inspectors were snooping around, the raid reportedly uncovered a myriad of abuses—falsification of documents, lack of veterinary certificates for meat sales, unlicensed vendors, sale of stolen goods, illegal transportation of goods from one area to another. Police found sacks of rice on sale which were obviously stolen from state warehouses. In four of the markets they found chickens from state farms being sold. They even discovered the sale of a type of bean that the state had imported and then withdrawn from circulation because of excess pesticide contamination.[12]

Through the rest of 1982 and well into 1983, the markets, while officially still open, stood virtually empty, except for a few flower vendors and a farmer here and there. After the arrests, even legitimate farmers (at least in the Havana area) became wary of the government and decided it was best to lie low and not bring their goods to market. "What the hell," one farmer told us. "We'll just go back to selling right from the farm like we used to do. It's even easier for us. We get about the same price we got at the markets, and we don't have to worry about transportation or waste time hanging around to sell."

The most outspoken critic of the markets turned out to be Fidel Castro himself, who strongly denounced the profiteering and the "new bourgeoisie" they engendered. He said the markets were "undoubtedly a capitalist method of solving problems," and as such, they "corrupt and contaminate us."

Most consumers were delighted that the *bandidos* got what was coming to them, especially since many had suspected all along that some vendors were not the farmers they made themselves out to be. But frequent customers in the farmers' markets now found themselves forced either to go without or to revert to buying on the black market. During the months following the clampdown, the black market returned with a vengeance, at prices even higher than before. Chickens that had sold for 10 pesos were suddenly selling for 15, and rabbits went from 15 to 20. The risk involved in black market sales, now heightened by increased vigilance, commanded a premium which came out of the consumer's pocket.

A major ANAP Congress in May 1983 provided the opportunity for intense debate of the private markets by farmer delegates from around the country, ANAP officers, and Mr. Castro, who took an active part in the sessions. The discussions provide fascinating insights into the whole question of private markets in a nonmarket economy.

On one side were the farmers, who wanted the law of supply and demand to reign. On the other side were perhaps the majority of Cubans, who wanted the government to regulate prices. But if prices were regulated, farmers would stop selling. There would be cheap prices, but nothing to buy.

The government offered a solution: it proposed not to limit prices, but instead to impose a 50-percent tax on sales. This way, prices would remain high but profits made at the market would not go solely for the personal enrichment of the farmer, but for the betterment of society as a whole.[14]

But the farmers were adamantly opposed to the idea. Some argued that high taxes would take away the strong incentive for greater production. Others said the tax would just be passed on to the consumer in the form of higher prices, increasing the already strained relationship between farmers and consumers.

It was clear that the ANAP Congress would not come up with a "magic formula" to reconcile the three points of view. But it was also clear that the congress was not a rubber stamp for the government's policies. The government's role, as President Castro explained, was "not to impose but to persuade or be persuaded." Take the question of the 50-percent tax scheme. "The

Congress has helped us change our ideas on this question and not say 'let's implement this idea' just because it was developed by a group of us and it seemed very good, and the state would receive 40, 50, or 60 million pesos," Castro concluded. "We have to go back and analyze all this again, taking the delegates' and the people's criteria into account."

These discussions prepared the way for the new farmers' market regulations issued in October 1983. In an attempt to eliminate the go-betweens, only ANAP members may now sell in the markets. This regulation excludes not only intermediaries but also the small percentage of farmers who for various reasons have never joined ANAP, as well as nonprofessional farmers—hobby and garden plot producers. The latter are excluded because it is difficult to distinguish many of them from illegal intermediaries.

To prevent the diversion of state produce to the farmers' markets, the local ANAP rather than People's Power would determine if a farmer had met his contractual obligations to the government purchasing agency. A 20-percent tax on gross sales—not the originally proposed 50-percent tax—was also added, in addition to the daily user fees charged under the original regulations.

Even more significantly, the government moved to expand its own role as a marketeer of foods on a nonrationed basis, building on the "parallel market" discussed in Chapter 4. Farmers' markets would not be closed down by decree, but by borrowing another time-honored capitalist tool: competition. New larger government markets were opened and existing ones were expanded, primarily in the Havana region at first. The array of foods available through government stores—meats (even beef), live animals, coffee, export-quality rum, tuna, candies, pastries, beans, rice, sugar, citrus fruits, and cigars—is unprecedented in postrevolution Cuba. The prices, however, are equal to or in some cases even higher than those that had prevailed on the black market and in the farmers' markets.

The explosion of food (and nonfood) items in government stores became *the* topic of conversation. Two newly opened emporia, one in the old Sears store (El Centro) and the other in what once had been the Havana market (El Mercado Unico), immediately became objects of great curiosity. Visiting both in

November 1983, we—like everyone else we spoke with—were struck by the high prices. Fillets of fresh swordfish and marlin were being sold for 7 pesos a pound, more than the daily average wage; rum for 14.40 pesos a bottle. Pork, initially on sale for 3.50 pesos a pound, was raised to 4.50 a pound because the demand was so great, even though at the end of 1981 the government had intervened in the farmers' market to place a 4-peso ceiling on pork prices. Beef was 8 pesos a pound, over ten times the ration price and equal to the black market price. Coffee, sold in two-ounce packets, was going for a staggering 36 pesos a pound; instant coffee, in cans whose labels perfectly ape Nescafe, sold for 10 pesos a pound.

Some of the new items for sale were previously destined for export. The tuna cans were labeled "product of Cuba" in English and French with the name of a Canadian distributor. Quite possibly the Canadian market was oversupplied or the deal had fallen through, but no Ministry of Commerce official we spoke with could tell us. Nor is it clear what has changed since a televised January 1982 interview in which the Minister of Food Industry had said that high-quality fish would not be sold to the Cuban public because it was needed for export. Yet the very fish he mentioned—snapper, grouper, swordfish, marlin—were now sold at the government markets. Also available were canned fruit juices labeled in Arabic (fortunately, with a picture of the fruit).

Most intriguing is that much of the food sold at these government stores comes from private producers. In its deliberations over the farmers' market crisis, Cuba's political leadership apparently decided to continue to encourage more food production by private producers (as they had hoped the private markets would do), but to make the government the marketeer. The government set its sights on beating the illegal intermediaries at their own game. It set the tax on private sales to the government at 5 percent, compared to the new 20-percent tax on sales at the private markets and offered to transport the goods free.

As a further incentive to sell surplus production to the government rather than on the private market, the government agreed to pay individual farmers or cooperatives significantly higher prices for that part of their production which exceeded their government quotas. Thus a bean farmer would get 25 centavos a pound for the beans he was obligated to sell as part of his quota and 55 centavos a pound for every additional pound he sold to the government.

The government has been trying to use its influence to get producer cooperatives to stop selling their surpluses on the farmers' market and sell only to the government. This reverses the earlier policy of pressuring the co-ops to produce and sell *more* at the farmers' markets to help bring prices down. In addition to the financial incentives, the government is also relying on "moral persuasion." And this moral persuasion has come from none other than the revolution's number one persuader, President Fidel Castro. He personally met for two days with the presidents of all the producer cooperatives, "asking but not telling" them to sell their produce to the government rather than on the private market, according to one ANAP official.[15] (Visiting a farmers' market in November 1983, we found the Bulgarian-Cuban Friendship cooperative still selling there. The cooperatives obviously do have a choice.)

The latest private market regulations, as already pointed out, allow non-ANAP farmers and gardeners to sell only to the government. And as the cooperative sector becomes larger, and if the cooperatives opt to sell their surplus to the government, the hope is that the parallel market will be so well-supplied that the farmers' markets will become at best marginal, even to those households with the extra money for a varied and higher-priced diet. Moreover, ANAP officials told us that each year a farmer's state production quota will be reassessed in view of the amount sold on the private market: the more sold privately, the higher the production quota next year.[16]

Nonetheless, as of our last visit to Cuba in November 1983, the farmers' markets, far from withering away, seemed to be coming back from their virtual shutdown the year before. In June 1982, few farmers were selling in the markets and the number of products being sold, by one count, had fallen to only 21. By the end of 1982, the number of farmer-sellers had increased and 44 different products were on sale. Yet this remains well below the level of activity before the crackdown. It also appears that the government's parallel market—plus, perhaps fear of another crackdown—has moderated the prices in the farmers' market.

For the consumer, there are pluses and minuses. The government stores tend to be centrally located (the largest one in Havana, El Mercado Unico, is on one of the busiest intersections in the city), while the farmers' markets are usually on the outskirts of town. The government stores also sell some popular items prohibited on the farmers' markets—coffee, beef, and sugar—as well as processed foods; some, such as El Centro in Havana, also sell clothing, toiletries, and household goods.

The long lines are one of the chief drawbacks of the government parallel market stores. While it was admittedly the day after payday for most Cubans, we saw two- to three-hour lines in front of Havana's El Centro one Saturday in November 1983. For the first time in many years, time translates into money: with time, you can spend half the day in line and get your groceries at a slightly lower price; at the farmers' market you might pay a little more, but you seldom encounter a line. (There have reportedly been police crackdowns on Cubans who set themselves up as professional shoppers, getting paid by saving someone else the time of standing in line at the new parallel market stores. Undoubtedly friends and neighbors must also informally exchange time in lines.)

Socialist societies are fond of talking about contradictions. The farmers' markets—this dash of capitalism in a socialist society—will surely keep Cubans talking for years to come.

CHAPTER 6

Reagan sent a spy team to Cuba to gather facts for his anti-Cuba campaign. The team returned several months later with much data but no conclusions. The President, furious at the waste of time and money, asked why.

"It's like this, Mr. President," explained the team leader. "In Cuba there's no unemployment but nobody works. Nobody works but they always overfulfill their production goals. All the goals are overfulfilled but there's nothing to buy. There's nothing to buy but everybody has all he needs. Everybody has everything but everybody's always complaining. Everybody complains but everybody goes to the square to pledge their lives for Cuba and Fidel, and then they go home and complain some more. So you see, Mr. President, we have lots of data but no conclusions."

CUBAN JOKE, 1984

Is Rationing Socialist?

 We have already discussed the problems of rationing from the consumer's point of view. But the ration system is also fraught with problems for the government. First there is the unproductive bureaucracy that rationing has spawned. Much time, energy and expense go into administering the system: providing every family in the country with a ration book and ensuring that each person's food "basket"—with all the variants by age and doctor-prescribed diet—is at a particular store at a particular time. On top of that, every birth, death, marriage, divorce, even a move from one block to the next, requires a change in the ration book. (In 1982, one out of every eight Cubans made such a change.) The system is not computerized and the paper work alone—with umpteen carbon copies sent to umpteen different places—is mind-boggling.

Rationing is also a drain on the economy, for foods are sold at prices way below production costs. With prices frozen from 1962 until 1981, Cubans were insulated from the effects of worldwide inflation, constantly rising import costs, and wild fluctuations in the price of sugar on the world market. Over the years, this protection of the consumer has translated into heavy government subsidies. Meat that the government calculates costs 1.24 pesos per pound to produce is sold to the consumer for 55 centavos. Beans were sold at 47 percent below government-stated cost and milk at 29 percent.[1] In 1980, the government estimated that food subsidies (taking into account both retail

79

sales and subsidized meals at workplaces) amounted to 25 pesos a month per person.[2]

In 1980 the Cuban government instituted a wage reform. The minimum wage went up by 14 percent and about 2.5 million workers (out of a total work force of 2.8 million) got raises. Many workers were also earning extra income through bonuses tied to increased productivity. Social security payments were raised, and farmers were getting higher prices for the goods they sold to the state. The average wage jumped from 148 pesos a month in 1980 to 168 pesos in 1981. The government calculated that with these measures there would be an extra 4 billion pesos in circulation during the period 1981–1985.[3]

It is no coincidence that within a year of the wage reform, food prices were raised for the first time since 1962. Prices went up an average of 10 to 12 percent. *Granma*, Cuba's major (and official) newspaper, carried a two-page explanation. Citing the need to absorb the excess money in circulation, the government announced three measures to be implemented simultaneously. One was to offer more goods and services for sale. Another was to encourage people to save. (For the first time in years, starting July 1983 Cuban banks began to pay interest on savings accounts, but at minimal rates ranging from 0.5 to 2 percent.) The third way was to increase prices.

Why the "need" to soak up money in circulation? "Without these measures, money would lose its value, since there would not be sufficient products and services to spend it on," *Granma* explained. "Excess money in circulation would logically lead to negative phenomena like absenteeism and a drop in productivity since there would be no reason to work harder and earn more money." It also hinted that if the government did not raise prices, the excess money would go instead to nongovernment channels such as the farmers' market and the black market.

Lest price hikes coming on the heels of the wage reform smack too much of capitalism, Humberto Perez, the head of Cuba's Central Planning Board (JUCEPLAN), made a distinction: "While in capitalist countries prices are constantly going up, reducing the workers' purchasing power, . . . in Cuba, after many years of constant prices, first the people's income was substantially raised and only afterwards were retail prices raised, but by much less than the increase in income."[4] The new food prices represent about 25 percent of the expected average increase in income from 1982 to 1985.

The 1981 price hike substantially cut the food subsidy, and government policymakers have called for the eventual elimination of subsidies. But if rationing is continued, it seems unlikely that complete self-financing will be reached in the near future. First of all, no spectacular gains in production are on the horizon (see chapter 10). Second, prices of imported foods are likely to continue to rise, and since it is doubtful that regular increases can be passed on to the consumer, part of these increases will be absorbed by the government.

One of the most troublesome effects of rationing for government economists is the "mentality" it has created. Many Cubans have come to see rationing not as an emergency response to distribute scarce goods equitably, but as a perpetual right to buy goods at prices that have nothing to do with costs. So imbedded is this mentality that consumers will buy this or that item on the ration simply because "it's coming to them" regardless of whether they really need it.

The across-the-board uniformity of Cuba's rationing system inevitably gives rise to "gray" market exchanges, while allocations of some popular items are so small that they foster a black market. The rationing system has also led to a lack of selection and of quality—take it or leave it is the rule. The result is that the goods the economy produces do not provide an incentive for people to work more and better.

The Debate on Rationing

Undoubtedly all these problems associated with Cuba's rationing system lay behind the government's decisions to open farmers' markets and to expand its own nonration, or parallel, market system.

But the role of the parallel market in Cuba's food distribution has still not been clearly defined. Two views of the parallel market's relation to the ration system have emerged among the leadership. Some believe the parallel market should sell only luxury goods while the ration continues to provide the basics; others think it should sell both luxury and basic goods, thereby eliminating the ration system altogether.

Proponents of expanding the parallel market to replace the rationing system argue that the egalitarian basis of rationing thwarts the development of socialism.[5] As they see it, the fundamental principle of socialism is "to each according to his or her work." Those who work harder and better should earn more. A number of measures since the early 1970s have aimed to put this principle into effect. For instance, wherever feasible, salaries have been made dependent on the quantity and quality of work. As Vice President Rodriguez told us: "It is no longer a question of just going to work, but getting the work done."[6]

But, this argument continues, the principle of more pay for more work makes no sense without offering more things for the workers to buy. Rationing, where all receive the same, runs contrary to the socialist principle of rewarding people according to the contributions they make. Rather, it is a form of communist distribution (to each according to his or her *need*), for which Cuba is not yet sufficiently developed.

These critics of the rationing system take pains to point out that, early in the revolution, rationing did help to justly distribute basic goods in scarce supply at a time when private speculation reigned. But the basic circumstances have changed and it is time to do away with rationing, they believe.

Policymakers who see the parallel market as merely supplementary to the ration also argue that, under socialism, goods should be distributed according to work. But these ration proponents hold that while the parallel market is necessary to help motivate people to work, it should only distribute rare or unusually high-quality products. Here, for them, socialism is distinguished from capitalism. "In capitalist countries the supply of *all* products is governed by the law of supply and demand," writes an official of the national planning agency. "In our society only a minimal part of our total supply of products is controlled by this economic mechanism, and *only after having satisfied the basic needs of the entire population*."[7]

This seems to be Castro's position. While calling rationing a "real nuisance" to be done away with as soon as possible, he is concerned about what the end of rationing would mean to Cuba's low-income households. During the 1983 Congress of the small farmers organization (ANAP), he said Cuba could easily do away with rationing and sell everything at private market prices, undoubtedly making many people happy. "But what about all the people . . . with low incomes?" he asked. "We can't do things that way. Capitalism does, but capitalism is one thing and socialism another."[8]

For Castro, the "socialist" way to eliminate rationing is by increasing production. He is among those government officials who fear that prices would tend toward the high levels of the parallel market if rationing were ended without a rise in food production. (To get a sense of what this might be like, we calculated what the monthly ration would cost at November 1983 parallel market prices. Food which costs 11.82 pesos on the ration would cost 53.22 pesos—almost five times as much.) Of course, the government now sets nonrationed market prices which do not necessarily reflect production costs or supply and demand; were rationing eliminated, the government could choose to set new prices somewhere between present parallel market and ration prices. But even so, an end to rationing would mean higher food prices. For those who cling to a vision of an egalitarian socialism, this is a problem. In short, there seems to be considerable high-level resistance to a course of action that might result in two very distinct diets based on income differences—one a monotonous diet of rice, beans, eggs and perhaps low grade fish and the other a varied, high-meat diet.[9]

In response, policymakers against rationing contend that banking on increased production to end rationing is not sufficient. They think that as long as prices are kept artificially low, demand will be inordinately high. Low prices, these critics contend, actually ensure the perpetuation of the ration system: they reduce the motivation to work harder, so that production declines, scarcity persists, and rationing is continued.

The way to eliminate rationing, they argue, is by increased production together with periodic price hikes. High prices make people work harder to earn more money. If you know, for example, that you can buy steak on the parallel market for eight pesos a pound, you might be inclined to work overtime to earn a few extra pesos. But if steak is sold only on the ration and at a mere 70 centavos a pound, you might prefer to go home and watch television instead. And if people work more and better (and watch television less), supply could catch up with demand and prices would fall. Then the rationing system, according to these critics, will be obsolete. Although prices will be higher than the ration prices, with increased worker productivity prices should be lower than they have been on the parallel market (or the black market).

Besides rationing, there are other ways to see that low-income households get at least the basic necessities. But with rationing the Cuban leadership appears to have locked itself into the broadest-shot and certainly most expensive system, one that was developed in an emergency and quite probably has long outlived much of its usefulness.

One approach Cuban policymakers debating rationing appear reluctant to consider (at least publicly) is replacing rationing with income supplements for those whose basic well-being would be threatened by an end to rationing. Such a program would appear to satisfy the concern of Castro and other leaders about the fate of low-income families. At the same time, compensating the poor for increased food prices would undoubtedly be cheaper than the present policy of subsidizing everyone through artificially low prices and the maintenance of the huge rationing system. In 1980 the government estimated spending on social assistance at 22 million pesos, while the whole range of food subsidies for consumers totaled almost three billion pesos.[10]

Already in Cuba there are a number of measures that especially help low-income households. For example, rents were set at 10 percent of the income of the head of a household, so that one family might pay 9 pesos a month for their apartment while another pays 35 pesos for a similar apartment in the same building. (Again, however, such a broad-shot policy means that some households that could pay their own way are being carried by the system: take, for instance, a household with three adults working outside the home, all with good salaries but the head of household getting the least. Such a household would wind up paying a mere 3 percent of its income for rent.) Since 1977, day-care fees have been calculated on a sliding scale (from 3 to 40 pesos a month), depending on the combined income of the parents.

Households with very low incomes (below 25 pesos a month per person) are exempted from paying for rent, medicines and meals in worker cafeterias. (While medicines prescribed in hospitals are free to all, those obtained in pharmacies, even with a prescription, must be purchased.) A step in the direction we are suggesting was taken in 1981, when the hike in the rationed food prices was accompanied by an increase in social security benefits.

Who is likely to win the debate on rationing—those who favor a quick frontal blow or the advocates of the long hard pull? The ration advocates have some important advantages. One is bureaucratic inertia. The huge administrative apparatus needed to keep the ration system going will be very hard to dismantle. At the same time the Cuban people have become accustomed to rationing and, as noted earlier, have come to see cheap food as their right, associating rationing with the ideals of social justice upon which the revolution stakes its claim to legitimacy. (Remember, more than half the Cubans alive today were born after the start of the revolution and do not know anything else.) The impression we get is that while Cubans say that rationing is a pain in the neck and they'd love to see it go, they would feel somewhat naked without it. This would be more difficult still if rationing were replaced by high food prices.

Either because the government enjoys most people's support or because it tightly controls public activity, it is unlikely that an end to food subsidies would spark the same outbreaks of rioting that have accompanied such moves in the Dominican Republic, Egypt, Tunisia, Morocco and Poland. But the groundswell of near universal discontent over the increase in restaurant prices in 1981 (subsequently rolled back) taught the technocratic planners a lesson they probably have not forgotten.

An important factor in favor of continued rationing is Cuba's low food output per capita. And judging from past experience, gains in food production could come slowly despite the new policies for increasing productivity we discuss in Chapter 10.

On the other hand, an end to rationing is squarely in line with the overall changes in Cuba's economic organization since the mid-1970s: greater emphasis on profitability and productivity. The "self-financing" of food production and distribution would be the logical corollary to these new policies.

Who knows which version of socialism will win out?

CHAPTER 7

Recent visitors to Havana report an outbreak of anti-Castro graffiti—most with the same message: "Better exploited under Batista than starving under Castro."

The revolution has met the basic needs of all. There is no one who goes hungry.

WAYNE SMITH, Chief of U.S. Interests Section in Havana from 1979 to 1982.[2]

Is There Hunger
in Cuba?

 As these reports indicate, there are conflicting answers to a central question of this book: Is there hunger in Cuba today?

Our own view, based on more than a dozen visits to Cuba by the three authors over the past fifteen years, plus the four-year stay of one of the authors (nutritionist Medea Benjamin), is that hunger has been eliminated in Cuba, with very few exceptions. Cubans may not have the kind of foods they want, or even as much as they want, but few suffer from lack of calories or protein.

Moving to Cuba after years of working with malnourished children in Latin America and Africa, Medea took one look at the Cuban population and realized—to her delight—that in Cuba her skills were obsolete. Even the 1982 report prepared for the Joint Economic Committee of the U.S. Congress acknowledged that Cuba had achieved a "highly egalitarian redistribution of income that has eliminated almost all malnutrition, particularly among young children."[3]

In our investigation of hunger in Cuba, we used three approaches to the question. First we looked at Cuba's total food supply. Then we examined key health indicators and patterns. Finally, we investigated studies on the incidence of malnutrition.

Food Availability

The most widespread nutritional problem in the world today is the insufficient intake of calories. (Only in exceptional areas where the dietary staple is not a cereal but a starchy food such as yams, cassava, or plantains is protein seriously lacking.) Are Cubans getting enough calories for an adequate diet? Is there more or less food available since the revolution?

The standard way of assessing a nation's food supply is through food balance sheets. These are created by adding up production, reserve stocks and imports, and then subtracting exports, food used for seed and animal feed, and losses during storage and transportation. The total food available is then divided by the population to get per capita availability. Theoretically, we could compare per capita figures before the revolution and today to see how the food supply has changed.

While that sounds straightforward enough, studies using this comparative approach come up with contradictory results. Some contend that the first decade of the revolution resulted in a serious deterioration of the food supply and that there has been a significant improvement only since the late 1970s. They claim that in 1958, the last year before the revolution, 2,870 calories a day were available per person and it was not until 1980 that this level was reached again. Others go so far as to state that the total supply of calories and proteins is less today than before the revolution.[4] Still others claim that a number of staples—rice, beans, *viandas*, many fruits, meat, and coffee—are less plentiful now than in the years immediately preceding the revolution, and that the only foods in greater supply are eggs, fish, and some dairy products.[5]

On the other end of the debate are scholars such as Swedish economist Claes Brundenius, who finds the scales to be balanced in favor of the revolution. According to Brundenius' calculations, the per capita availability of food and beverages increased by 33 percent between 1958 and 1980.[6]

How can we explain such different and even contradictory conclusions? First of all, there is the issue of statistical reliability. Data from before the revolution are exceedingly unreliable. No single government office was charged with gathering statistics and what data the government did publish relied on tax reports—

faulty sources of information even with governments less corrupt than the Batista regime. With the revolutionary upheaval, many statistical records were destroyed or lost and most of the few trained statisticians left the country. Gradually the new government, with its emphasis on central planning, improved the data base (except for the ultraleft period during the late 1960s when accounting was judged a bourgeois activity). Today Cuban and foreign scholars alike agree that by the late 1970s Cuban statistics had become considerably more reliable.[7]

Then there is the problem of how to compare different periods when some basic definitions have been changed. Before 1963, for example, production totals were calculated by multiplying estimated average yields by the area under cultivation. Since then, however, production statistics have been based on sales to the government purchasing agency. The latter method is likely to be much more realistic because it is based on performance. However it excludes food consumed on the farm, bartered, or sold privately to consumers (both legally and on the black market) and therefore underestimates total production.

Another problem is that some analysts take the quantity of food Cubans can buy through the rationing system as synonymous with the total quantity of food available to them.[8] Such an assumption is way off the mark since it disregards food distributed through restaurants, workplace cafeterias, schools, self-provisioning and the other sources outside the rationing system we discussed in Chapter 4.

But more fundamental than discrepancies in the calculation of total food availability is the erroneous assumption that such aggregate figures can demonstrate something about nutritional status. Even if a nation has enough food available to feed its people, this does not automatically mean the people are well-fed. Far more important than *how much* food is theoretically available is how equitably—or inequitably—it is distributed. Consider the case of Mexico. While per capita food availability in Mexico is well above the nation's requirements, the Mexican health ministry reported in 1983 that 40 percent of the population suffers from a deficient diet. As *Food First: Beyond the Myth of Scarcity*[9] documents, countries whose people go hungry may have plenty of food—it just doesn't get to those who need it.

Statistics on per capita food availability in prerevolution Cuba masked huge gaps between the diets of the rich and the poor. Today, however, Cuba is one of the few countries where per capita figures are likely to approximate actual distribution, thanks to what one analyst of Cuban food policy has referred to as "the equity imposed by wage policy and food rationing."[10]

To illustrate the difference between the Cuban diet before the revolution and today, let's look at Cuba's consumption of eggs and meat. In 1958 four eggs were available per person per month; in 1982 there were nineteen.[11] But more important than the higher per capita figure is the difference in distribution. In his 1945–46 study of rural conditions in Cuba, Lowry Nelson found that most rural families had hens but were too poor to eat the eggs; instead, they sold them to buy more filling, if less nutritious, staples. The 1956–7 Catholic University Association survey indicated that only 2 percent of agricultural workers and their families ate eggs on a regular basis. In contrast, a 1979 study by the Cuban Consumer Institute found that 96 percent of all Cuban households ate eggs regularly.

Beef is another story, with per capita consumption statistics down considerably since the revolution. Before the revolution, per capita beef consumption was estimated at 48 to 66 pounds per year, depending on the study.[12] During the first years of the revolution, consumption shot up and the national herd was being slaughtered at such an alarming rate that strict rations had to be imposed. Today the Cuban government estimates beef consumption at only 39 pounds per year per person.[13]

But actual consumption before the revolution was very unequal. For Cuba's poor, beef was a great luxury, eaten only on special occasions. The difference between rural and urban consumption of beef was great. A 1955 study showed that residents of Havana ate eight times more beef, per person, than rural dwellers.[14]

Today, since most beef is sold through the ration system or eaten in workplace and school cafeterias, everyone tends to get about the same amount. While households with higher incomes can consume more by eating in restaurants or buying on the parallel and black markets, no family goes without beef, unlike the situation before the revolution.[15]

According to the UN Food and Agriculture Organization, Cuba's daily per capita caloric intake in 1980 was 2,795 calories,

TABLE 2 Caloric Content of Ration

FOOD	WEIGHT	CALORIES/DAY
Average allocation for one month, one person		
Beef	1 lb. 4 oz.	84
Chicken[a]	1 lb. 11 oz.	40
Rice	5 lb.	275
Cornmeal[b]	4 oz.	14
Beans	1 lb. 4 oz.	66
Oil	8 oz.	68
Lard	1 lb.	136
Sugar	4 lb.	242
Milk (fresh)[c]	4 qt.	86
Milk (canned)[d]	3 qt.	55
Coffee	4 oz.	0
Bread[e]	15 lb.	624
Tomato Sauce	8 oz.	3
Other[f]	—	150
According to Supply[g]		
Viandas	6 lb.	35
Fruit (orange)	1 lb.	7
Vegetable (tomato)	3 lb.	10
TOTAL calories/day		**1,895**

(a) Figure presented is the monthly average, although meat is distributed every nine days (either 12 oz. of meat or 1 lb. of chicken). See Table 1 for calculations.

(b) Cornmeal is the only fixed ration item that is not always available. It seems the goverment is not very concerned about fulfilling this quota because people are not anxious to buy it.

(c) The 4 qt. figure was obtained by multiplying the milk ration for children under seven by the percentage of the population under seven.

(d) The 3 qt. figure was obtained by multiplying canned milk allocations for different population groups (6 cans per month for 7–13 age group; 3 cans/ month for 13–65; 6 cans/month for over 65) by proportion of population in each age group.

(e) Officialy part of the ration but often so readily available that it is sold off the *libreta*.

(f) Mayonnaise, sweets, cooking wine, baby food, etc.

(g) Fruits and vegetables are seasonal and the ration varies according to supply. This is a rough estimate.

well above UN standards.[16] In 1983 the Organization of American States reported that Cuba ranked second in per capita food availability in Latin America (Argentina was number one). Cubans are guaranteed about four-fifths of these calories through the ration. Table 2 gives a breakdown of the ration's caloric content. While it varies somewhat from month to month, the ration provides around 1,900 calories a day.

In addition to the average ration, groups with special needs— young children, pregnant women, the elderly and sick—get extra rations to ensure they have an adequate diet. Cubans generally receive another 800 calories or so from any number of the nonrationed food sources we discussed in Chapter 4. Most, if not all Cubans, are therefore guaranteed a diet sufficient in calories. While "per capita food availability" may not have changed significantly since the revolution, distribution surely has.[17]

Changes in the Patterns of Health

Another way to address the hunger question in Cuba is through changes in health patterns. The infant mortality rate measures the number of babies, for each 1,000 born alive, who die before their first birthday. In young children especially, a vicious interaction exists between malnutrition and infection: malnutrition weakens the body, making it more susceptible to infection, which in turn leads to further malnutrition since the infected intestines cannot properly absorb nutrients. Coupled with virtually nonexistent health care, this cycle of malnutrition spells death for forty thousand people a day in the third world, according to UNICEF estimates.

Figures on infant mortality before the revolution were little more than "guestimates." Since about half the women gave birth at home, particularly in the rural areas, the births and deaths of many children went unrecorded. Infants who died before being registered as born were not recorded.[18] Spanish law, still in effect in Cuba until 1965, held that only a baby who had survived 24 hours could be counted as born.[19] The Batista dictatorship claimed an infant mortality rate of 33 deaths per thousand, while some researchers estimated it as high as 125.[20] See p. 219

Regardless of the figure one uses for the prerevolution period, it appears that during the first decade of the revolution there was actually an *increase* in the infant mortality rate—from 34.7 in 1959 to 46.7 in 1969, to cite the government's own figures.[21] This increase has been attributed to the exodus of about half of Cuba's doctors during the early 1960s as well as the U.S. embargo against Cuba, which reduced the availability of medical equipment, spare parts, and medicines. Also significant was the departure of large numbers of middle- and upper-class families with low mortality rates. But perhaps the most important explanation lies, ironically, in the rapid extension of free health services. Especially in rural areas and poor urban neighborhoods, these new services meant that for the first time every birth and death was registered.

By the 1970s, more hygienic living conditions, a better diet, and free and accessible health care for all Cubans led to a dramatic decline in infant deaths. By 1983, the infant mortality rate had been brought down to the astonishingly low figure of 16.8.[22] Compare this figure with that of the neighboring country of Haiti, where the 1975–80 estimate of infant mortality rate is 126.9.[23] Cuba's rate is now the lowest in Latin America and on a par with the most industrially developed countries in the world. (In fact, it is lower than the rate for the black population in the United States, which in 1982 was 18.1.)[24]

Cuba's ongoing success in lowering infant mortality rates has become a matter of national pride. Six-month updates make the front page, and a surprising number of Cubans can tell you what the current statistics are.

There are still significant regional differences. The western province of Matanzas, for example, has a rate of 12.2 while the easternmost province of Guantanamo has 21.6. These differences reflect historical differences in the level of development between the eastern and western parts of the island, but the gap is definitely narrowing.[25]

Another sensitive index of the nutritional well-being and health of a population is the physical growth and development of children. As the social welfare of a population improves, the children born into that population become taller. In 1972, the Cuban Ministry of Health carried out a growth study, one of the most comprehensive ever undertaken in any country, using a sample of 56,000 children from ages 0 to 20.[26]

The study found that, while the growth curve for Cuban children under ten was the same as the British curve, in the older age group (10 to 20 years) the British children averaged almost three centimeters taller. This finding suggests that younger Cuban children showed more growth than older ones because, since they were born after the start of the revolution, they have benefited from the generalized improvements in health services and nutrition. A 1982 follow-up study (to be completed in late 1984) is expected to show that Cuban children of all ages are growing as well as, if not better than, the children studied in London.[27]

Cause of death is another revealing health indicator. The leading causes of death in Cuba of the 1980s are different from those of the 1950s. Acute diarrhea and tuberculosis—diseases associated with poverty—no longer figure among the top ten causes of death. Infectious and parasitic diseases caused 13.3 percent of deaths in 1962, but only 2 percent in 1980.[28] As some Cuban officials are proud to note, the principal causes of death in Cuba today are similar to those causes in developed countries: heart disease, malignant tumors, cardiovascular disease, and accidents. "Cuba now faces the same health problems as advanced industrialized countries—the predominance of chronic diseases such as cancer, heart disease, pulmonary disease, diabetes and asthma," concluded a group of U.S. health professionals visiting Cuba in 1980. "These diseases have replaced infectious disease as the main causes of morbidity and mortality."[29] As a result of these changes, life expectancy has risen—from 57 years in 1958 to 73.5 years in 1983, comparable to expectancies in advanced industrialized nations. Cubans are dying from diseases associated with older populations.

Why does Cuba, admittedly an economically underdeveloped country, have the disease pattern of developed countries? The first reason is equitable food distribution. Seasonal unemployment, which had left many Cuban families hungry for a part of the year, was eliminated. The "floor" in food consumption provided by government rationing and subsidies has helped eliminate most undernutrition. Second, Cuba's extensive health-care system—which, according to a 1982 U.S. Congressional Report, is "superior in the third world and rivals that of numerous developed countries"[30]—has led to the elimination of such curable diseases as tetanus of the newborn, diphtheria, malaria, and polio. Third, improved sanitary conditions, with a better distribution of basic foods, have reduced the incidence of such infectious diseases as acute diarrhea and tuberculosis.

The Evidence of Malnutrition

Finally, to determine if there is hunger in Cuba today, we need to look at available studies on the incidence of malnutrition. (While the term malnutrition technically applies to both overnutrition—obesity—and undernutrition, we will use its common definition, which refers only to the latter.)

Malnutrition continues to be the number-one killer of young children in the third world. A study of the causes of death of over 35,000 children in fifteen countries of Latin America during the 1970s found malnutrition to be the direct cause of 7 percent of the deaths and the indirect cause of 46.2 percent.[31]

There is little data on malnutrition in Cuba before the revolution. But the few studies that do exist reveal malnutrition to have been widespread. Nutrition patterns reflected the inequities within the society at large, so that the rural areas were worse off than the cities, the lower classes worse off than the upper, and nonwhites worse off than whites.

A 1956 study of sixth-grade children found that 43.7 percent of the public school children studied were underweight, as opposed to 10.4 percent of private school children. "Since the private school children probably represent the irreducible minimum of underweight in a population group having adequate food supply, the proportion underweight in this group would seem to indicate that about a third of the public school group is not receiving sufficient nutrients to maintain normal weight," the study concluded.[32] This study did not even cover over 50 percent of Cuba's children, those who were too poor to attend school and who undoubtedly had the most serious nutrition problems.[33]

The 1957 Catholic University Association survey claimed that 91 percent of agricultural workers were malnourished. While we have shown that this figure is inflated,[34] it nevertheless conveys the magnitude of rural malnutrition. The 1951 World Bank study quotes an eminent Cuban physician: "Although we have no master statistics, it is possible to estimate that more than 30 percent or 40 percent of the city population, including Havana, suffers from hyponutrition [undernutrition]. . . . In the rural zones that percentage is doubtless more than 60 percent."[35]

During the first decade of the revolution, no national nutrition studies were made, only a few local surveys. In 1969 a survey of the isolated rural community of San Andrés de Caiguanabo, on the northwestern tip of Cuba, reported that 42 percent of preschool children had first-degree malnutrition and 6 percent second-degree and that their diets were deficient in protein, vitamin A, and vitamin B. A nutritionist involved in the study told us San Andrés was one of the poorest areas in Cuba and so isolated that inbreeding was common. A 1967 study of the sugar region of Alquizar reported that 25 percent of the preschool children had first-degree malnutrition and 5 percent second degree. They also observed widespread calcium and vitamin A deficiencies.

Some academics avail themselves of these studies to make general statements about the nutritional status of the Cuban population today, drawing such conclusions as "malnutrition affects at least one of every four Cuban children."[36] But these studies, conducted in the 1960s and in depressed areas, cannot be used to describe the nutritional status of Cubans in the 1980s. By the 1970s malnutrition was apparently reduced to a very low level, as the 1972 child-growth study indicates. This study was more comprehensive than either of the earlier two studies: it examined 56,000 Cuban children from all over the country. It found no incidence of second- and third-degree malnutrition and only 3 percent of the children with the milder first-degree malnutrition.[37]

Cuba's attempts to deal with the problem of malnutrition throw light on the general problems of effective public policy in this field.

In 1960, nutrition rehabilitation centers (*hogares de recuperación infantil*) were set up to treat malnourished children. By 1973 there were 52 such centers throughout the country. But one by one they closed down, and by 1980 there were none left.[38] One reason for closing them was diminishing need, as the number of malnourished children decreased. Another reason was that they were not very effective. A study of 239 children discharged from 11 centers found that, despite an exceptionally lengthy average stay of 113.7 days, 60.3 percent were still underweight.[39] Just as in many other countries where such centers have been created, it was found that placing malnourished children in an artificial environment for a few months is not an effective means of combating malnutrition.

Much more effective has been Cuba's emphasis on *prevention* of malnutrition through a nutrition surveillance system. As part of this system, the weight gains and hemoglobin levels of all pregnant women are monitored. The women are provided with special food rations, counseled on the importance of a balanced diet and given free vitamin and iron pills throughout their pregnancy.

All Cuban babies get monthly checkups during their first year. (Remember, all health care is free and mothers are given time off from work to take their children to the doctor.) Babies' heights and weights are charted. Underweight children are given special rations and, in severe cases, hospitalized.

Low birth weight, however, is a continuing problem. "We licked polio in four years, diphtheria and tetanus of the newborn in six years, malaria in seven years, but with low birth weights you're up against 'historical hunger'," an official of the Ministry of Health told us. By "historical hunger" he meant that mothers who previously suffered from chronic malnutrition tend to have underweight children.[40] With 99 percent of births now taking place in hospitals, the weight of virtually all newborns is carefully checked, especially infants with low birth weights (under 2.5 kg). The number of low birth weights in Cuba remained high through the mid-1970s and began to fall in 1978. It wasn't until 1980 that they fell to under 10 percent of all births, the level considered acceptable by World Health Organization standards.

There are still isolated cases of malnutrition. The Cuban nutritionists we spoke with attributed these cases to a variety of factors: children of alcoholic or very young mothers, children not living with their mothers, families who have recently migrated from the countryside and are living on the periphery of the cities, lack of breastfeeding, and lack of early weaning.

In the next chapter we will look at the content of the Cuban diet and how satisfied people are with it. What we have seen is that hunger is a thing of the past. While to us in the United States this may not seem to be a startling accomplishment, let us remember that no other country in all of Latin America—including those with greater per capita food supplies—can make this claim. In our view, it is the single most unassailable achievement of the Cuban revolution.

CHAPTER 8

The best thing I can say about Cuban food is that it is filling.

ANONYMOUS CUBAN DIPLOMAT

Split Peas Again?

 The fact that Cuba has eradicated malnutrition does not mean it has eliminated nutritional problems or that the people are satisfied with their diet. But before we look at the remaining problems—and even at "new" ones—let us describe what most Cubans eat during the course of a typical day so that we can better consider how the Cuban diet contributes to those problems.

What Cubans Eat

Breakfast is generally nonexistent or else a piece of toast with butter and *café con leche* (coffee with milk). Cubans rarely eat eggs in the morning; a 5,000-family survey by the Cuban Consumer Institute found that only 1 percent of the households ate eggs for breakfast. Nor do they drink fruit juice, which is difficult to obtain.

Midmorning and midafternoon snacks are usually sweet: a piece of cake or pie, yogurt with plenty of sugar, soda, or an ice cream cone. Or it might be a buttered roll, a roll with a croquette, a fried meat patty, an omelette, or sometimes a sandwich of just plain mayonnaise.

Lunch and dinner differ little one from the other. Most common is a plate of black beans or split peas, rice, some kind of meat, chicken, fish or eggs, *vianda* (if available), and bread. The most common desserts are cream cheese with guava jam, custard, bread pudding, and rice pudding.

The menu for festive occasions—whether at the workplace, neighborhood committee, birthday, or wedding—is standard: *congri* or *moros y cristianos* (beans and rice cooked together), pork, yucca, tomato salad (optional), bread, cake, soda, and beer.

The old saying *"sin arroz no hay comida"* (without rice, it's not a meal) still holds true for the majority of Cubans. When rice quotas were cut in 1966, Cubans went to the extreme of cutting spaghetti into tiny pieces to resemble rice. The rice tradition came to Cuba from Africa (through the slave trade), Spain (through the colonizers), and China (through the contracted workers).

The U.S. embargo, a sharp decline in rice production in the first years of the revolution, and the cutoff of rice imports from China in the late 1960s made wheat more important. Spaghetti and macaroni made from imported wheat have become staples in the Cuban diet since the revolution. And bread and crackers, previously identified with wealthy urban diets, are now daily fare for everyone.[1]

Cornmeal, once an important staple in the rural Cuban diet, is now spurned as "poor man's food." Cornmeal was the traditional food for slaves, and during depressions poor people often lived on three meals a day of corn gruel. The Consumer Institute survey found that 44 percent of Cubans dislike cornmeal and consider it bad for their health.

The preferred meat is beef, eaten as thin steaks fried with salt, garlic, onion, and lemon. As we have seen, the ration of beef is quite limited, and only in late 1982 was beef available on the parallel market at a very high price. Chicken is often a Sunday dish or a dish to serve guests, while pork is *the* dish for holidays and special occasions.

Beans are also part of Cuban tradition. Cubans prefer black, red, and pinto beans, but the bean ration is usually divided between these preferred types and the unpopular (imported) split peas. While Cubans can eat black beans every day with no complaints, they have developed an aversion to split peas. Split peas are served ad nauseam in institutional settings (school, work, military). Cubans say you can't cook split peas without some kind of meat, preferably bacon or sausage, and lots of spices. They complain that split peas cooked at cafeterias are often tasteless.

The revolution has made eggs one of the mainstays of the diet. On a per capita basis, Cubans consume a tremendous number of eggs. The Consumer Institute Survey reported that 33 percent of the households consume eggs every day and another 50 percent two to three times a week. Eggs are quick to prepare, readily available, and cheap. The revolution has changed the old Cuban saying "when there's nothing else, we'll eat taro" to "when there's nothing else, we'll eat eggs."

Fish consumption has also increased dramatically since the revolution. The Consumer Institute study found that 44 percent of Cuban households ate fish at least once a week and 43 percent every two weeks. Cubans have been called "people with their backs to the sea" since, strangely enough, fish was never part of the traditional Cuban diet. Domestic consumption has jumped from 10.6 pounds per person per year in 1958 to 33 pounds in 1978,[2] and by 1979 fish was being sold off the ration. Refrigerated fish stores have been set up all over the island, bringing fish to rural areas where it was previously unknown.The Cuban government sees the increased consumption of fish as one of the achievements of the revolution, but some Cubans are not so delighted. It seems that before the revolution, those who did eat fish ate what they considered high-quality fish and seafood—lobster, shrimp, crab, snapper, bass, grouper—from the island's coastal waters. Since the revolution, Cuba's domestic catch has increased eight-fold, but most of the higher-value fish and seafood is exported. Meanwhile, Cuba imports low-priced fish to help meet the growing internal demand. This makes economic sense: according to FAO estimates, Cuba could import five times the amount of fish it exported and still come out with a profit.[3] But it has meant limited variety and less satisfaction for Cubans.

Most of the fish now available in Cuba is frozen fish from the Soviet Union or Cuban fresh-water fish. Cuban fresh-water fish come from irrigation canals and aquaculture projects. The Ministry of Food Industries turns out fish sticks, patties, and packages of chopped fish meat, all sold off the ration at low prices. Once in a while, squid, a well-liked seafood, is sold. But whereas fish was once a treat, today it is eaten for lack of other choices. Nitza Villapoll, Cuba's "Galloping Gourmet," told us that when friends come to dine they are shocked to see her preparing fish. "Most Cubans think fish is only to be eaten as a last resort!" she told us.[4]

A list of most Cubans' favorite fruits would include mamey (chocolate-colored exterior with an orange flesh and the texture of very rich pudding), mango, guava, avocado, and plantains. Before the revolution, citrus fruits were eaten mainly by higher-income households. Over the years, citrus production has increased, and although the bulk of the crop is exported, domestic consumption has still increased.[5]

While demand for oranges and lemons is high, beautiful grapefruits (when not exported) lie rotting because most Cubans believe they lower your blood pressure and make you weak and dizzy.

Raw vegetables are considered "rabbit food," and traditional prejudices against eating them remain strong. Lowry Nelson, describing rural Cuba in the late 1940s, found "green and yellow vegetables almost totally absent from the rural diet."[6] The only vegetables most Cubans will eat raw are lettuce, tomatoes (green), cucumbers, and watercress. Still, one sees gorgeous bunches of watercress sitting on store counters for days until they finally wilt and are heaped into the garbage truck.

One thing that Cubans cannot and do not get enough of is coffee. Vice President Rodriguez called Cuba's traditional coffee consumption level "irrational" and claimed it was higher than in Europe or anywhere else in Latin America. Rationing has dealt a severe blow to coffee consumption. Supply still falls way short of demand, although there is now more coffee available at cafeterias and snack bars, mixed coffee for sale off the ration, and, as of 1983, pure coffee for sale at a very high price on the parallel market.

The favorite alcoholic beverages are beer and rum. While Cuban rum is famous the world over, Cuba also makes five different brands of beer that rival many European brews in quality. Beer was in short supply during the 1960s but is now more readily available and at moderate prices. But the best Cuban rum, Havana Club, is hard to come by since most of it is exported. Lower-quality rums are sold but are quite expensive (12 pesos a bottle). While the high cost of alcohol has undoubtedly cut down on its use, it has also encouraged the consumption of ethyl alcohol. Sold in the pharmacies for 40 cents a pint, it is mixed with three parts water, a handful of sugar . . . and down the hatch.

The Diet in Terms of Nutritional Content

The Cuban diet is high in total calories.

By 1980, 2,860 calories worth of food were (statistically) available for every Cuban every day, well above the internationally recognized minimum requirement of 2,500. Plans call for increasing this figure to 3,155 calories by 1985.[6] Cuba sets its nutritional standards higher than the United Nations recommendations, which it believes are set artificially low as a concession to many governments who fear political repercussions if a large percentage of their populations are judged undernourished.

The Cuban diet is high in fat, especially saturated fats.

Cuban nutritionists we interviewed believe that fat consumption in Cuba is considerably lower than in the United States. Fats provide about 30 percent of total calories in Cuba as opposed to over 40 percent in the United States and fall within the FAO recommended guidelines, they told us. Our own observations, however, led us to believe that fat consumption is higher than 30 percent and on the rise, especially now that extra cooking oil has been made available for sale off the ration.

Most Cuban food is fried. Chicken is usually fried, meat is fried, fish is fried, beans and stews are prepared with heavy doses of oil, and *viandas* are inevitably fried or, as in the case of cassava, boiled and then doused in a sauce of oil and garlic. The only way most Cubans will eat potatoes is French fried. Even rice is cooked with a generous wad of lard to make the kernels separate and shine. Many households do not have ovens, just stoves with two or four burners, and those which do have ovens rarely use them for anything but baking desserts.

Oil for frying is used again and again until every drop has been consumed. Lard is usually the first item used up in the monthly ration, and it is probably only thanks to the ration that it is consumed somewhat sparingly. Given the importance of lard and other animal fats in the diet, the Cuban diet is exceptionally high in saturated fats. While in the United States about 40 percent of fats are saturated, in Cuba the figure is over 60 percent.[7]

The Cuban diet is high in carbohydrates.
A typical Cuban meal may combine rice, French fries, bread, and a starchy dessert like rice pudding. Or a typical meal at a pizzeria would be an individual cheese pizza (the equivalent of about two large slices in the United States), plus a bowl of spaghetti and a fried doughy dessert.

The typical Cuban diet is particularly high in empty calories from refined sugar. Sugar is one of the coveted ration items, and the four pounds per person per month (or six pounds in the eastern provinces) is quickly consumed. Cakes, pies, candies, ice cream, and soda are typical snack foods at work and school cafeterias and often substitute for meals. It is common to see high school students skip lunch at school and run down to the local ice-cream parlor, Coppelia, for the only "salad" Cubans really like—an *ensalada* consisting of five large scoops of ice cream! All drinks—fruit juices, coffee, tea—are usually heavily sweetened. At snack bars people ladle tablespoon after tablespoon of sugar into small glasses of yogurt. (Some say yogurt, widely introduced since the revolution thanks to a Bulgarian aid project, has caught on only because it is served in cafeterias and snack bars with a sugar bowl—which allows sugar addicts to stoke up on the unrationed, free sugar.)

The Cuban diet is adequate in protein.
In 1980, 74.5 grams of protein were theoretically available per person per day in Cuba, more than enough according to any of the commonly used standards.[9] But the government believes more is needed and hopes to increase this level to 81.7 grams by 1985.[10] It also hopes to increase the percentage of protein from animal rather than vegetable sources.

The Cuban diet is low in fiber.
The diet most Cubans eat (and want to eat) is lacking in high-fiber foods such as unprocessed cereals and fresh fruits and vegetables. Most visitors immediately notice one effect: constipation.

The Cuban diet provides adequate vitamins and minerals.
What Cubans typically eat gives them basically enough vitamins and minerals, although low consumption of fruits and vege-

tables, especially at certain times of the year, may lead to specific deficiencies.

Obesity: A Growing Problem

Cuba's major nutritional problem today is not undernutrition but overnutrition. A 1973 study found that 20.2 percent of children in Havana's day-care centers were obese.[11] A 1977 survey of 16- to 18-year-old adolescents revealed that 14 percent were obese.

Obesity is a serious health problem. It is a risk factor for numerous diseases, including diabetes, hypertension, and heart disease. All the Cuban health officials and health workers we talked with inevitably brought up the problem of obesity, whether or not we asked about it.

From what we have seen of Cuba's typical diet (high in calories, high in fat), it is not surprising that obesity is prevalent. But obesity is also one of the most difficult problems to combat because of its cultural significance as a measure of prosperity. A comfortable roll still remains a sign of well-being. While in the United States you'd probably gain an enemy by telling a friend how much weight he or she has gained, in Cuba there's no greater compliment. *"Qué gorda estás,"* ("How fat you are!,") really means "You're looking great." And *"Estás flaca,"* ("You're thin,") translates more like "You don't look so good these days." The same is true for babies. You can tell someone how cute his or her baby is or what pretty eyes she has, but if you really want to please, you say how fat she is.

One of the authors was unfortunate enough to have a skinny child while living in Cuba. While pediatricians in the United States who examined her just shrugged their shoulders and said, "Don't worry, she'll eat when she gets hungry," the Cuban pediatricians declared she was severely malnourished and needed hospitalization. On the mother's insistence, they finally backed down and agreed not to hospitalize the child on the condition that she follow a strict diet to fatten her up. This one-year-old was given an extra meat ration (filet mignon) and *viandas* (eight pounds a week), prescribed six meals a day, and loaded down with vitamin and mineral supplements, as well as the notorious "formula." It seems that almost all Cuban children, at some point in their lives, are given an "appetite enhancing" formula which includes an antihistamine called cyprohistadina and B vitamins. If the "formula" doesn't do the trick, there are numerous home remedies such as a shot of wine in the morning, an egg yolk, an herbal tea concoction, or else the antihistamine by itself in the stronger pill form. Contrary to the attitude in the United States that appetite is regulated naturally by the body's needs, Cubans are not about to leave such an important issue as their children's weight up to the whims of nature.

How Do People Feel about Their Diet?

It should be clear that the Cuban diet is far from ideal as far as health is concerned. Ironically, as the variety of foods has increased in recent years, people's diets have deteriorated. Cuban nutritionists we spoke with agree that in the early days of the revolution, when there was little food available off the ration, people had a more balanced diet. For example, now that beer is more available in restaurants, it is common to see people starting off the day with a couple of bottles for breakfast. The greater availability of cakes, pies, cookies, ice cream, and candy has surely increased sugar consumption, just as the new nonrationed cans of cooking oil and pork lard on the free market have increased fat consumption. Unfortunately, as Nitza Villapoll lamented, "people do not always *like* to eat what is best for them." This brings us to another aspect of nutrition, the question of what people *want* to eat and how satisfied they are with their current diet.

While many complain the diet is monotonous and they don't get enough of the foods they want, Cubans' satisfaction with their diet depends largely on their situation before the revolution.

How did the revolution affect the diet of the rich? Most of Cuba's country-club set didn't stay around long enough to be affected, having left for Miami during the early 1960s. Those who stayed behind tried to keep up their previous standards by hoarding and eating out in restaurants. Many received compensation payments for nationalized property and thus could afford to eat out regularly and pay someone to stand in line for their rations. The Cuban film *The Survivors* is a parody of a bourgeois family just after the revolution who, fearing a drop in their standard of living, have truckload after truckload of food sent to the house. And the book *Inconsolable Memories*, also about the early years of the revolution, describes the Cuban bourgeoisie turning into "an endless intestine: obsessed by food."[12]

An American visiting Havana during the early 1960s recalled sitting next to an upper-class Cuban woman at a coffee shop at lunch time one day. "I noticed the woman had just finished a large bowl of potage (a thick bean soup) and was well into her main course, a beef stew made up of beef chunks, string beans, and potatoes, accompanied by an avocado salad, three slices of bread, and a large plate of black beans and rice. . . . Then she began her dessert: a large wedge of layer cake topped with a scoop of ice cream, followed by the customary Cuban expresso." The American, astounded at the quantities of food this woman was consuming, was even more astounded to hear her say that she was on her way to the United States "because I'm not going to die of hunger here!"[13]

Perhaps most affected by the early shortages were reasonably well-off professionals, civil servants, unionized workers, and rural technicians. Before the revolution, these groups had enough money to eat well and plenty of food was available. With rationing, food became more of an issue in their lives.

In contrast to these groups, the revolution improved the diet of the vast majority—the urban poor, the agricultural workers, and even the private farmers, for they had access to government stores selling at low, fixed prices. For Cuba's poor, the revolution meant more quantity, variety, and, perhaps most important of all, regularity.

But people's perceptions of these improvements vary—and most often the complaint is monotony. One night we overheard a group of elderly men over a game of dominoes. "Before the revolution the stores were overflowing with food from all over the world," one of the men reminisced, his eyes sparkling. "I remember one supermarket where you could buy about thirty different kinds of meat—salami, ham, ribs—you name it. Now you've got to take whatever there is, like it or not." "But who could afford to buy in those fancy stores?" responded another. "Rich folks from Vedado, not poor slobs like us. I remember working twelve hours a day and then not having enough money to buy my kid a decent meal on her birthday. So don't give me that crap about fancy supermarkets!"

We found that young people were more likely to complain about the monotony of the diet than older people. This is logical, given that they have no memory of life before the revolution nor of the hardships of the 1960s.

The Cuban government seems to look at the diet in narrow terms of calories and proteins. The policy of making enough food available to cover requirements, laudable as it is, often disregards the question of satisfaction. While black beans and split peas contain similar nutrients and are both excellent foods from a nutritional point of view, the fact remains that Cubans like black beans and don't like split peas. And although eggs and fish are splendid sources of protein, Cubans want beef and pork. Government planners have also overlooked many small items, such as onions and garlic, so essential to the question of satisfaction.

The Role of Food in the Revolution

In the early days of the revolution, equality in eating was an important factor in forging national unity, especially in times of difficulty. Everyone knew that what was on their table each day was on the table of all others, and that what was missing for one was missing for the rest. All Cubans—from an important state functionary to an unskilled worker—received the same ration. An observer of the early years of the revolution noted that the slogan "Everyone eats the same," launched by Fidel Castro when rationing was established, "had an immediate echo among the people and was later adopted as appropriate for . . . different situations when privilege or inequality was being fought." [14]

Food also became an issue of national pride. Billboards in the early 1960s read *"Chicle, no; taro, si."* Chiclets, the symbol of U.S. penetration the world over, was out. "Good riddance," the Cubans said. "We'll chew on taro." The disappearance of another universal symbol of U.S. penetration, Coca Cola, was hailed in song: "If you want to drink rum but *without* Coca Cola, Cuba's the place to go." [15]

Foreign imports were scorned. "Why should we eat peaches?" Fidel Castro asked the people. "We were made to think that peaches were the best thing going, and when we'd visit someone's house they'd offer us peaches. So we all thought that . . .

peaches were better than mangoes, but peaches are expensive and foreign and mangoes are sweeter, cheaper and much better. . . . I remember that on one of my first trips after the triumph of the revolution, everywhere we went they'd give us pear juice or peach juice or other fruits [*sic*] juices from California and I'd ask them: 'What's with the pear juice?' And on the next trip they'd give us guava juice, tamarind juice, and mango juice. Tamarind juice is marvelous."[16]

Cubans were encouraged to sacrifice, to put off consumption today for a better future tomorrow. They were constantly reminded of the tradeoffs between consumption and investment. "Investing in development necessarily implies not consuming everything we might consume," Fidel explained. "A good example for us: our foreign exchange. If we spend it all on consumer goods and nothing on a single machine, irrigation equipment, or machinery to build drainage systems or water conservation projects, the sure result is all too clear. We would eat today, but it is certain that we wouldn't be able to eat next year, and as time went on, there would be less and less food. . . . In other words, with foreign credit we can buy bulldozers or powdered milk, one or the other."[17]

Foreigners were often amazed by the willingness of everyday Cubans to sacrifice and to do so with a sense of high purpose. "How does Castro do it?" a tourist asked a visiting U.S. journalist. "He delivers bad news—and everybody claps." The tourist was referring to Fidel's announcement that the coffee ration would have to be cut from two ounces to a half ounce a week in order to save foreign exchange. The journalist concluded that "This generation of Cubans does not expect a chicken in every pot, let alone a car in every garage; what they confidently look forward to is an educated, industrialized, self-sufficient nation."[18]

Not only did Fidel Castro call on Cubans to make sacrifices for Cuba's sake, but for people all over the world. A poignant example is his speech at a 1972 mass rally in solidarity with the people of Chile. He explained that Chile needed more sugar than it could pay for but that Cuba could not afford to renege on any of its prior sales commitments, so that "anything our country gives away must be taken from what we consume." He then went on to propose that each month, Cubans donate part of their sugar quota to Chile, for a people's heroism is not only measured by its willingness to "give its blood for its brother" but also by "its willingness to share its food."[19]

In 1968, when the adult milk ration was cut, there was a rumor going around that Cuba was sending milk to Vietnam. Fidel made a speech discounting the rumor, but emphasizing the real point: "The Vietnamese have never asked us for milk, but if the Vietnamese should ask for milk, our fitting response, our most basic duty, would be to send it to them! A part or half or, if necessary, all of it. Because the Vietnamese are giving something more for us and are giving something more for the world!"[20]

But by the 1970s, the revolutionary symbolism of food had declined. The shift from moral to material incentives has meant a decreased emphasis on egalitarianism. Revolution is no longer conceived of as "everyone eats the same." And while sending food to countries poorer than Cuba is still hailed in theory, government leaders are well aware of the people's reluctance to continue making sacrifices.

Efforts to Change Diet

The Cuban diet is far from ideal on a number of counts. It is not particularly healthful. It is also quite bland and monotonous. Much of that is a result of scarcity (few condiments available, little variety of dishes). But traditional Cuban cuisine is not particularly exciting either, especially compared to other Caribbean cultures.

Neither is the diet appropriate for the Cuban climate. The standard Cuban meal of beans, rice, meat, *vianda*, bread, and dessert, eaten at midday when the temperature hovers around 100 degrees, goes down like lead.

The present-day Cuban diet is also not economical for the nation. The emphasis on wheat automatically involves massive imports. The emphasis on milk entails expensive production and substantial imports which must be bought with hard currency.

In Cuba, diet is controlled much more directly by government decisions than in most countries. The government also assumes direct responsibility for the nation's health. It is interesting, then, to consider the government's attempts to change the country's nutrition and dietary habits.

One way the government influences diet is simply by the foods it makes available, both on and off the ration. The decision to give priority to high-protein foods (milk, eggs, and fish) has undoubtedly influenced nutrition levels. So has the introduction of new foods, such as yogurt. The government saw yogurt, along with ice cream, as a way to increase milk consumption among the adult population. It made yogurt available in snack bars, work and school cafeterias, and milk stores, and per capita consumption soared from less than 0.1 kilogram per person per year in 1963 to 5 kilograms in 1980.

Not all new foods have met with such success. Brown bread, also previously unheard-of in Cuba, was introduced in 1980. It was not made available *instead* of white bread, but rather alongside it and off the ration. A few health-minded people, especially foreigners, eagerly bought the brown bread up. But to most Cubans it became known as *pan de diabéticos*, diabetics' bread, to be eaten only by the sick.

The government also influences people's habits through price mechanisms. Smoking and drinking, for example, are discouraged by high prices. On the other hand, the consumption of certain foods, such as fish, is encouraged through subsidies.

The government can also decree changes in the food processing industry which, like all other industries in Cuba, is state-owned. Thus in the late 1970s, on the basis of recommendations from the Department of Nutrition, a decision was made to reduce the sugar content of baby foods and processed fruit juices.[21]

But such changes are not always successful. In our interview with the vice president, he told us of their attempt to reduce the fat content of Cuban milk from 3 percent to 2.8 percent. The result was an onslaught of complaints that the milk had been watered down.

The government does make attempts at nutrition education. There are radio and television shows, as well as newspaper columns, devoted to promoting good nutrition. Nitza Villapoll does television programs on the need to switch from saturated to unsaturated fats, and Cuba's largest circulation magazine, *Bohemia*, recently began a series of full-page nutrition ads on such topics as how to retain nutrients when cooking. Mass organizations and clinics also give talks on nutrition. But the ineffectiveness of the country's nutrition education was made clear in a 1979 survey conducted by the Institute of Consumer Demand. The study showed that only 13 percent of Cubans knew what foods contain carbohydrates and only 27 percent knew what foods are high in calories. A mere 4 percent of those questioned had any idea how the body uses the different nutrients.

While the government tries to influence people's nutrition— through health measures, education, price, distribution, etc.— our overall impression is that Cuban dietary problems have been attacked piecemeal rather than with a comprehensive strategy.

Obesity, for example, has not been attacked through diet but by a campaign against sedentary living. Cubans will wait in the sweltering heat for a crowded bus rather than walk a few blocks. Beginning in 1980, a barrage of advertising on radio, television, and in newspapers encouraged physical activity. Exercise programs sprouted up throughout the island, and work centers were encouraged to turn their coffee breaks into aerobics classes.

But while physical activity is an important part of reducing, so is eating less. A popular health booklet put out in 1983 says, "The easiest way to lose weight is through more physical activity"; eating less is only mentioned as a minor issue.[22]

A campaign against smoking was also begun in the early 1980s. Cuba has always been a nation of cigar and cigarette smokers. The image of Fidel Castro with his long beard and army fatigues would be incomplete without a big cigar clenched in his teeth. But those days are over; as part of the campaign, Castro pledged not to smoke in public.

Compared to the exercise and anti-smoking campaigns, and countless others the revolution has undertaken over the years, the "nutrition campaign" seems quite feeble. As to the reasons why, we can only speculate. One reason might be that government leaders themselves are not totally convinced that the diet needs changing. Many of the officials we interviewed seemed to accept uncritically the "modern" western diet as superior. Take the question of animal versus vegetable protein. We discussed this in our interview with Vice President Rodriguez, and while he recognized that animal protein may not be better nutritionally or economically, he saw it as associated with development.

"We don't support the idea that has been tossed around in international circles that developed countries are going to have animal protein while developing countries get vegetable protein," he told us.[23]

Perhaps the government is reluctant to encourage changes in the diet until there is a stable supply of alternative foods. How can you tell people to eat fewer sweets and more fruit, for example, when fruit is only available a few months of the year and even then in short supply?

With continued scarcity, making changes in diet is a politically volatile issue that the government might just as soon avoid. The goal was set at the beginning of the revolution, for example, that every child under seven would get a liter of milk a day. Since then, the government has been told time and again by nutritionists that children do not *need* a liter a day, that half a liter would do fine. But, the vice president told us, before we can tell people they don't need so much milk, there must be plenty of milk available for everyone. "If we did it before that," he explained, "the people would say: 'Here they come with technical arguments, when all they want to do is take away half a liter of milk from the kids.' These are political problems," the vice president stressed, "and the people's feelings must be taken into account. We can't be 100 percent scientific because politics won't allow it."[24]

CHAPTER 9

Our idea was to convert the swamp land into enormous rice paddies. Talking to a local worker (in the area), Fidel stressed that the "prognosis" for the region's development was rice. . . . The worker, looking perplexed, stared at Fidel. Then he took off his hat and said, "Say, that prognosis you're talking about, do you eat it with rice?"

ANTONIO NUÑEZ JIMÉNEZ, *EN MARCHA CON FIDEL*[1]

Sugar vs. *Viandas*

The Cuban revolution has been remarkably successful in achieving equitable food distribution. Cuba has become one of the few countries in the third world to eliminate hunger. But what about food production? It is now twenty-five years into the revolution. Still, beans, rice, and *viandas*, not to mention beef, chicken, and dozens of other foods that Cuba seemingly has the potential to produce in great quantity remain in very tight supply. Cuba is dependent on imports for much of the food basic to its diet. Of all fats and oils, 94 percent are imported; more than 80 percent of beans; 40 percent of rice; and 24 percent of milk.[2] Dependence on food imports continues despite strong pressures for Cuba to supply its own food needs: the complete embargo imposed by its former major food supplier; the great distances from its current principal food suppliers; the repeatedly announced expectation that the revolution would bring about material advances; and the nagging popular desire for a more bountiful food supply.

Also disappointing to some observers is the fact that sugar production in postrevolution Cuba seems even more central to agriculture and export earnings than in the 1950s. Sugar cane covered 75 percent of cultivated land in 1982, compared with 60 percent in 1958.[3] Sugar export earnings increased from 80 percent of total foreign exchange in 1957 to 83 percent in 1982.[4]

In fact, Cuba has achieved a feat which no one perceived as a

116

priority of the revolution in 1960: More than any other Caribbean nation, Cuba has modernized its sugar industry. This con-
trasts sharply with the neglect and outright disinvestment under
previous Cuban regimes.

The inability to increase food production and throw off sugar's
domination of the economy represent serious shortcomings of
the Cuban revolution. These shortcomings are the product of
twenty-five years of decision making by the revolution's leadership—decisions which they themselves admit have often been
short-sighted, utopian, or even contradictory. An understanding
of Cuban agriculture today requires a sense of the pivotal policy
shifts and the accompanying achievements and disappointments
of the past.

The First Years: More Food, Less Sugar

*Either the Republic will overthrow sugar cane, or sugar cane will
overthrow the Republic.*

—JOSÉ COMALLONGA, 1946

As early as the 1790s, Cuban policymakers and patriots, scholars
and social critics advocated de-emphasizing sugar production in
favor of a more diversified and smallholder agriculture.[5] A mid–
twentieth-century representative of this long "antisugar" tradition wrote: "Sugar cane, the industry that exploits it, and the
system that has developed around it . . . represent something
foreign to our country, . . . like a parasitic body which, although
attached to us for centuries, still serves foreign rather than national interests."[6]

Nurtured in the antisugar tradition, many of the Cuban revolution's leaders viewed sugar cane as only the dead season, under-
employment, unplanted lands and uncut cane, economic stag-
nation, political corruption by wealthy sugar companies, and
subservience to the United States. Che Guevara recalled in 1964
that many of the revolution's leaders had "a fetishistic idea [that]
connected sugar with our dependence on imperialism and with
the misery in the rural areas."[7] New policy was designed to
"undo" what imperialism had created. "Imperialism meant a one-
crop Cuba; therefore, diversify," an American economist and ad-

visor to the new government, Edward Boorstein, explained.[8]
After all, even such less-than-revolutionary sources as the World
Bank had called for decreased reliance on sugar.[9]

Thus it was no surprise when the revolution's leaders first proposed cutting back on sugar cane acreage in favor of crops for
domestic consumption and nonsugar agricultural exports. The
strategy was to diversify not only on a national basis but on
a local basis as well. Each of the large cane estates and cattle
ranches expropriated under the first agrarian reform law (May
1959) was to develop—virtually overnight—mixed cropping
where before there had been monoculture.

The strategy was not to abandon sugar production but to increase yields so that sugar output would not drop off despite less
acreage in cane. The leadership believed that reforms placing
the big sugar estates and mills into the hands of the workers
would rapidly increase productivity. This confidence was reflected in Cuba's 1959 request to increase its U.S. sugar quota.

The first three sugar harvests of the revolution were good,
particularly the first "people's harvest" of 1961; with 6.7 million
tons produced, it was the second biggest harvest in history.
These good harvests resulted in part from favorable weather, but
even more from living off past investments. The 1961 harvest
was exceptional because for the first time in history, all the cane
was cut. But the underlying antisugar mentality expressed itself
in neglected weeding and replanting. And diversification plans
led to the plowing under of more than two hundred thousand
acres of cane following the 1961 harvest.[10]

René Dumont, the well-known French agronomist and an early
adviser to the revolution, advocated diversification on every estate with the hope that the land would be more fully utilized,
that there would be more year-round employment, and that
greater revenues would be generated. He called for the "libera-
tion" of half the land on each sugar cane estate—20 percent for
forage crops and 30 percent for a wide range of vegetables, as
well as industrial crops such as cotton, sisal, peanuts (for cooking oil), and soybeans (for oil and feed). All estates were to combine crops with livestock: cattle raising would provide more
meat for Cubans and generate export earnings, while crop byproducts would help feed the livestock.

Food self-sufficiency was the principal short-run objective (except, of course, for wheat, for climatic reasons).[11] Plans were hastily drawn up for boosting the production of commodities imported from the United States. Priority was assigned to rice, hog raising, beans, and cotton.[12] Together these items accounted for 60 percent of the foreign exchange Cuba had spent on agricultural imports in 1958.[13] Euphoric projections boasted that long lines and other emerging food supply problems would be eliminated by the end of 1962.[14]

This was a tall order: calculations revealed that Cuba would have to nearly double the amount of land cultivated, given 1958 average yields, to achieve food self-sufficiency.[15] Not only was cane acreage cut back, but massive investments went into reclaiming swampland and clearing maribu, a thorny tropical weed. By 1962, perhaps as much as 440,000 acres of "new lands" had been cleared or reclaimed and planted with the "crops of diversification."[16] The volume of land, labor, and capital resources invested in agriculture noticeably increased in 1960 and 1961.[17]

It was a time of unbridled optimism for Cuba's revolutionary leaders and their advisers. The inner councils were divided, with the pessimists projecting a 13 percent annual growth compared to the optimists' 15 percent![18] In a forecast characteristic of these heady times, one Cuban economist declared that by the end of the decade, Cuban per-capita consumption would be higher than in any Western European country.[19] At the same time Fidel Castro declared: "There is no excuse for the shortage of *viandas*; and we pledge that they will never be scarce again. . . . Between now [August 1961] and February, the production of chickens will increase sevenfold; . . . we promise to overcome, during the rest of the year 1961, all the organizational deficiencies in production and distribution."[20]

During the first two years, the optimism was fueled by impressive production gains. Rice, potatoes, tomatoes, onions, garlic, and *viandas*, and some nonsugar industrial crops all advanced, several to unprecedented levels.[21] The area under rice cultivation doubled between 1958 and 1961. Production increased 60 percent, representing a major advance in the direction of Cuba's goal to free itself from U.S. imports. The potato crop area also doubled in 1958, and plans were drawn up to diminish the need for imported potato seed to achieve greater self-reliance.

To substitute for imported lard, as well as to improve the nutritional quality of fat consumption in the national diet, soybean, sunflower, and peanut production were expanded. Major investments were made in large U.S.-style chicken raising, including efforts to develop an independent genetic capacity. (Cuba had been spending more than $10 million annually on imported eggs and poultry, since the entire commercial chicken industry had been based upon shipment of day-old chicks from Florida.) The fish catch almost doubled from 1958 to 1960, when it reached 68 million pounds.In addition to food self-sufficiency, the plan was to diversify agricultural exports. Che Guevara predicted that the investments being made in citrus, pineapple, bananas, tobacco, and coffee would "triple the present level of exports."[22]

A combination of factors contributed to the early successes: weather conditions were favorable; growing domestic demand gave farmers incentive to increase production; newly created state farms expanded the land under cultivation; and large private farmers cultivated previously idle land to protect themselves from expropriation.[23]

The optimism continued through 1961. But in that year, and to a more alarming extent in 1962, came signs of impending crisis. The output of *viandas*, beans, rice, vegetables, and several industrial crops fell, in some cases sharply. "Our people can be absolutely sure that they can continue to eat 130 pounds of rice per capita," the government's chief agricultural production official promised in May 1962. But six months later, the rice ration was set at seventy-two pounds per person.[24] While agricultural diversification was generally not going well, sugar output was also declining in 1962 and 1963. The 1963 harvest was little more than half the 1961 harvest.

What Had Gone Wrong?

Many factors led to the declining harvests. One was the weather. Less than normal rainfall in the final months of 1961 turned into a full-scale drought in 1962.[25] Vegetables and *viandas* withered. Cattle became thin and bony, further reducing the supply of milk and meat just as more money in the hands of the poor led to an increase in demand.

Another problem was an exodus of trained technical and administrative personnel to the newly opened doors of the United States. The revolution's leaders also chose to replace some technically qualified persons with technically inexperienced ones who had proven themselves sympathetic to the socialist goals of the revolution. "Who should manage a farm?" Castro asked rhetorically. "A revolutionary. What were the prerequisites? That he be a revolutionary."[26]

The Eisenhower administration's 1960 embargo on most exports to Cuba was a tough blow to production since the island's agriculture had become dependent on the U.S. for farm machinery and spare parts, fertilizers, pesticides, and even seeds. "Not only did we have to pay higher than world prices for seeds, but there was obvious tampering with their variety and quality," Cuban Vice President Carlos Rafael Rodriguez told us.[27] Virtually all of Cuba's farm machinery was of U.S. origin, and spare parts were extremely difficult to obtain elsewhere. The lack of a single inexpensive part could bring an entire operation to a complete halt. By mid-1961, the official estimate was that over one-third of the country's tractors were out of service.[28] Soon a shortage of functioning trucks meant that substantial quantities of farm products were lost in the countryside simply because there was no way to get them to market.[29] Diversification was also obstructed by the de facto ban on U.S. exports of breeding hens and other animals.[30]

Internally, the new government lacked the organizational resources to design and implement sweeping agricultural and industrial changes. Che Guevara's analysis of the disappointments in this period emphasized that the simultaneous effort to change the structure of agriculture and to diversify proved overwhelming.[31] Organizational shortcomings made for costly bottlenecks in the distribution of seeds, pesticides, and fertilizers.

The government's organizational deficiencies made for pseudo-planning. "Planning" consisted of targeting desired production levels with little calculation of the necessary inputs, especially of labor, equipment, seeds, and fertilizers.[32]

Usually only land requirements were calculated, and even

then by the rather naive method of dividing the desired output by an assumed average yield. In the case of taro, almost two hundred thousand acres were prepared for sowing while there were seeds for only half that area. Carlos Rafael Rodriguez, then head of the government agriculture and agrarian reform agency, called this an "instructive mistake."[33] Unfortunately, such mind-boggling mistakes were all too commonplace and often on a grand scale.[34]

The policy of introducing mixed agriculture on the local level exacerbated these organizational and material problems. State-controlled cane farms were instructed to diversify into a wide range of crops and livestock without any studies of soil, rainfall, climate, or economic prospects such as demand, transportation, and proximity to markets. Workers and managers experienced only in cane production were expected to oversee the diverse tasks of mixed and truck farming as well as livestock rearing. "People's farms," moreover, often were amalgams of numerous scattered farms, making efficient management even more difficult.[35]

Poor planning also led to clearing of more land than could be cultivated. The use of heavy bulldozers frequently destroyed thin topsoils, leading to severe erosion and a rapid falloff in yields.[36] Clearing maribu and forests not only was very expensive, but often other places more suitable for cultivation could have produced much more at less cost.[37]

Agricultural production was also affected by an entirely new phenomenon in the Cuban countryside—a labor shortage. The reasons for this shortage were many: the opening up of new employment opportunities, many of which appeared more attractive than farm labor; the land redistribution, which allowed growing numbers of rural dwellers to grow their own crops instead of hiring themselves out;[38] and the mass mobilization for the 1961 sugarcane harvest to the neglect of other agricultural work. The labor shortage especially affected the harvest of taro and other food crops that require a good deal of stoop labor, the least desirable work. It was also one of the principal reasons why promising cotton production was completely abandoned; cotton picking is particularly unappealing work.[39]

Sugar production was especially affected by the labor shortage. Cutting cane by machete is hard work and available only a few months a year. The fact that more and more canecutters turned to other work demonstrates a certain success of the revolution: the early reforms had undermined the old motivators— poverty and economic insecurity. The employment alternatives opening up on the diversified "people's farms," on rural construction projects, in the military, and in the cities were higher paying, less arduous, and steadier. By the 1963 harvest, nearly one-half of Camaguey province's eighty thousand cane cutters were otherwise employed.[40]

Many experienced *macheteros*, moreover, found that their income from cutting cane was dwindling in 1962 and 1963 since their earnings were tied to the weight of cane they cut daily. With the downgrading of sugar production in favor of diversification, the quality of many cane fields had dropped off. Some of the best canelands were plowed under to make way for other crops, while cane was left on some of the poorer-quality lands. With little acreage replanted, sugarcane, a perennial, suffered falling yields as the average plant age increased. The labor shortage left weeding and other cultivation practices increasingly neglected, resulting in lower yields which attracted still fewer workers.

The mobilization of volunteer workers to cover for the labor shortage probably accelerated the withdrawal of experienced cutters from the fields. As the inexperienced volunteers often cut the fields poorly and disrupted the organizational routine essential to high volume output, the professional *macheteros* could not cut as much daily and therefore earned less.

The Return to King Cane (1963–1970)

Behold: here is sugar without tears;
to say,
I have returned, do not fear;
to say,
Long was the journey, and bitter the road.
>   —NICOLÁS GUILLÉN, "EULOGY TO JESÚS MENÉNDEZ"

By 1962, a balance of payments crisis began to overshadow other economic questions. Cuba, which had always exported more than it imported, found its trade surplus transformed into a $170 million deficit. Without oil, hydroelectric power, and several other key natural resources, Cuba relied on imports for its energy and other vital needs. Yet the output of sugar—the principal traditional export to offset these costs—was plummeting. Cuba would not be able to fulfill even its existing sales contracts with the Soviet Union, China, and other socialist countries.[41]

And nothing was taking sugar's place as a net foreign-exchange earner. When the vital question became how to obtain the foreign exchange to purchase machinery, fuel, and other basic commodities, a return to sugar was the obvious answer.

In 1964, Che Guevara succinctly stated the leadership's changed view of sugar: "The entire economic history of Cuba had demonstrated that no other agricultural activity gives such returns as those yielded by the cultivation of sugar cane. . . . Hard facts have shown us both the errors and the road toward their correction. . . . Sugar now has first priority."[42]

This was traditional comparative-advantage thinking at work, now that labor and land were tight. "It had been one thing to diversify at the beginning of the Revolution when idle labor and land abounded," Boorstein recalls. "Now using the resources for one purpose meant not using them for another."[43] A few rapid surveys were done comparing the costs and benefits of using a given amount of land for sugar or for other products. Prime Minister Castro illustrated these studies' conclusions in a comparison of sugar with rice. "To become self-sufficient in rice," he said, "we would have to use some 333,000 more acres of irrigated land and invest in them our scarce water supply. . . . Undoubtedly, it wouldn't make sense for our country to stop producing one and one half million tons of sugar—which is what we could produce on 333,000 acres of irrigated land planted to sugar cane and which could increase our purchasing power abroad by more than $150 million—in order to produce on this land, with the same effort, rice valued at $25 million.[44]

Other calculations also lay behind the decision to shift back to a concentration on sugar. Several studies indicated that Cuba could produce cane sugar far more cheaply than Eastern Europe and the Soviet Union could produce beet sugar. Accordingly, Cuba could become the main source of sugar for Soviet-bloc socialist countries.[45] Other studies concluded that Cuba spent less money importing sugar inputs, per dollar earned, than any other export commodity with the possible exception of tobacco.[46] In short, increased sugar output seemed to offer the soundest and speediest way of attacking the balance-of-payment crisis. Finally, world market sugar prices in 1963 were almost double the 1962 average price.[47]

The leadership hoped that the "return to sugar" would not just be a return to the ways of the past, but something new—"sugar without tears." For one thing, a good part of foreign sales would no longer be subject to the ups and downs of the world market but would be sold at fixed prices through long-term contracts with the socialist countries (including China). The price would be a good one, it was argued. Not only would the socialist countries bend over backwards not to exploit Cuba's lack of an alternative major buyer (due to the U.S. government embargo), but also their own beet sugar production costs were so high that a good price was justified.[48]

The "return to sugar" was also seen by policymakers as a break from the prerevolution sugar domination of the economy because sugar production would be tied to future economic development. For the first time, the sugar production—and its profits—would no longer be controlled by foreign corporations. Now sugar production, it was thought, could be "used to advance, instead of hold back, the rest of the economy, to buy machinery and equipment required for broad agricultural and industrial development," as Boorstein saw it.[49]

The leadership planned a substantial mechanization of sugar harvesting if, with Soviet help, Cuba could design a mechanical harvester. No longer did mechanization threaten unemployment. In addition, agriculture would not have to compete for resources with industrialization as it had done during the first years. A momentous lesson had been learned: Cuba could not modernize its agricultural base and industrialize at the same time.

Agriculture would come first and receive the highest priority. Industry would come later and only as linked to agriculture in the production of inputs such as fertilizer and mechanical cane harvesters and in the processing of agricultural production.

10 Million Tons

Expansion of sugar output became "the first aspiration of the agricultural economy of the country."[50] A goal was set to harvest 10 million tons of sugar in 1970, over two and a half times the

1963 harvest and considerably more than Cuba's largest harvest of 7.2 million tons in 1952.

Achievement of the ten-million-ton goal became an obsession with Fidel Castro and consequently with the media, the army, the Party, and such citizen organizations as the neighborhood Committees for the Defense of the Revolution. Castro elevated the ten-million-ton harvest to "a yardstick of the Revolution." Achieving the harvest, according to Castro, would show how ineffective the U.S. embargo was and would improve Cuba's international credit rating. The harvest would be the decisive turning point in breaking the foreign-exchange barrier and sounding the "open sesame for great progress in the future."[51] Virtually the entire nation was brought into a campaign in which Fidel Castro himself took charge. Over 1.2 million workers from other sectors of the economy, along with one hundred thousand members of the armed forces, were mobilized to cut and lift cane.[52]

While only 8.5 million tons was finally harvested, it was nonetheless an all-time record—18 percent greater than the previous record. As such, it might have constituted a success. But the costs to the rest of the economy were staggering. Losses and setbacks in other productive areas probably surpassed the gains in sugar production. Even the casual visitor could see that the rest of the economy from management to workforce had been neglected. Not only were many workers taken from their regular jobs but the single-mindedness of the drive toward 10 million tons meant that even during the period preceding 1970 the sugar industry monopolized investment funds, transportation, steel, fertilizers, etc. The all-out preparation of the fields and mills for the 1970 harvest helped make the 1969 harvest the second worst of the revolution.

Food output was directly and negatively affected. The plan for beans, formulated in 1965, had called for expanding cultivation by 1970 to 160,000 acres; instead, the area in beans *decreased* to only 27,000 acres. Bean production dropped to only 10 percent of what it had been in 1962.[53] *Vianda* production declined, some items such as taro and cassava drastically.[54] Dairy production, although defined as a priority, fell to practically the lowest level since the 1950s. Fruit production dropped 25 percent below the level of 1968 and less than half of the planned acreage for citrus was planted.[55] Meat production was also off.[56]

The drive for 10 million tons which, in the words of Castro, "led to a multiplication of our problems,"[57] became the subject of intense and prolonged analysis by the Cuban leadership. Once again the Cubans had made production at any cost the watchword. No one had asked if the earnings from the additional tons of sugar would be greater than the cost of its production (including extra fuel for field machines and mills, fertilizers, labor, the wear and tear on machinery, and the neglect of other productive work).

The 1970 harvest marked what the Cuban leadership now commonly refers to as the end of the days of "idealism." The early attempts at immediate diversification and the later effort to harvest 10 million tons were both overambitious. It was now time to come down to earth. Looking back on this period, President Castro admitted: "It is not that revolutionaries should have neither dreams nor indomitable will. Without a bit of dream and utopia there would have been no revolutionaries. . . . But the revolutionary also has to be a realist . . . must also know how to learn from the facts and the realities."[58] The revolution had come of age. *according to the authors?*

— Go to p. 145

+ See quote p. 112 &Xnow —put here?

State dairy complex in the Picadura Valley. Cuba has made some of the heaviest investments in dairy develoment, of any tropical country. By the 1980s fresh millk output had tripled and milk was being sold in Havana province in unrestricted amounts. Unfortunately, large dairy complexes near Havana have often displaced bean, *vianda*, and vegetable farms. Cuba's emphasis on improving the breed of milk cow and not on pasture development has made for a dairy industry dependent on massive and costly imports of feedgrains. Over forty percent of Cuba's national milk consumption must still be imported as powdered milk.

The Cuban-manufactured *combinado*, or sugarcane harvester. The pride of Cuba's farm mechanization program, the combine reportedly does the work of 30 canecutters. In 1983, 60 percent of Cuba's cane was mechanically cut and 100 percent machine-gathered. Far from displacing labor, mechanization has filled in for a labor shortage. Cuba is now the world's largest manufacturer of sugarcane combines and is looking to export them.

Harvesting sugarcane by hand. Traditionally all cane was laboriously cut and gathered by hand, requiring an enormous pool of farmworkers. Most farmworkers were unemployed, however, during the long "dead season" between harvests. For many years into the revolution thousands upon thousands of students, urban workers, and soldiers had to be mobilized to supplement professional canecutters during the annual harvest of sugarcane, still by far Cuba's principal crop.

Machetero, or professional canecutter. Many are descendants of the hundreds of thousands of African slaves brought to Cuba by colonial plantation interests. While advances in mechanization since the early 1970s have greatly reduced the size of the labor force required in the sugar harvests, a core of highly productive and well-remunerated *macheteros* will be essential to Cuba's sugar production for a long time to come.

Junior high school students from Havana harvesting *malanga*, a root crop, as part of their annual six weeks' work in the countryside. All junior high students—urban and rural—provide needed labor for Cuba's state and private farms. But policymakers suggest that students learning to appreciate the hard work as well as the dignity of farm work is even more important than their economic contribution.

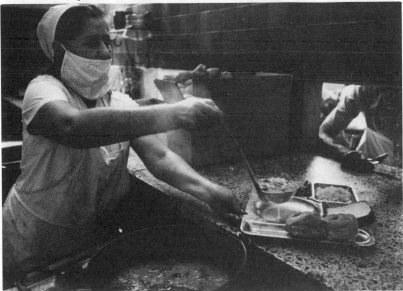

Kitchen in a *comedor obrero*, or workers' cafeteria, in a Havana factory. Just under one half of Cuba's workforce daily eats one hot lunch and two *meriendas*, or snacks, in their workplace *comedores*. Typical lunch fare is rice, bread, split peas or beans, eggs or fish, a starchy vegetable, and a sweet dessert. Lunch at the *comedores* was free until the mid-1970s, when a flat charge of 50 centavos was introduced, considerably less than a comparable meal in a restaurant.

Shoppers returning home from a farmers' market in Havana. In 1980, markets were opened where private producers, once they had fulfilled their government production quotas, could sell to the public at unregulated prices. The stated intention was to improve the variety and quality of foods available. Within two years a range of problems prompted a virtual government shutdown of the markets.

A Havana supermarket, one of a couple dozen in Cuba. Formerly belonging to the Rockefeller-owned Mini-Max chain, this supermarket today serves as a large *bodega* selling the grocery ration to neighborhood households. It also sells some non-rationed items to the general public. Shelves are never empty: several items, mostly canned goods from Eastern Europe, are stacked in as many as a dozen places in the store.

A *bodega*, or grocery store, in Old Havana. Every Cuban household is assigned to a specific *bodega* for its guaranteed monthly grocery ration. *Bodegas* also sell some non-rationed items. Since 1968 all stores are government owned and operated. This shopkeeper's t-shirt boasts "Cuban sugar, the best sugar in the world."

Buying grapefruit at a *"Feria del agro,"* or government non-rationed produce market. These markets were opened in 1980 and sell surplus produce from state farms. Prices are much lower than those in the farmers' markets, but consumers consider the quality of produce generally inferior and their availability erratic.

Farmers market (1980). Garlic and other condiments fetch high prices because of low state farm output of such labor-intensive "minor crops" which are greatly prized by most Cubans for adding zest to their favorite foods.

A Havana *carniceria*, or butcher shop. The meat ration per person is three-quarters pound of beef or beef products every nine days. Frequently one pound of chicken is substituted for the beef ration. Since 1983, as part of an unprecedented increase in the number of foods for sale in unlimited quantities, special stores have sold meats, but at very steep prices, roughly equivalent to those on the black market.

A Havana lunch-counter in what was once Woolworth's. A wide variety of snack bars, cafeterias, and restaurants supplements the ration and adds variety to the Cuban diet. Since 1968, all eateries are publicly owned and operated by municipal governments.

A school *comedor*. Most school children have half-day sessions and eat only a mid-session snack in school. However, over 100,000 children in day-care centers and over 500,000 students in boarding schools (mostly junior high schools in the countryside) receive two hot meals and two snacks a day at school. Cuba has made itself the only country in the hemisphere without undernourished children.

Floridita Restaurant in Havana. Cuban restaurants can be quite posh, with tuxedoed waiters, linen table cloths, wine lists and live musicians. For most Cubans, restaurant meals are a special treat. Restaurants get most crowded toward the end of the month when monthly rations are running out. Restaurant prices tend to be high, service slow and waits long.

A pizza stand in Santiago. Numerous and very popular, pizza stands offer spaghetti and a few other items in addition to the basic tomato and cheese pizza. "Fast food" is also available at a chain of fried chicken restaurants. And a favorite hangout in every Cuban city is the local "Coppelia" ice-cream parlor.

State farmworker enjoying a break for a hot lunch. Wages of Cuban farmworkers, especially unskilled fieldhands in non-cane agriculture, remain low even by Cuban standards.
Benefits, however, such as hot meals, snacks and refreshments served in the field, full
health care, paid vacation and maternity leave, daycare and schooling for children and
adults, cultural activities, and subsidized housing with electricity and running water,
would be the envy of farmworkers throughout Latin America and even the United States.

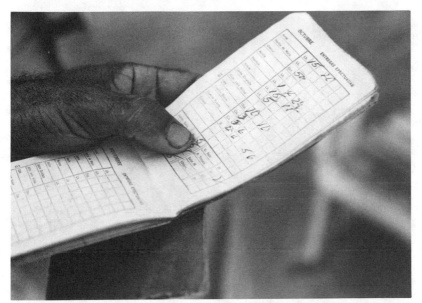

One family's *libreta*, or ration book. Each purchase of an allotted item is noted. Since 1962 every Cuban is entitled to a fixed monthly "food basket." Prices are low and heavily subsidized. The ration supplies only part of the basic diet for most Cubans; the remainder is purchased through non-rationed sources. Some items, including eggs, spaghetti, and fish, have been "liberated" from the ration and now can be bought in unlimited quantities, generally at low prices.

Wendy Watriss

State dairy farm near Havana. These two workers, once independent small farmers, receive rent for their land which has been absorbed into the state dairy complex where they are now salaried employees. They also retained a small piece of land to grow food for their families. Since 1980 it has been legal to sell the food they produce to the public, generally for very good prices.

A feast of pork, rice, black beans, and *viandas* in the home of a member of a sugarcane cooperative in Matanzas province. These are Cuba's traditional and favorite foods. Today they are more readily and abundantly available to small farmers and agricultural cooperative members who have the advantage of their own food production plus the government ration.

New housing for state dairy farmworkers in the Picadura Valley. Multi-family, concrete structures on state farms and cooperative contrast sharply with single-family, thatched-roof, dirt-floor *bohíos* still to be found in the Cuban countryside. Families in the new communities have electricity and plumbing and live closer to schools and medical services

New members of an agricultural cooperative near Mariel at work on the cooperative's housing project. Agricultural cooperatives have been promoted since the late 1970s through a variety of incentives. Though there is a national housing shortage, cooperatives have priority in purchasing scarce building materials. Unlike individual small farmers, agricultural cooperatives can purchase new farm machinery, have priority in the distribution of fertilizers, seeds, pesticides, and receive lower-interest loans. Today increasing numbers of rural young people with technical training are staying in the countryside and seeking to join cooperatives, attracted by cooperatives' modernized farming and good living standards.

Individual private farmer, Cuba's vanishing species. The revolution's agrarian reform made landowners of many thousands of Cuba's sharecropper and tenant farmers, accounting for two-thirds of the nation's small farmers. But by 1983, only 9 percent of Cuba's agricultural land remained in the hands of individual small farmers. Few farmers' children have chosen to inherit their parents' lands and become individual private farmers. Moreover, in the late 1960s some twenty thousand farmers sold or permanently leased their land to the government for large-scale agrulcultural schemes. Since the late 1970s more and more farmers have decided to pool their land in agricultural cooperatives (which comprised 11 percent of agricultural land by 1983). Many private farmers and cooperative members enjoy higher incomes and have more consumer goods than most other Cubans.

A *puesto*, or shop selling both rationed and non-rationed fresh produce. Produce is the most variable part of the ration. Prices are low, especially when seasonal produce abounds. In this *puesto* unlimited potatoes are available for a mere one centavo a pound at harvest time. But at other times of the year, potatoes are strictly rationed or unavailable.

CHAPTER 10

Farming looks mighty easy when your plow is a pencil, and you're a thousand miles from the corn field.

DWIGHT D. EISENHOWER[1]

A Shaky Balance

The Vice Minister for Sugar takes pleasure in ticking off the dimensions of sugar production in today's Cuba. Sitting at an imposing desk, he looks for all the world like a corporate executive—and the Sugar Ministry is by every measure the biggest corporation in Cuba and quite possibly in the Caribbean. The 1976–1980 harvests, he notes, averaged 7 million tons, almost 50 percent more than any five-year period before or after the revolution. Moreover, the harvests have been far steadier from one year to the next. The goal is 14 million tons yearly by the end of the 1980s, more sugar than Cuba produced in any two consecutive years during the 1950s and 1960s.

Not only is there more land under cane cultivation, but greater emphasis is placed on boosting yields (averaging over eighteen tons per acre as of 1981, compared with eleven in 1958). Large investments have brought irrigation to one-quarter of Cuba's cane fields. Cane cutting is now 60 percent mechanized, compared to none before the revolution.[2] Cuba is now the largest producer of cane combines in the world and is looking to export them. The ministry has three research institutes, and new cane varieties as well as fertilizers and herbicides are constantly being tested. In 1981 the government announced the construction of two new sugar mills—the first since 1924—and plans call for fifteen new mills with the latest computerized technology.

Despite the emphasis on sugar, Cuban officials say the country has struck a balance between sugar and food production. They also claim great strides have been made in nonsugar agricultural

144

exports. A careful look at the trends in other crops gives a revealing view of the revolution's nutritional and economic priorities.

— buts recent miyeal (?) — See below

Citrus

Citrus production grew little in the 1940s and 1950s, despite the excellent conditions provided by the island's frost-free climate and the nearness of the North American market. During the first decade of the revolution, there was little increase in production, although acreage was expanded.[3] Beginning in 1970, citrus production began to register dramatic gains. Production was 20 percent higher in 1970 than in 1957 and by 1983 had increased eight-fold, reaching six hundred thousand tons.[4] Quality has been good enough for two-thirds of the crop to be exported. The remaining two hundred thousand tons available for internal consumption, equivalent to 44 pounds per person, compares favorably with the prerevolution figure of 13 pounds per person.[5]

While citrus expansion is hailed as a way to diversify exports and decrease dependency on sugar, citrus exports still account for a mere 2 percent of Cuba's foreign exchange earnings,[6] compared to sugar's 83 percent.[7] About 90 percent of the citrus harvest is exported to the Eastern European common market.[8] Some early-season fruit has also been exported to Western Europe and Japan,[9] and the Cubans would like to increase these exports to earn convertible currencies, that is, currencies which can be exchanged for dollars. If the U.S. government embargo on trade were lifted, Cuba could become a tough competitor to Brazilian orange exports, which have made inroads in the U.S. frozen juice market.

Tobacco

While citrus's share of export-oriented agricultural land increased from 1 percent in 1946 to 7 percent in 1980, the share of Cuba's second most important agricultural export crop, tobacco, dropped from 6 to 3 percent over that period.[10] The 1978 public acknowledgement of the need to recover and surpass prerevolution levels has been frustrated by disease and weather difficulties. The "blue mold" virtually wiped out the 1980 tobacco crop.

Rice

When asked about growing food for local consumption, Cuban officials point to rice production as a major step in the direction of self-reliance. Before the revolution, Cuba was a major world importer of rice. Rice producers in the southern United States benefited from Cuban tariff concessions in return for U.S. concessions to Cuba on sugar exports. Sharp increases in rice prices finally made domestic production more appealing in the 1950s. Large credits were given to Cuban farmers to plant rice, and production quadrupled in the decade before the revolution.[11]

Today rice is Cuba's second most extensively cultivated food crop after sugarcane. Land under rice cultivation has increased 40 percent since the start of the revolution.[12] Huge irrigation investments now allow for two crops a year in many areas, and rice has probably become Cuba's most highly mechanized crop, even more so than sugar cane. Seven state farms specialize in rice production, using some of the latest "green revolution" varieties.

In the mid-1970s, the year 1980 was targeted for self-sufficiency in rice. Yet 1983 production still covered only 60 percent of national consumption. Cubans were once said to eat more rice than any people outside of Asia, and current consumption is probably artificially low since rice is rationed. Rice was one of the most desired items in the farmers' markets. With the 1983 expansion of the government's parallel market, rice imports had to be increased.[13]

In discussions with government officials, we learned that irrigated rice land was sacrificed to expanded cultivation of sugar cane in 1978 and 1979.[14] Cuba, it seems, is caught between its costly high-tech rice production—irrigation requirements are three times those of cane[15]—and the less costly expansion of its sugar production. The vice president of Cuba's Academy of Science told us that it still costs Cuba more to grow its own rice than to import it.[16]

Corn

Corn, the nation's traditional basic grain, is the revolution's forgotten food crop. Before the revolution, corn was grown on more farms than any other crop. Small holders, tenants, and sharecroppers—all grew corn as a last line of defense against hunger. Cultivated on the island before Columbus, corn took on the stigma of those who depended upon it; corn was (and remains) low status, poor folks' food, a dead-season crop, a food of hard times.

We have been told that corn has been a low priority because it cannot be produced economically on a large scale in Cuba. Corn acreage has shrunk to only a third of what it was before the revolution.[17] Most is grown by private farmers whose yields have shown little improvement over the years. (Cuba's corn yields today are considerably lower than those of several other Caribbean countries.)[18] A staggering 97 percent of all corn is imported, mainly for the chicken and egg industry.[19]

Potatoes

Potatoes are also cited as evidence that food production marches ahead even if sugarcane is still king. The numbers, at least from the mid-seventies onward, are impressive. Total potato cultivation increased from an average of twenty thousand acres in the decade preceding the revolution to thirty-four thousand in the early 1980s, with yields said to be substantially higher. The 1982 harvest was a record 258,000 tons, or 60 pounds per person, nearly three times the 1970 production level.

But prerevolution potato production was already quite advanced. Domestic production covered 70 percent of consumption (or 40 pounds per person), making Cuba the fourth largest producer in Latin America, with the highest yields.[20] It took fifteen years before record potato production levels were recovered because of tremendous inefficiencies in organizing state production and the radical shifts in policy on food self-reliance.

Cuba's potato self-sufficiency is undercut by its highly seasonal supply: periods of glut (when potatoes are practically given away) are followed by long stretches in which potatoes are rationed or unavailable. The problem is that Cuba still does not have much refrigerated storage capacity. In the tropical climate, much of the potato harvest would rot were it not for the "great potato swap." Each year, Cuba ships part of its potato harvest thousands of miles to East Germany and the USSR during their off seasons in exchange for potatoes during Cuba's off season. When the potato shipments arrive, they cannot be distributed gradually, but instead are dumped on the market. Moreover, those outside the Havana region don't see many potatoes since production and distribution are concentrated in Havana province.

Viandas

The traditional root crop of Cuban agriculture is not the potato but any one of the several *viandas*. Unlike potatoes, cultivation of *viandas* makes few demands on foreign exchange. While Cuba must still import two-thirds of its seed potato, *viandas* require no imported seed. The imported high-yield seed potatoes are vulnerable to pests and require a great deal of imported pesticides and fertilizers. The local varieties of *viandas* flourish with fewer chemical inputs.[21]

Before the revolution, *viandas*, like corn, were generally grown by small farmers. But unlike corn they are very popular foods. In Chapter 2 we saw that increased buying power early in the revolution created an extraordinary demand for such favorites as taro and how Castro pledged to increase production and eliminate shortages. Yet twenty years later, only half as much land is planted in *viandas* as in 1946[22] and taro is available neither on the ration nor on the parallel market, except for those with medically prescribed diets.

Government publications show *vianda* production doubled from 1970 to 1980.[23] But 1970, the year of the drive for 10 million tons of sugar, was a particularly abysmal year for *viandas*, the production of taro collapsing to less than 5 percent of what it was in the first year of the revolution and to one-sixth of what it was in 1961.[24] The reality is that absolute production of *viandas* remains low, certainly far short of consumer desire. *Viandas* were, however, plentiful in the farmers' markets, suggesting that small farmer production is considerable and that part of it is not recorded in official production statistics. There are also indications that output during the early 1980s is finally going up in both the state and nonstate sector.

Why are *viandas*, the beloved food of Cubans, in short supply? Since they do not earn foreign exchange, the government assigns them a low priority. (If the U.S. trade embargo were lifted, however, Cuban *viandas* might find an attractive market among the

Cuban population in the United States.) Here, then, is a clear example of unbalanced agricultural production favoring King Cane at the expense of consumer desire. If Cuba were blockaded and thereby forced to grow more of its own food, one agricultural official told us, contingency plans exist to plow up cane and plant more *viandas* as well as other food crops on prime agricultural land. But barring such a dramatic change imposed from the outside, *viandas* are unlikely to have their day. *Vianda* yields are much lower than those of the high-yielding potato varieties now being cultivated. The growing season is notably longer for *viandas*, and they require a great deal more hand labor. When we asked a Spanish agronomist living and working in Cuba to comment on the low *vianda* output, his reply was immediate: "*Viandas* don't fit into the government's vision of agriculture— modern and mechanized as in the United States."

Beans

As highly prized as *viandas*, but perhaps even more slighted, are beans. If potatoes are the success crop to tout, then beans are the "failure" crop to keep quiet about. This is unfortunate since Cubans, as we have seen, are wild about beans, especially black beans and red beans, and beans are a good source of protein. Cuba imports 80 to 90 percent of its beans and produces fewer beans now than in the years immediately before the revolution. Per-capita bean production is down by 30 percent, and the area planted has been cut by about one-third.[25]

Despite their popularity, the government agricultural planners do not prioritize bean production. Rice yields (with fertilizers and irrigation) are about 2,200 pounds per acre, compared to only 670 pounds for beans. Beans are particularly susceptible to pests; and, worse still, they do not lend themselves to mechanization and thus require lots of hand labor.

A high-ranking agricultural ministry official discussed the "bean problem" in terms of soil erosion and plant diseases as well as the "backwardness" of the small farmer producers. He thought the solution lies in large-scale state farm bean production using full mechanization and bean varieties that respond to fertilizers and irrigation. Unfortunately, these varieties, fertilizers, and irrigation are all very expensive, as are pesticides which are available mainly for dollar-convertible currency. Policy makers are unlikely to meet popular demand for black and red beans. According to this official, state farms will assign highest priority not to black or red beans, but to soya beans, because of their low-cholesterol oil and usefulness in feed concentrate for the poultry industry.

Meat and Eggs

In the field of "protein" foods, the revolution's major success has been with eggs. In 1982, Cuba produced over five times more eggs per person than before the revolution.[26] Eggs are low-priced and have been off the ration since the mid-1970s. As we noted in Chapter 8, Cubans say they are getting enough eggs—and then some. In this sense, Cuba is "self-sufficient" in eggs—but virtually all of the corn and other feed grains for the highly industrialized production of eggs are imported.

Most Cubans want more chickens and fewer eggs. Yet despite sizeable investments in agribusiness-style poultry production, chicken is still rationed (less than 2 pounds per month) and 22 percent of consumption is imported (principally with scarce dollars).[27] In 1979 Cuba had difficulty fulfilling the ration because a "fraternal" (socialist) country, widely thought to be Bulgaria, reneged on delivery of thousands of tons, as President Castro revealed in a closed-door address to the National Assembly of People's Power. This failure was especially critical because chicken was being substituted for the beef ration due to disappointing beef output.

Beef has fared even worse than chicken. For years, Castro touted beef as Cuba's next big foreign-exchange earner, along with sugar. The "plan" called for beef exports based upon feedlot operations in which cattle were to be fattened on a mixture of molasses and Peruvian fishmeal. Among the many serious problems that developed were molasses toxicity and difficulties in obtaining the fishmeal. Beef is no longer considered a future export. But Cuba hopes to be self-sufficient in beef production by the year 2000, although it is not clear whether that goal is based on current levels of consumption which, as we noted in Chapter 8, are considerably below what most Cubans would like.

Milk

What greater evidence of Cuba's priority on dairy production than a milk cow as a national personality? "Ubre Blanca" (White Udder) was nothing less: for weeks in 1981–82, she was daily front-page copy, a subject for songwriters, the occupant of an air-conditioned suite with special catered meals, even the recipient of a nationally televised visit from the head of state (who, according to Reuters, "seemed ecstatic as he whispered endearing words while circling and admiring her").[28]

Why such renown? Ubre Blanca is reputedly the world record holder for milk production: 241.4 pounds of milk in three milkings in a single day.[29] (Such prodigious productivity led many Cubans to joke that, just like a record-breaking canecutter, Ubre Blanca had been awarded a Lada, the Soviet-made Fiat automobile.) But the real story is twenty years of unflagging determination to achieve dairy self-sufficiency—something never before accomplished in the tropics. It remains, however, an unfinished story.

Before the revolution, extensive cattle raising was a major economic activity but these were mainly beef cattle, primarily Zebu, an animal of Asian origin well-adapted to the tropical heat, diseases, and the long dry season when most of the natural pasture withers. Following the revolution, the leadership (with Castro, son of a rancher, very much involved) boldly opted to develop a new, improved breed, a "dual purpose" animal producing both beef and milk. Costly investments were made in crossing imported Holstein from Europe and Canada with the traditional Zebu. The dual-purpose animal eventually convinced the Cubans that specialization in either milk or beef was more productive: dairy became the priority. Large-scale government dairy farms were established, often displacing bean and vegetable farming near Havana. It was a largely uncharted course since tropical dairying was a poorly studied field.

Milk output increased threefold from 1962 to 1979, with the most impressive gains in the most recent period.[30] In 1980, milk was sold off the ration for the first time in Havana province where over a third of production is concentrated. But domestic production still lags considerably behind consumption. In addition to the 800 million liters produced in 1982, 600 million liters of powdered and butterfat milk were imported.[31]

From Here!

The costs of milk production have been ominously high and prices to consumers continue to be heavily subsidized. Foreign dairy consultants say that Cuba concentrated on breeding technology and neglected development of better pastures (planting improved varieties of grasses, irrigation, etc.) and feedgrain growing. Huge amounts of feedgrains are purchased with hard currency from Canada and Europe. With requisite dollars scarce, particularly when sugar earnings are low, Cuba's specially bred cows are not given enough feed concentrate during the island's frequent long dry spells. ("It's like paying for a high performance engine and then not putting in the gas," a visiting U.S. dairy farmer commented.) As a result, Ubre Blanca's celebrated output, if true, is light years ahead of the national average, which hovers around 8 to 9 liters a day, although it can go to 12 liters in the spring when pastures are often in better shape.

The Future of Sugar

King Cane is not likely to decline in the foreseeable future. Sugar accounts for 85 percent of Cuba's export earnings. Plans are to invest 1 billion pesos in renovating sugar mills and building new ones, ensuring that sugar will remain the key factor in determining what gets produced in the Cuban economy. (By 1983, 1 billion pesos had already been invested.)[32] But what are the risks of banking on sugar so heavily?

Cuba is far and away the world's largest sugar exporter, accounting for 28 percent of world sugar trade.[33] Its nearest competitor is France, whose sugar exports (from sugar beets) make up 9 percent of world trade.[34] But most of the world's cane and beet sugar production is consumed in the countries where it is produced. Western Europe does have a sweet tooth, but the European Common Market (EEC) is not only self-sufficient but a net exporter. The world's two biggest importers, the United States and the Soviet Union, also rank among the world's biggest sugar producers.

A significant factor for a large sugar exporter is that most of the world's sugar trade goes through "closed" markets. Sugar-importing nations favor selected exporting nations with artificially high prices. This leaves the exporter dependent on the continuing favor of the importer. In 1982–83, the United States covered two-thirds of its sugar imports by granting quotas at a price several times the open-market price to the Dominican Republic, Brazil, Guatemala, Argentina, Panama, El Salvador, and Colombia. Nicaragua was abruptly cut off early in 1983 as part of the Reagan administration's efforts to destabilize the Sandinista-led government. Cuba, cut out of the U.S. quota since 1960, has long-term delivery contracts with the Soviet Union at a price that in 1982 was reportedly six times the world rate. (It is difficult to judge dollar equivalency accurately since, as previously noted, a barter agreement virtually ties sugar revenues to imports from the Soviet Union and Eastern Europe.) Since these closed-market arrangements are based on the importer's foreign policy, they offer little advantage to more efficient, lower-cost producers who are not favored.

Only 10 to 20 percent of world sugar consumption is traded on the open or "free" market. The open market covers variations in production resulting from good or bad harvests or changes in import needs and trade agreements. For example, if the USSR or its major supplier, Cuba, have a bad crop year, the USSR turns to other suppliers on the free market, such as the European Common Market (EEC), Brazil, the Philippines, Thailand, or Argentina, as it did for 2 million tons in 1981. (The political stripe of the government seems to play no role.) This in turn drives up the free-market price.

Because the free market is so small and the variables so many and unpredictable, it is subject to the wild price gyrations characteristic of most commodity markets. Over the ten years 1973–83, for instance, free-market prices fluctuated between a low of 6 cents and a high of 74 cents a pound. It is to this highly unstable market that Cuba must turn to sell the sugar not contracted by the Soviet Union. These sales earn dollars or dollar-convertible currencies for payments on debts to Western banks as well as imports of Western (and Japanese) capital and consumer goods.

While this free market is essential for Cuba, it does not augur well for the future. Little increase in consumption is expected in high-income countries, where population growth is slow and sugar consumption has long reached a high, stable level. Many importers are likely to cut back to protect domestic producers. (The United States cut its sugar imports by 25 percent in 1982.)

Competition among suppliers is likely to become sharper. World production is projected to continue to outstrip consumption. A number of third world countries, many with foreign aid loans and grants, have been increasing their sugarcane production capacity, some for internal consumption, some for export. Even Cuba has been helping, aiding a rival exporter, Nicaragua, to open up the largest sugar plantation and mill in Central America.

Worse still, there is a major dark cloud on the horizon: corn sweetener. In the affluent countries, the predominant sugar consumer is the food processing industry—for soft drinks, baked goods, ice cream, breakfast cereals, practically everything edible in a jar, bag, box, or can. "Grocery sugar"—the granulated sugar bowl variety—accounts for only one-third of total consumption.[35] For manufacturing uses, corn sweetener (also called high-fructose corn syrup) is an option. Since the Japanese discovery in the early 1960s of an enzyme that converts corn starch into a high-fructose syrup, corn sweetener is considered equivalent in sweetness and calories to sucrose from cane or beets. Its reputed advantage is a more stable and therefore predictable price. During the big surges in free-market sugar prices (such as in 1974), corn sweetener manufacturers captured a significant share of the food processor market. U.S. corn sweetener interests also love to wave the flag about their product, boasting that "it's refined entirely from corn, America's most plentiful crop." Once they have converted to corn sweetener, many food processors cannot readily retool, even to take advantage of drastic drops in cane sugar price.

Can't sugar exporters pull together? How about a sugar OPEC? Cuba and other members of the International Sugar Organization have tried to establish sales quotas for exporting members in an attempt to establish floor and ceiling prices. While many exporting and importing nations have joined the group, their efforts have not been very successful, especially since the European Common Market, which exports even more sugar than Cuba, has refused to join. Indeed, F. O. Licht, the respected German sugar market analyst, noted that the highly taxpayer-subsidized beet sugar production in Western Europe has dashed the hopes of third world sugar exporters more than any other factor.[36]

During the writing of this book, the free-market sugar price hovered around a depressed 7 cents a pound, well below the supposed International Sugar Organization floor of 13 cents. It is estimated that no sugar producer can cover its costs at prices below 10 cents a pound.[37] Although the Cuban sugar ministry would not reveal its productions costs, we believe they run around 11 cents, substantially lower than the other Caribbean and Latin American producers, who would all suffer from an even deeper financial crisis were it not for the preferential U.S. quota price many of them receive.

Over the past decade, the "terms of trade" between third world countries and industrialized countries have deteriorated. The Cuban government has made some sobering calculations. For example, in 1976, one ton of sugar could buy 0.49 tons of red beans; but by 1981, only 0.39 tons. A ton of sugar would buy 0.28 tons of beef in 1976; by 1981, only 0.11 tons. The same ton of sugar could buy only one-third the ammonium sulfate fertilizer in 1981 that it could in 1976. During the same period, wheat prices went up almost 50 percent; and powdered milk by 175 percent, or $677 a ton—and Cuba imports sixty thousand tons a year.[38]

Given such realities, it is not surprising that Cuban officials praise their socialist trading partners for indexing the price of agricultural commodities with industrial goods in order to maintain stable terms of trade. But Cuba also needs dollar-convertible currencies to import an array of industrial and consumer goods, including food and agricultural inputs, of the type or quality available only from capitalist countries. It is highly unlikely that Cuba's considerable planned expansion of sugar output is destined principally for the Soviet Union (which, according to some international sugar trading sources, is aiming to be self-sufficient in sugar).[39] Free-market prospects are therefore crucial. Even at current levels of sales on the free market, a one-cent price drop costs Cuba a staggering $70 million. That one-cent difference would be enough to import seven chickens a year for every Cuban, almost a third the annual chicken ration.

To P. 159

The Future of Food Production

After investigating Cuba's food policies over a five-year period, we have come away feeling that there is a renewed commitment to increased and improved food production. More important, it seems that the current approach is much more pragmatic, methodical, and likely to endure than the grandiose food plans launched at several points over the first two decades of the revolution.

At least two factors seem to lie behind the government's commitment to get more food produced and to make available a greater variety of foods. One is the widespread feeling that sacrifices have been made long enough. As the revolution passes its 25th birthday, belt-tightening is ever less acceptable, especially when it can no longer be blamed on *force majeure* such as a hurricane or sabotage by a foreign enemy. Two, the government's determination to stimulate productivity means that food, beyond a spartan diet, has now become one incentive among others to promote "more and better" work.

As of 1980, sugar-cane cultivation is no longer the responsibility of the Ministry of Agriculture.[40] Now the Ministry of Sugar oversees cultivation of cane as well as the milling and marketing of sugar. The Sugar Ministry can now exercise a more integrated and hopefully more efficient vertical control. With this change, the human resources of the Ministry of Agriculture are no longer tied up several months of the year in overseeing the planting, weeding, and harvesting of cane. The head of agricultural planning told us that previously everyone in the ministry got sucked into some problem or other with sugar production, no matter what one's crop responsibility was. Now, the Ministry of Agriculture's reputation rises and falls with success and failure exclusively in food production—not cane production.

Another important development is that state farms are now growing their own food for the first time in almost twenty years. In 1980, there were a few experiments in this direction, though specialization was still the watchword of the day. By 1983, self-provisioning, as we noted in Chapter 4, and spread across the island to every state farm in cane and noncane agriculture. Only two years before, such a policy would have been ridiculed as "antieconomic," taking away human and material resources from the main production of each farm. This policy change appears to represent greater pragmatism and greater decentralization as well as a response to the popular demand for more food.

Ironically, the Sugar Ministry is more advanced than the Agriculture Ministry in implementing the self-provisioning policy. Three years into the program, enough food was being produced to cover 40 percent of sugar workers' meals. With as many as thirteen hundred workers in each operation, this is no small achievement. In addition to *viandas*, beans, rice, and other staples, the sugar plantations produce pork, beef, mutton, milk, chicken, and eggs, whenever possible using byproducts from cane production, such as torula yeast, molasses, and processed cane fiber as animal feed. Several sugar enterprises by 1983 were self-sufficient in meat and milk and many others are expected to become so within a few years.

On the question of national self-reliance, the Cuban government argues that their island is as self-reliant as it needs to be, for it participates actively in the self-reliant socialist common market. Stable long-term agreements among these trading partners, the government argues, guarantee Cuba's food supply. When we expressed fears that external developments beyond Cuba's control—such as war in the Middle East—could shatter this fragile multinational self-reliance, we were told that Cuba has contingency plans for ripping up cane and producing food.

Cuban officials are confident that food production can be significantly increased but not at the expense of lower sugar output or even reduced cane acreage. They foresee steadily advancing productivity in both sugar and nonsugar agriculture, through improved techniques and not through gung-ho campaigns. In November 1983 Vice President Carlos Rafael Rodriguez went as far as to tell us, "Right now Cuban agriculture is in a phase of successful, systematic and continued development. I am convinced we are not going to have any problems in the future."[41] Optimism reigns in Havana but, as everywhere, only time will tell.

CHAPTER 11

I had friends who were car dealers. One of them worked for Chrysler. As soon as the revolution triumphed I told him: "Look, change your job quick. Instead of selling Chryslers, get a job with one of those tractor companies, 'cause that's where the action's gonna be."

MARUJA IGLESIAS[1]

The Agrarian Revolution

During the days of the guerrilla war in the Sierra Maestra mountains, Fidel Castro and his rebel army gradually won the hearts and minds of the peasants. The rebels treated the peasants with respect and, unlike most armed groups, paid for all the food and supplies they used. Gradually the guerrilla army was transformed into a peasant army—by 1959, three-fourths or more of the soldiers were peasants.[2]

Having lived among the peasants, the revolution's leaders were vividly aware of the enormous disparity between city and countryside. They knew that the majority of Cuba's peasants lived in isolated thatched-roof shacks with no electricity or running water, no land security, no schools, no medical facilities. They also knew that the average farmworker earned only 91 pesos a year, in contrast with the nationwide average income of 374 pesos.[3]

Once in power, the revolutionary government instituted a series of reforms designed to improve life in the countryside. All land rents were abolished. Tenant farmers, sharecroppers, and squatters were given title to the land they worked, along with guaranteed fixed prices for their produce and low-interest loans. Many seasonal workers were given full-time employment. Rural salaries were raised. People's stores were created to bring cheap consumer goods to the countryside. In 1961, the government initiated a massive literacy campaign, sending urban students to

159

the countryside not only to teach reading and writing, but to gain an understanding and appreciation of rural life. For the first time, rural communities were provided with schools, clinics, and recreational and cultural activities. Teams of projectionists traveled to remote villages showing movies, free of charge, to people who had never seen a film. The documentary, *Por Primera Vez* (*For the First Time*), which captured the faces of villagers watching their first movies, is vivid testimony to the revolution's efforts at improving the quality of rural life.

The Cuban peasant, previously downtrodden and abused, acquired a new status after the revolution. As Fidel said in a speech just after the promulgation of the agrarian reform, "From now on when a peasant goes to the city . . . no one will laugh at him, no one will make jokes about him, for the peasant is now a hero and will be treated with respect. From now on when a peasant goes to the city, no one will watch to see how he walks, how he eats, how he picks up a knife, what he buys, what color his wife's dress is. . . . Why? Because now that feeling of hostility against the peasant, . . . that timidity of the peasant who was always mistreated by the Rural Guard, by the big landowners, by the politicians . . . is gone forever."[4]

The revolution's leadership assumed that private individual farming would eventually disappear.[5] Many farmers, perhaps most, would move out of agriculture altogether. Others would join agricultural cooperatives, or sell their land to the state and take jobs on state farms. Both state farms and cooperatives (in that order) were thought to be superior to small private farms in terms of both productivity and the social benefits they could offer their workers. Ideologically, state farms were considered superior to cooperatives, since they were not privately owned and the wealth they generated benefited the public at large.

But paradoxically, by giving land titles to tenants, squatters, and sharecroppers, the agrarian reforms helped make small farmers more secure. Small farming represents virtually the only private sector that still exists in Cuba. Since Fidel Castro has personally and categorically promised that small farmers will never be forced to give up their land, the state finds itself in the awkward position of having to guarantee the existence of islands of small farmers in a sea of large state farms. A look at the evolution of state versus private agriculture should give us a better understanding of how this relationship stands today.

The First Agrarian Reform

The revolutionary government instituted its far-reaching land reform law just five months after taking power. Symbolically, it was signed at the former headquarters of the rebel army in the Sierra Maestra. The maximum land area one person could own was set at 1,000 acres, with exceptions made for particularly productive farms. Land ownership was so concentrated that by expropriating twelve thousand large farms, the government gained control of 44 percent of farm and ranch land.[6] State farms became key to Cuban agriculture for both domestic and export production.

For those with too little land to make a living, a "vital minimum," defined as the amount of land needed to support a family of five, was set at 67 acres. Peasants with less were given that amount free, plus the right to buy another 100 acres.[7]

Whether they owned the land or not, farmers were still a minority of the rural population. Wage-earning farmworkers on large estates outnumbered them four to one. Most observers, both foreign and Cuban, assumed the government would divide the large estates among the laborers who had worked them. Traditional wisdom among socialist thinkers was that even if the eventual goal was to collectivize agriculture, the first step was to divide up the land among the workers, then at some later point encourage them to pool their resources and work together. In the Soviet Union, China, and all of Eastern Europe, land reform programs were all based on this principle of "land to the tiller."[8]

But the Cuban land reform did not divide up the large estates among the workers, converting them instead into state farms and cooperatives. Why? "I found upon the victory of the Revolution that the idea of land division still had a lot of currency," Fidel explained years later. "But I already understood by then that if you take, for example, a sugar plantation of 2,500 acres . . . and you divide it into 200 portions of 12.5 acres each, what will inevitably happen is that right away the new owners will cut the production of sugar cane in half in each plot, and they will begin to raise for their own consumption a whole series of crops for which in many cases the soil will not be adequate."[9] Castro believed dividing the land would lead to a decline in production, which would be disastrous for the whole country.

Castro offered the same explanation for not dividing up the large cattle ranches. During the guerrilla war, the rebels had confiscated herds and distributed them among the peasants. Within a few months, practically all the animals had been eaten. "The majority of the *campesinos* had killed their cows because they preferred the immediate benefit of being able to eat them to the longer-range value of having the milk," Castro explained. "This naturally fortified my conviction that the land of the *latifundistas* should not be divided."[10]

Cuba's leaders understood that circumstances in Cuba were different from those of other countries which carried out significant land-reform programs. The workers on large estates in Cuba were not small farmers who aspired to own their own land, but rather a rural proletariat whose main concerns were job security, better working conditions, and a higher standard of living. Thus the decision to create cooperatives rather than divide up the land did not encounter resistance from the farmworkers.[11]

How Was the Law Implemented?

Even with the exemptions for particularly productive land, the agrarian reform law still called for the expropriation of half of Cuba's cultivated land. The National Agrarian Reform Institute (INRA) was to determine where to start and how fast to move.

INRA had to walk a thin line. If it moved too slowly, it would alienate the poor peasants and allow the rural elite more time to react—perhaps by sabotaging production. If INRA moved too fast, it would take on more land than it could administer properly and production would fall.

INRA's first moves were timid. In ten months, only six thousand small farmers received redistributed land. French agricultural economist Michel Gutelman noted that, with one hundred and fifty thousand small farmers to be dealt with, "At this rate, it would have taken twenty years" to complete the redistribution.[12] But as the large owners (both Cuban and American) began to actively oppose the reforms, INRA was forced to adopt a more radical position.

One example of systematic opposition was provided by the cattle ranchers. The cattle industry was set up so that the small farmers bred the calves and sold them as yearlings to middle-size farmers, who then sold them to the large ranchers. Threatened with expropriation, the ranchers not only began slaughtering more cattle but also stopped purchasing new yearlings, thus affecting both middle and small farmers. INRA tried to assist the small farmers by purchasing their calves, but soon found that it lacked sufficient pasture to maintain them. It was thus forced to accelerate the expropriation of the large ranches and within a year and a half controlled almost 90 percent of them.[13]

The expropriated cattle ranches were converted into state farms (called *granjas del pueblo*). Ranches used so few laborers that if they had been handed over to the workers, there would have been a few rich workers owning thousands of heads of cattle. The solution, the government reasoned, was to have the state administer the ranches and pay the workers a fixed wage.[14]

Since one-fourth of the best land in Cuba was owned by U.S. companies, agrarian reform placed the Cuban government in direct conflict with U.S. interests and set into motion a series of moves and countermoves that eventually led to the Bay of Pigs invasion in April 1961. (Cubans themselves see the passage of the agrarian-reform law as "the beginning of the end" of Cuba-U.S. relations.)[15] With history moving at lightning speed, the legal text of the agrarian reform law was soon left behind. In fact only one-quarter of the land taken over was actually taken under the terms of the law itself. The majority came from the nationalization of U.S.-owned sugar mills and agricultural enterprises after the U.S. cut its sugar quota and from the confiscation of land owned by persons who left the country or engaged in efforts to bring down the revolutionary government after the Bay of Pigs invasion.[16]

Two years into the reform, nearly half Cuba's total land area had been affected.[17] More than 100,000 peasants—mostly tenants, sharecroppers, and squatters—had gained title to the land they worked. But having made the decision to keep the large estates intact, the big winner was the state, which now controlled 44 percent of the land.[18]

The State Sector

Apart from the ranches, the rest of the state's land was converted into "cooperatives." The cooperatives set up by the first agrarian reform were more akin to state farms than to traditional self-administered cooperatives whose members receive a share of the profits. Cooperatives were accountable to INRA and had little autonomy. Production targets were set by INRA and produce was sold to the state purchasing agencies. The cooperatives selected their own coordinator, but the administrator was appointed by INRA, creating a two-tier power structure in which the appointed administrator had the upper hand over the elected coordinator.

Workers reportedly were not enthusiastic about the creation of cooperatives. Their experience as farmworkers left them ill-equipped to take on administrative responsibilities.[19] While their monthly wage was theoretically an advance on their share in the year's profits, in practice it was simply a wage. (Since no accounts were kept, it was never known if there was anything left at the end of the year to distribute.)

The cooperatives also posed two challenges to the government's commitment to equality. One was the increasing difference between rich and poor cooperatives. Some co-ops had advantages—in particular, fertile land and high value crops such as tobacco—that gave them higher revenues independent of the work of the members. The other problem was the friction between cooperative members and temporary workers. Temporary workers received higher wages than members (3.00 pesos a day vs. 2.50), since cooperative wages were supposed to have been supplemented by yearly dividends. Cooperative members, though, had a host of other advantages, such as free health care, housing, schools, sick leave, and accident insurance. Temporary workers became, in the words of Fidel Castro, "second-class citizens."[20]

By 1962, the cooperatives were converted into state farms. Like the cattle ranches, they were called *granjas del pueblo*. In part, this move was merely an acknowledgement of existing reality. But there were some important differences. Workers no longer even theoretically shared the farm's profit but received a fixed wage. All workers received the same wage. Planning and investments were made more centralized than before. Since state farms were often formed by combining cooperatives, purportedly to take advantage of economies of scale, the average size was larger.

From the start, state farms received priority over private farms. Beside taking advantage of economies of scale, the government wanted direct control over rural investments and agricultural production. Vice President Carlos Rafael Rodriguez, formerly the head of INRA, saw the existence of state-controlled agriculture as "a guarantee that, unlike the situation that prevailed for a time in a number of socialist countries, Cuba's economy will not be dependent on the will and actions of the individual peasants."[21] Fidel Castro held that the state farms were superior in both economic and social terms: "You can utilize the land in an optimum way . . . determining at each moment that whatever crop benefits the nation shall be produced. And you guarantee the workers a satisfactory income, housing, schools, roads—all those social benefits that are needed as much by the man who is planting sugar cane as by the man who is planting tobacco or tomatoes or sisal grass."[22]

In a short period of time, the life of the farm workers vastly improved. On a 3,000-acre former cattle estate in Pinar del Rio province, just a few months after it became a state farm, 200 families moved in to work the land, and a new town was built with modern concrete housing, a school, a "people's store," a clinic, and a cafeteria. School children were given clothing, free lunch, and free transportation. A visiting Chilean economist observed, "Of course, it was not possible to multiply this experience in each of the People's Farms across the country. There simply were not enough resources to do so. But the importance of this experience is that it reveals the ambitious ideas of the revolutionary leadership."[23]

The Private Sector

While the state sector was being created, the private sector was being transformed. By giving titles to former tenants, sharecroppers, and squatters, the agrarian reform added about one hundred and ten thousand peasants to the already existing forty-five thousand small farmer-owners. Thus two-thirds of Cuba's small farmers became farm owners thanks to the revolution.[24]

The private sector included both small and large farmers. Defined as those with under 165 acres, the small farmers constituted 94 percent of the private farmers. Large farmers, while in the minority, still held 42 percent of the land in the private sector.[25] Together they were important producers not only of food but also of foreign exchange, accounting for 85 percent of tobacco production, 80 percent of coffee, and 33 percent of sugar cane.[26]

The small private farmers reaped the benefits of the government's first agrarian reform. With land rents abolished, their incomes grew dramatically. They were given low-interest loans, guaranteed fixed prices for their crops, access to low-priced "people's stores," schools for their children, free medical care, and more. Freed from exploitative intermediaries and price fluctuations—harvest prices were now fixed and guaranteed before planting—small farmers improved their material conditions considerably.[27]

In May 1961, on the second anniversary of the agrarian reform law, the National Association of Small Farmers (ANAP) was formed. Membership was voluntary and restricted to farmers with fewer than 165 acres and larger farmers who had proven allegiance to the revolution. ANAP was to coordinate small farm production, mainly through the allocation of credit. Before the revolution, government credit was largely confined to the estates and large farms. Many small farmers were forced into the hands of loansharks charging up to 30 percent interest. Now small farmers were given credit at 4 percent annual interest. (From 1967 to 1978, no interest at all was charged on loans.)[28]

Excluding the larger farmers from membership in ANAP represented a critical step in differentiating the remaining large farmers from the small ones. Rich farmers were few in number; two years after the first agrarian reform law, only 592 farms over 1,000 acres remained. (The number of holdings between 165 and 1,000 acres had grown from 9,752 to 10,623, their ranks swelled by former large owners.) While small farmers received special support from the state, large private farmers were excluded from the mainstream of agricultural planning.[29] With the nationalization of the banking, transport, and distribution systems, it became increasingly difficult for these farmers to obtain supplies and deliver their goods to urban markets. "Discrimination against this group of farmers was apparently official policy of the revolutionary leadership that wished eventually to nationalize these properties," according to Canadian economist Archibald Ritter. "It refrained from doing so immediately due to a scarcity of INRA administrators and to political factors, i.e., the wish to avoid creating another body of opponents to the regime."[30]

But while the government made it difficult for large farmers both to produce and sell their goods, the increase in national consumption coupled with the inexperience of the newly created state sector made these farmers more important than ever in supplying the nation's food. Rather than sell to the state at fixed prices, these farmers preferred selling their produce privately to the highest bidder.

In an effort to force the farmers to sell to the state, serious errors were committed. A number of farms were illegally expropriated. The large farmers used these errors to make even small farmers fear expropriation. To quell the fears of the small farmers, the government was forced to hand back lands taken illegally. Fidel said at the time, "If the return of illegally confiscated farms is going to restore peace and quiet to thousands of people who must go along with the revolution, then they will have to be given back."[31]

Although the government considered the remaining rich farmers incompatible with the revolution, it did not want to precipitate their downfall and affect the economy adversely. The idea was to organize the state sector for several years and then deal the death blow to the remaining large farmers. But once again, the course of events forced the revolution to speed up its plans. Many rich farmers sabotaged production. Others, particularly in the Escambray mountain region, were directly involved in counterrevolutionary activities. Perhaps even more critical were their efforts to convince small farmers that the government was out to do away with all private farmers, big and small alike. These problems, coupled with the need to control food supplies in the face of ever-growing demand and shortages, led the government to promulgate a second agrarian reform.

The Second Agrarian Reform

In October 1963, the second agrarian reform was instituted, expropriating the land of all farmers with more than 165 acres. The government believed that state farms would guarantee food for everyone as well increased exports. They would make resurgence of capitalism in the Cuban countryside impossible. INRA took over about ten thousand farms, comprising approximately 20 percent of the nation's farmland.[32] This left the state in control of about 63 percent of the cultivated land,[33] as well as all agricultural credit, inputs, and marketing facilities.

Now the small farmers were the only significant private sector remaining in the entire economy. The government went to considerable lengths to reassure them there would be no "third agrarian reform" and that all future steps at collectivization would be strictly voluntary. Fidel Castro himself made a strong and highly visible political commitment towards the small farmers and their style of production. Not until a small farmer personally believed it was advantageous to farm collectively would his farm be joined with others in a cooperative, Fidel promised. If a farmer chose to live out his years as an individual farmer, this was fine. Fidel even promised that the farmer could be buried on his individual plot of land. "It is better to be patient as long as is necessary rather than have it be said in the future that our revolution forced a peasant to join a cooperative," Castro told the farmers. "We must be patient. If we have endured the ranches, the corrals, the latifundia and the minifundia all these centuries, what does it matter if we wait ten, fifteen, twenty, thirty, or fifty years for isolated cases? And if the owner of a minifundium wants to have it become a museum piece, then let him."[34]

When the government offered to buy out small farmers in the early 1960s, four thousand immediately rushed forward to sell, and the government was forced to retract its offer. It decided to purchase land only from those farmers who were old or unable to work. "If a young, able-bodied farmer wants to sell, we'll have to tell him no. We need him to stay on the land and keep producing," Fidel later said.[35]

During the late 1960s, however, there was a big push to persuade farmers to sell or lease their land to the government for its ambitious agricultural projects. (Undoubtedly the deal was attractive to some; others, we have been told, felt forced more than persuaded.) Between 1967 and 1970, the government purchased about twenty-thousand farms, then slowed down to buying fewer than fifteen hundred a year.[36]

Land in Cuba cannot be privately sold; it can only be sold to the government or to cooperatives. Land can be inherited, if the heir is within the family and personally willing to continue farming it. The law is enforced flexibly to keep people on the land, the head of ANAP's legal department told us. For example, a farmer's daughter can inherit the land if her husband agrees to farm it.[37] If a farmer dies or retires without heirs who want to work the farm, the farmer's family must sell the land to the government. In the twenty years following the second agrarian reform in 1963, the percentage of land in the private sector diminished from 37 to 20 percent.[38]

Private farmers are private only in the sense that they own their land and live mainly off the sale of their produce. But unlike private farmers in capitalist countries, they cannot freely sell their land, they must respond to the government's request as to what to grow, they are dependent on the government for inputs, and they must sell part of their produce to the government at prices the government sets.

While there are no statistics available on private farmers' incomes and there are still poor private farmers, farmers seem to enjoy higher incomes and better standards of living than most other Cubans. Indeed many would say they are pampered. A private tobacco farmer we met in Pinar del Rio in 1978 said he earned 10,000 pesos that year—five times the national average and considerably more than the salary of the minister of agriculture. "You know some farmers are millionaires," Castro said in 1982. "In keeping with the measures taken by the Revolution, the prices set by the Revolution and the markets and opportunities it has provided, some farmers have hundreds of thousands of pesos."[39]

Virtually all private farm families are better off in food terms than other Cubans. Not only are small farmers able to grow much of their own food, but along with all other Cubans they purchase foods inexpensively through the ration system. In addition to receiving guaranteed prices for their crops and low-interest credits from the government, private farmers can take advantage of food shortages to sell part of their produce through nongovernment channels (mainly the black market) at high profits. Many farmers also have leased part of their land to the government in return for a lifetime monthly "rent check"—often higher than the average monthly wage. And all farmers and their families reap government benefits from free education and free health care. Little wonder that many joked that Cuba's small capitalist farmers were exploiting the socialist state.

The Small Farmer Dilemma

Though individual farmers can make lots of money from their farming, they have not necessarily produced up to capacity. While they are required to produce certain quantities for sale to the government, these contracted amounts have apparently been based on state-farm yields, which tend to be low; most private-farm families could easily fulfill them. Farmers who have failed to fulfill the contract have seldom been penalized. At a certain point the revolution had provided so much for the farmer that "he did what any normal human being would do: relax and take life easy," Vice President Rodriguez told us.

As we have previously noted, it is impossible to determine how much the private farmers really produce because official statistics only take into account sales to the government. If private consumption, barter, black-market, and free-market sales were recorded, the picture could change considerably. When the farmers' markets were created in 1981 and suddenly much more food was legally available for sale, it was obvious that black-market sales had been substantial and that probably, given the right incentives, private farmers could produce more.

Why weren't the farmers producing more? In part, it was because private farmers had the lowest priority for buying scarce agricultural inputs, such as fertilizers, irrigation equipment, and farm machinery and vehicles, that would have enabled them to produce more. During our visits to the countryside, we met farmers who could not buy even such a commonplace implement as a hose for watering vegetable crops.

Why weren't the farmers selling more to the government? Private farmers could make far more money selling their extra production directly to consumers. To control these sales without

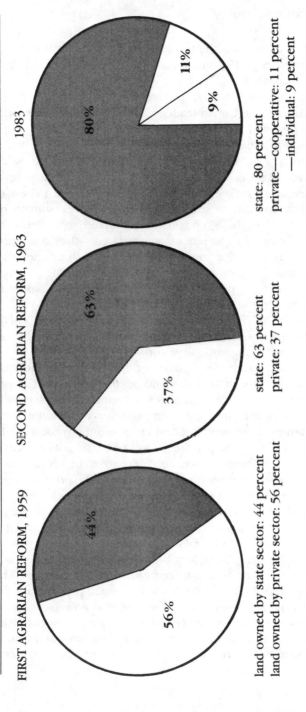

FIGURE 1: 100 percent = total cultivated land
DISTRIBUTION OF LAND: PRIVATE VS. STATE SECTOR*

FIRST AGRARIAN REFORM, 1959   SECOND AGRARIAN REFORM, 1963   1983

land owned by state sector: 44 percent   state: 63 percent   state: 80 percent
land owned by private sector: 56 percent   private: 37 percent   private—cooperative: 11 percent
                                                                                      —individual: 9 percent

*Varying figures appear in both official and secondary sources. Land surveys, especially before the revolution, were far from accurate. Another problem is that some figures refer to total land area, others to cultivated land.

formally restricting the farmers, the government limited buyers to purchases of 25 pounds or less.[40] But this restriction has been hard to enforce.

The existence of the private farmers continues to pose a dilemma for the Cuban leaders. The private farmers' production is still essential. Twenty years ago officials predicted that private production would be insignificant by now. But in 1982 it still accounted for 25 percent of Cuban-grown beans, 28 percent of the taro, 42 percent of the onions, 92 percent of the peppers, 52 percent of the coffee, and 18 percent of the sugar. (These official statistics, for the reason already noted, underestimate private production, perhaps considerably.) Given incentives—as the farmers' market experience demonstrated—they could produce even more. But the more they produced, the richer they became, and the greater the inequality—among the private farmers, between the private farmers, the cooperatives, and the state farms, and in the Cuban population as a whole.

In the 1980s, a series of measures was taken to encourage private farmers to produce more and sell more to the government, while at the same time curbing their incomes. The government raised the prices it pays for contracted production. Anything sold to the state above and beyond contracted amounts is now purchased at a higher price. Farmers' contracts with the government are enforced, with penalties for nonfulfillment. Private farmers must now honor their government contracts before selling either on the private market or to the government at the higher price. Furthermore, contracts are to be reevaluated each year in view of the amount of surplus sold the previous year. The idea seems to be that if records show a farmer met his contract and was able to sell an additional sizeable amount on the private market, the next year the amount he is contracted to sell to the government should be raised accordingly.[41]

To make private-market sales less tempting, taxes on these sales were raised to 20 percent for individual farmers. There is also, as of 1983, a progressive tax (5 to 20 percent) on the private farmer's gross income. Farmers will now have to pay for their own crop insurance (previously the government picked up the tab). And those who want to sell their land to the state will no longer be offered generous lifetime monthly payments but one lump sum.

It remains to be seen whether these new measures will work in the ways the government desires or be a disincentive for most farmers to produce.

But the most significant recent move concerning private farmers was the 1975 decision to encourage individual farmers to join together in agricultural production cooperatives. In the next chapter, we'll look at cooperatives which, along with state farms, are Cuba's two "superior" forms of agricultural production.

CHAPTER 12

Authors: *Are state farms really superior to cooperatives?*
Co-op member: *Of course.*
Authors: *Are they better organized?*
Co-op member: *Oh, no.*
Authors: *Are they more efficient?*
Co-op member: *Definitely not.*
Authors: *Are they more profitable?*
Co-op member: *No way!*
Authors: *Then what makes them superior?*
Co-op member: *(shrug)*

A Superior Form
of Production?

 Agricultural-production cooperatives are the new wave in Cuban agriculture, constituting in impact and significance a virtual "third agrarian reform." Before the 1975 decision to push cooperatives, most small farmers were engaged in individual production. The exceptions were 45 cooperatives surviving from the more than 300 cooperatives created in the early 1960s. (In fact, these were called "agricultural societies" for fear the term cooperative would scare away small farmers.)[1]

Why the dramatic shift to cooperatives after more than ten years of soft-peddling them? First of all, the small farmers were not pulling their own weight, producing far below their potential while burdening the government with the cost of low-interest credits, crop insurance, and social services. The new emphasis on cooperatives thus fell squarely in line with Cuba's emerging system of economic management, which stipulated that all productive sectors must pay their own way.

The government had also gained considerable political leverage with the farmers, having delivered on its early promise not to force collectivization. In the meantime, the government had built up a strong small-farmers' association (ANAP) with the organizational capacity and political clout to promote cooperatives. Finally, by 1975, experience with state farms had shown that huge investments in such inputs as irrigation and machinery were slow to pay off. Cooperatives were seen as a way of increasing productivity through smaller government investments.

The shift to production cooperatives was part of the government's effort to move Cuban agriculture towards increasingly "superior" forms of production. In its view, the most backward form of production is the individual small farmer—characterized by low levels of technology and social isolation. Next on the ladder are credit and service cooperatives (CCSs), in which farmers join forces to solicit material, financial, and technical assistance from the government.[2] Agricultural production cooperatives (CPAs) are considered more advanced than credit and service cooperatives because the land is owned and farmed collectively. But they are also held to be inferior to state farms, which in theory belong to all the people and not just those working there.

The number of cooperatives grew from 44 in 1977 to 725 in 1979 and 1,480 by 1983.[3] In 1983, cooperatives counted 78,000 members (27 percent women) and represented 53 percent of land in the private sector (or the "nonstate" sector, as government statistics now call the private sector).[4] The goal is to have 90 percent of private farmland in production cooperatives by 1990.[5]

To form a production cooperative, individual farmer-owners pool their land and resources—oxen, plows, and other implements—which become common property. The farmers are reimbursed for their property out of cooperative profits in ensuing years. Members do not receive wages but a share of the profits. Since profits are calculated yearly, members get a monthly advance determined by the amount and type of work they do. At the end of the year, after the repayment of debts, loans, and taxes, net profit is determined. Of that profit, 40 to 50 percent is divided among the workers; 25 to 30 percent is used to repay members who contributed land, animals, tools, etc.; up to 10 percent goes for productive investment; another 10 percent for social investment (housing, schools); and 5 percent for cultural events, sports, and recreation.

The emphasis on cooperatives does not mean a greater emphasis on food production. Like state farms, cooperatives reflect the nation's overall agricultural priorities. Fully one-third are cane cooperatives, followed by tobacco and coffee co-ops. Together these foreign-exchange-earning cooperatives account for half of all production cooperatives. In contrast, bean-producing co-ops are among the least numerous—only 26 in all.[6] Generally production cooperatives specializing in one crop are more diversified than state farms.[7]

Incentives to Join

The major incentive for small farmers to join cooperatives is better living conditions. The early cooperatives received housing and infrastructural improvements free of charge from the government. This proved to be more than the government could afford, and cooperatives must now pay their way. Cooperative members now buy construction supplies from the state and build houses themselves, each member paying the full cost of his or her home.[8] But cooperatives still enjoy priority in scarce construction materials and for such improvements as electrical service (73 percent of cooperatives had electricity in 1983).[9]

Recalcitrant older farmers are sometimes forced to join cooperatives under pressure from their families, who want to be closer to schools and medical care, to live in houses with electricity and running water and, perhaps most of all, to enjoy the social life cooperatives offer. The prospect of living in a community instead of the small farmer's traditional isolation is often an incentive in itself, especially for women and young people. For women, the cooperatives also offer the possibility of paid work, often a bone of contention with traditional husbands who want them to stay at home (and out of sight of other men).

New equipment is another powerful incentive for joining cooperatives. No matter how much money an individual farmer has, the government will not sell him a new tractor, which are reserved for the state farms and production cooperatives. Joining a cooperative gives farmers access not only to tractors, but also to the latest irrigation rigs and even the pride of Cuban manufacture: the sugar combine. One particularly rich cooperative we visited boasted an impressive row of 30 Soviet and Eastern European tractors. Cooperatives also get priority in fertilizers, pesticides, and seeds, as well as lower-interest credit (4 percent for cooperatives, 6 percent for individuals).

Cooperatives are also eligible to use state land free of charge.

In the complex land adjustments designed to create single cooperative units out of many small and disparate plots, the government often helps out by adding some of its own land into the
bargain. A total of 10 percent of cooperative lands have been
provided by the state.[10]

In 1983, two new incentives were added to the list. One is the
new social-security system, which covers only farmers in production cooperatives. Since many private farmers are old, it is
worth their while to join a cooperative and have a guaranteed
fixed income in their old age. The social security system also
covers maternity leave, accidents, disease, and payments to needy
families of deceased cooperative members.[11]

The other incentive is the new tax system. While the tax rate
is progressive, ranging from 5 to 20 percent, the individual
farmer's tax is calculated from gross income while the cooperative's tax is based on net income. With net income averaging 33
percent of gross revenues, the difference in the tax base is substantial. As a further incentive, cooperatives are exempt from all
taxes for the first three to five years after their founding.[12] (Free
market sales are taxed separately.)

Despite the many incentives and advantages offered by the
production cooperatives, we met many small farmers who just
weren't interested. A common theme ran through their refusal
to join: "*Mandar lo suyo*" or "Be your own boss." They tend to
be older farmers, and the government assumes that this group
will eventually be won over or simply die out.

State versus Private Farms: Size

The higher status accorded to production cooperatives, however, does not mean that Cuba's emphasis on state farms has diminished. The state sector outweighs the "nonstate" sector in
terms of land area (four to one, as of 1983), number of workers
(615,000 to 200,000), use of inputs, and total production. According to government figures in 1982, the state sector produced 82 percent of the nation's sugar, 66 percent of the non-
cane agriculture, and 80 percent of the livestock.[13]

The most striking difference between state and private farms
(both individual and cooperatives) is size. Over the years, state
farms have been merged into fewer but larger units. In the early

1960s, the 12,000 middle and large farms that existed before the revolution were incorporated into 920 state farms and ranches. By 1983, they had been further consolidated into 427 units.[14] The average state farm today covers 50,000 acres. If we recall that the first agrarian reform defined large farms as those over 1,000 acres, Cuba's state farms today are not large, but gigantic.

Cooperatives were also encouraged to grow in size. In 1979, José Ramirez, head of the small farmers' association, spoke of the "indisputable socioeconomic advantages" of uniting smaller cooperatives into larger units which afforded "greater development possibilities and more efficient use of technical resources."[15] From 1979 to 1983, the average size of cooperatives more than tripled, going from 350 acres to 1,300. Still, this left the average state farm 38 times the size of the average cooperative and 2,000 times the size of the average individual farm. State farms employed an average of 1,440 workers per farm, while CPAs averaged 52 members.

But is big necessarily better? The Cubans seem to say yes: the bigger the farms, the higher the levels of mechanization and the greater the economies of scale. As Cuban officials see it, "appropriate technology" is appropriate only if you want to stay underdeveloped. "We are not interested in the development of traditional agriculture, but of *modern* agriculture," Vice President Rodriguez told us. "And modern agriculture is based on two complementary elements, technicians and technology."[16] Another official summed up Cuba's position by saying, "Small-scale production means just that: small production."[17]

Large farms are also consistent with Cuba's highly centralized planning and decision-making system. In addition, while Cuba has trained thousands of agricultural technicians and professionals, there is a shortage of competent managers. One high government official with impeccable revolutionary credentials complained to us that the new generation lacked the "entrepreneurial spirit" so important in any enterprise, state or private. Larger, and therefore fewer, farms call for fewer managers.

The Cuban leaders' penchant for large-scale, high-tech agriculture has usually been attributed to Soviet influence. They have also, however, been strongly influenced by the international prestige of large-scale agriculture in the United States.[18] But for years, studies of U.S. agriculture has shown that bigger is not necessarily better, that economies of scale are usually reached on farms far smaller than the largest ones.[19] A comparison of the productivity of state and private farms in Cuba seems to draw the same conclusions.

State versus Private Farms: Productivity

It is difficult to compare productivity of private and state farms using official statistics. Production data for the private sector include only what is sold to the state and therefore substantially underestimate private production. The most meaningful official statistics on crop yields are for sugar, since all cane must be sold to the state for processing. Comparative yields show that despite less use of irrigation, nitrogen fertilizer, and mechanization, private production has been consistently higher than on the state farms (13 percent higher in 1982).[20,21]

In our visits to numerous state farms, cooperatives, and individual farms, the latter two invariably appeared to have higher yields than the large state farms. On one state farm, for example, the administrator himself told us that for onions, their number two crop, the private farmers in the same area had 50 percent higher yields than the state farm.[22]

But the most telling differences are in production costs. While cooperatives' costs averaged 62 centavos for every peso's worth of production, those for the state farms run over a peso. The vast majority of state farms run at a loss and keep functioning thanks to state subsidies. At one of the state farms we visited in Granma province, production costs were over 2 pesos for every peso's worth of production. Vice President Rodriguez admitted to us that while "almost all of the cooperatives are profitable, almost none of the state farms are."[23] Of course, whether or not the state farms are profitable depends on what the government pays for their production, and some state farm managers suggested to us that the government is not paying enough. But the cooperatives can make a profit with the same prices. Clearly, the government finds itself in an embarrassing position when the "superior" form of farming cannot pay its own way.

Popular participation in decision making could help account for the greater yields of the cooperatives. One cooperative we visited told us that at their monthly meetings they discuss every peso spent over the past month. "The members know that the success of the cooperative depends on our profits," he said. "So you often find that the president of the cooperative proposes a new idea, and the farmers get up and argue against it because it won't be profitable for such-and-such reasons."

The state farms are not only less participatory in their internal structure, they also enjoy less autonomy in making decisions. One state-farm manager, for example, complained to us that the money his farm gets from the state is allocated according to specific projects. If he and the workers on the farm believe that funds would be better spent on other projects, they cannot make that decision. "Those who give credit look at the investment from a national point of view," he said. "We look more narrowly at what it means for our state farm. And the two do not always coincide."

What Motivates the Workers?

One of the major problems on the state farms has been worker motivation. In theory, since the farm belongs to the people as a whole, people work for the benefit of the nation, not for their own selfish interests. (That's why state farms are said to be superior to cooperatives.) But while the theory is lofty, over the years the Cubans have seen that without individual material incentives, productivity suffers.[24]

This was especially evident during the "idealistic" period of the late 1960s, when all connections between salary and output were eliminated. Workers were encouraged to work extra hours for no extra income, and bad workers received the same paycheck as good workers. The results were disconcerting levels of absenteeism and a concomitant sharp drop in productivity. Even during the big push for the 10-million-ton sugar harvest in 1970, absentee rates among the professional and volunteer canecutters ran almost 29 percent.[25]

In the 1970s, great efforts were made to reduce absenteeism and increase productivity in all workplaces. Reversing previous policy, managers now have the power to suspend or dismiss workers without having to request authorization from workers' councils. The planning ministry undertook "time and motion studies" to determine how long it should take an individual or a work team to complete a particular task. Wherever possible, wages are based upon work completed and not time logged.

On the state farms, this meant that the more tomatoes workers planted, the more money they made. The policy, however, did not take into account the *quality* of the work. This was changed in 1981 and wages were tied to yields whenever possible. According to Vice President Rodriguez, this change in policy has led to increased productivity and decreased losses.[26]

With the new system, the more productive a worker, the higher the wage. On one of the farms we visited, the less productive field workers earned as little as 4 pesos a day; the more productive nearly doubled this. There were also different wages for different types of work. Machine operators earned from 8 to 10 pesos a day, depending on productivity. The highest wage was the manager's, who earned 16 pesos a day, and even his salary was tied to the farm's productivity.[27]

For sugar workers, monetary incentives are greater. Basic wages in both the mills and the field are 15 percent higher than for equivalent work in nonsugar activities. Sugar workers are paid extra for night work and particularly strenuous jobs. Older workers receive extra pay as an incentive not to retire. In addition, the best canecutters are allowed to purchase Cuba's most prized commodity, a new car, and have greater access to new housing, appliances, and vacations to Eastern Europe. In agriculture, the average nonsugar wage in 1982 was 135 pesos per month compared to 185 per month for sugar workers.[28] In industry, the average wage is about 170 pesos per month, compared to 230 per month in the sugar industry.[29]

There are also collective incentives in both the sugar and nonsugar sectors, tying workers' incomes not only to their own productivity but to that of the farm as a whole. One result is a new awareness of economic constraints and the need to cut costs. Once again, attitudes are in striking contrast to the late 1960s, when talk about production costs or profits—anything related to money—was heresy. Vice President Rodriguez recalled having taken a group of visiting Soviet dignitaries on a tour of state farms during that period: "At each farm I'd ask the administrator what the production costs were, and each time the answer was the same: 'Production costs? What's the difference, if money's unimportant?' I could have killed them. Today the state farms have to be self-financing, and everyone can tell you exactly what production costs are."

For the members of cooperatives, profits are even more directly related to income than on state farms. The monthly advance for unskilled workers on most co-ops is quite low, 4 or 5 pesos a day. Depending on profits at the end of the year, their earnings can range from this level to 20 to 28 pesos a day, four times the average national wage.[30]

There is also a wide range of incomes within the cooperatives, depending on the kind of work and the skill of the worker. Women's earnings, for example, seem to be substantially lower than men's. At a cooperative we visited in Santiago, the highest-paid man made 4,096 pesos per year, twice the average yearly income, while the highest-paid woman made 30 percent less. There are still many distinctions between "women's work" and "men's work" in the field, and "men's work" is often more strenuous for better pay. Women usually work fewer days than men (taking time off to care for sick children and do household chores) and fewer hours during the day (leaving work an hour before lunchtime to prepare lunch for the family, getting off work early to pick up children from school and prepare dinner).

At one very successful cooperative we visited we asked the manager what motivated the members: material incentives, moral incentives, or the right combination of both? "Look at our backgrounds," he replied. "We are all farmers, we all have a love for the land, for our work. That's probably the number one factor. If there's a job to be done, we don't look at the clock to see if it's after five, and it doesn't matter to us if it's a Sunday or a holiday. Our work comes first."

Perhaps with this view in mind, in the 1980s more and more state farms began dividing the land into smaller plots and making workers completely responsible for production on that plot. The result is to make the farmworker more like a small-scale farmer and to make it easier to tie wages to output.

Who Will Be Tomorrow's Farmers?

Before the revolution, most rural children worked in the fields and either became farmworkers themselves or took over the family farm. The revolution has brought them a new future; it is now common to find the children of farmworkers or farmers studying to be engineers, doctors, or technicians. But as Cuba's population becomes more sophisticated and better educated, who will be left to work on the farms?

Even as far back as the 1960s, the new job opportunities created by the revolution resulted in a labor shortage in the countryside. For the sugar harvest, thousands upon thousands of students, urban workers, soldiers, and others were mobilized. These workers' lack of skill and experience in agricultural tasks led to low productivity in the field, while the rest of the economy suffered as their regular jobs went unattended. For sugar cane, mechanization was the answer, and the bulk of the work—even during the harvest—is now done by the permanent labor force. When extra help is needed, the farms call on a select group of veteran canecutters from the city.

For other crops, labor mobilizations continue, but on a much smaller scale. The Federation of Cuban Women, together with the small farmers' association (ANAP), assembles brigades of unemployed women to work on the state farms during peak periods. More common is the use of students in the field. The majority of the work on the citrus plantations on the Isle of Youth is done by junior-high-school children. At one of Cuba's largest vegetable farms, we found that the permanent labor force of 2,000 accounted for only 40 percent of the labor needs. The rest is supplied by 15,000 students who come from the city each year in batches of 2,500 for forty-five days of farm work. In addition, the 3,500 high school students in the area work on the farm three hours a day, four days a week.[31]

The use of students in farm work is consistent with Cuba's principle of linking physical and intellectual work. The government loses money by sending urban students to work in the countryside, but an awareness and appreciation of manual work is considered an essential part of the students' education. As for the modern boarding schools in the countryside, the cost of the schools surely exceeds the students' economic contribution. But while the use of student labor has ideological underpinnings, it is also true that without their help the rural labor shortage would be even more critical.

Another combination of ideology and economics saw urban workers asked to give up their only free day, Sunday, to go work in the fields. It was a way to link the cities with the countryside, to make urban dwellers appreciate all the work that goes into providing them with food, and it was completely voluntary. One of the authors, Medea Benjamin, who participated in numerous such Sunday outings, remembers them this way:

> My work place would ask if anyone was willing to go to the countryside on Sunday to pick potatoes. The volunteers were told, "Be at such and such a place at 6 a.m. sharp. If you're not there on time, the bus will leave without you." We'd wake one another up at dawn, get to the meeting place at 6 a.m., and end up waiting till 8 a.m. for the bus to arrive. Already the grumbling would start: "Why can't the damn bus ever get here on time. You'd think after all these years . . ." Then the bus driver would get lost and circle around and around until he finally found the farm we were headed for. By that time it was 10 a.m., time for the morning snack of cake and soda. By 10:30 we'd be ready for work, but more often than not there'd be no one around to tell us what to do. On numerous occasions we'd find that they'd sent us to a field that had already been picked. So we'd feel around in the dirt a bit, fishing for a stray potato here and there. Little by little we'd lose interest and head back for the bus, for we were supposed to leave before noon so the farm would not have to provide us with lunch. On the bus back there'd be lots of laughing and joking, and the oft-repeated phrase: "You'd think that after all these years . . ."

Although not all experiences were so extreme, the overall productivity of such labor was so low that by the late 1970s, such Sunday outings were eliminated.

There is a shortage of skilled as well as unskilled workers in the countryside. At one of the state farms we visited, the manager said the need was such that they hired all skilled workers who applied there.[32] The labor shortage also affects private farmers. With their children away at school, they often hire outside labor to help out during peak periods. In the 1980s, a new policy allowed farmers to hire workers directly rather than through the ministry of labor. But it is still difficult to find workers since most Cubans, even in the countryside, have steady year-round jobs. Some of those willing to do seasonal work for the private farmers are retired people such as the 65-year-old former sugar worker we met who said his 75-pesos-a-month pension wasn't enough to get by on. Others hold state jobs at low wages. A night watchman said that his 98-pesos-a-month salary was not enough to maintain his family of five. Such workers were the poorest people we came across in Cuba.

The government recognizes the problem of these workers: an ANAP official told us that the only person in Cuba who is still exploited is the one who works for the private farmowner. Great efforts have been made to reduce the number of such workers, with the aim of eliminating them altogether. The policy of constantly increasing the minimum wage, coupled with the growth of cooperatives in the private sector, have been particularly effective. From about one hundred and fifty thousand in 1962, this sector was reportedly reduced to somewhere between thirty and sixty thousand in 1966[33] and dropped to sixteen thousand by 1977. This figure, however, undoubtedly does not take into account much of the "informal" hiring not reported to the government.

Labor shortages are particularly acute with labor-intensive foreign-exchange earners such as coffee and tobacco. The vice minister of agriculture has called these "crops of underdevelopment."[34] Unlike sugar cane, they are difficult to mechanize and, therefore, do not lend themselves to large-scale agriculture. Coffee farmers often live in mountainous areas in isolation from each other, making it difficult for the government to bring electricity, running water, and other conveniences of modern life. In the past these poor living conditions led to an exodus from the rural areas to the cities. The government is emphasizing the creation of cooperatives in the mountain areas to stop farmers from abandoning the land. This seems to be meeting with some success already. In the mountainous region of San Cristobal (Pinar del Rio), for example, we were told that between 1976 and 1980, 370 farm families had migrated to the plains. By 1982 there were twelve cooperatives and the exodus had stopped.

The Future

If the current rate of conversion continues, Cuba is likely to achieve its goal of turning 90 percent of privately held land into cooperatives by 1990. The insignificant portion of land left in private hands would dwindle even further as the old farmers die off and there is no one to take their places.

The cooperative movement is bound to gain greater strength.

Visiting Cuba's cooperatives, one gets a sense of optimism for the future. Members see cooperatives becoming more and more profitable, and they are confident that their living standards will continue to improve.

At one of the cooperatives we visited, we asked the elected officers, who were obviously quite proud of their cooperative, if state farms were truly superior forms of production. "Oh yes," they all readily agreed. We asked if they were better organized. "Oh no." Were they more efficient? "Definitely not." So what made them superior? Nobody could tell us. And when we asked if their cooperative would one day "graduate" to become a state farm, they were unenthusiastic. "Maybe many years from now," they said. "But by that time, we'll all be dead and buried."

Vice President Rodriguez argues that yearly government subsidies to state farms are getting smaller and that soon the huge investments made to modernize the state farms will begin to pay off. With their flair for dialectics, Cuban leaders insist that cooperatives and state farms are not in conflict but are complementary to one another. The cooperatives, with their lower production costs, act as an "economic model" for the state farms, they say. The state farms, with their high levels of mechanization, serve as "technical models" for the cooperatives. The two are now engaged, the leadership concludes, in a friendly competition ("emulation") to see who can produce the most at the lowest cost.

And if time proves that cooperatives are more productive than state farms, will the farms be converted to cooperatives? Fidel once made that suggestion to a group of farmers, so we asked Vice President Rodriguez if he was serious. "Turn the state farms into cooperatives?" he laughed. "Fidel was just kidding around. You just don't understand the Cuban sense of humor."

CHAPTER 13

---

*There's been much said about my anti-Communism. Well, I am
an anti-Communist if you talk about Communism for the United
States. . . . But I never thought it was necessary for us to impose
our form of governments on some other country. . . . So far as I'm
concerned, we can live at peace in the world together.*

> PRESIDENT RONALD REAGAN,
> Press Conference after Trip to China, May 2, 1984

*The United States and Cuba must renew their friendship and their
ties. We must talk with each other, not at each other. We must turn
to each other, not on each other. . . . We must forgive each other,
redeem each other—go on and give peace a chance.*

> REVEREND JESSE JACKSON,
> Press Conference after Trip to Cuba, June 26, 1984

Our Menu in Havana

 The Cuban revolution confirms the principal conclusion of President Carter's Commission on World Hunger: in every country, hunger could be eradicated if only there were the political will to do so.

With all the authority of hindsight, it is important to analyze and criticize the methods Cuba has chosen to eradicate hunger—its marketing policies, agricultural priorities, farm organization, and so forth. But we should never lose sight of the fact that the Cuban revolution declared, from the outset, that no one should go malnourished. No disappointment in food production, no failed economic take-off, no shock wave from world economic crisis has deterred Cuba from freeing itself from the suffering and shame of a single wasted child or an elderly person ignominiously subsisting on pet food. No other country in this hemisphere, including the United States, can make this claim.

Ending hunger is not the revolution's only accomplishment. The streets of Old Havana are no longer lined with prostitutes. A former slave society with many blacks and a history of discrimination, Cuba is now the most racially harmonious society we have ever experienced. The rate of violent crime is among the lowest in the world. The streets are safe at any hour of the night. Ask a Cuban about rape and she or he may recall a case in such-and-such town so many years ago. Illiteracy has been virtually eradicated and the current campaign is to ensure everyone, even the oldest small farmer, at least a ninth-grade education. Health care is free, and Cuba's health indicators are perhaps the best in Latin America. Every effort is made to guarantee full employment. All this makes for a society with a pervasive sense of dignity and confidence in the future—a sharp contrast from the shame and hopelessness one finds in much of the third world.

Even the revolution's opponents admit its material successes. The Washington-based and corporate-funded Overseas Development Council's Physical Quality of Life Index ranks Cuba the highest in Latin America.[1] A 1982 study prepared for the Joint Economic Committee of the U.S. Congress cites the accomplishments of the Cuban revolution as follows:

- A highly egalitarian redistribution of income that has eliminated almost all malnutrition, particularly among children.

- Establishment of a national health care program that is superior in the third world and rivals that of numerous developed countries.

- Near total elimination of illiteracy and a highly developed multilevel educational system.

- Development of a relatively well-disciplined and motivated population with a strong sense of national identification.[2]

But the report goes on to say that these achievements have only been possible thanks to "continuous, massive, economic and military aid from its principal patron, the USSR."[3] It contends that the Soviets have been propping up the Cuban economy to the tune of $3 billion a year, most of it through subsidized prices.[4] They pay Cuba more for sugar and nickel than world market prices and sell oil to Cuba at prices substantially lower than the OPEC price. The report concludes that Cuba's economic ties to the USSR represent "the epitome of a client-patron relationship."

But Cubans argue otherwise: the Soviets are not propping us up, they say, but merely paying fair prices for our goods, unlike the terms of trade on the "free" world market. Nor are they milking our economy like the Americans used to do: they own no property in Cuba, remit no profits from investments in Cuba, and don't buy cheap and sell dear. A poem by Cuba's national poet, Nicolás Guillén, sums up the view from Havana:

Never have I seen a Soviet trust in my country.
Nor a bank
a five and dime store
a sugar mill,
a naval base,
or a train.
I've never once found
a banana plantation
where on passing you might read:
MASLOV AND COMPANY, INC.
WHOLESALE BANANAS. OFFICES IN CUBA:
CORNER OF MACEO AND SUCH-AND-SUCH A STREET.[5]

Whether we characterize Soviet relations with Cuba as a friendly embrace or a bear hug, we must recognize two undeniable facts: first, while Cuba was dependent on the United States, there was hunger and massive unemployment. Second, many countries—the Philippines, El Salvador, Pakistan—receive "continuous, massive economic and military aid" not from the Soviet Union but from the United States. Yet which of them can boast the same accomplishments as Cuba?

Look at Puerto Rico, an island nation with a history very similar to Cuba's. While Puerto Rico receives more than $4 billion in U.S. aid every year—four times more, per capita, than Cuba receives from the USSR—what does it have to show? Its economy has lost its agricultural base without anything as substantial in its place; it has become totally dependent on food imports; 25 percent of its people cannot find work; more than half live (ever more precariously) from food stamps and public assistance; and since the 1950s nearly a third of Puerto Rico's entire population has emigrated to the United States, many in search of employment and security.[6]

Finally, what are the origins of Cuba's close ties to the Soviet Union? Early in the revolution, the U.S. efforts to isolate Cuba economically and politically—cutting off its sugar quota, breaking diplomatic relations, expelling it from the Organization of American States, imposing an economic blockade and pressuring other Latin American and Western countries to join the blockade—gave Cuba no choice but to seek assistance from the Soviet

Union. When reporters asked revolutionary leader Che Guevara in 1960 "how far" the Cuban revolution would go, he replied that it was U.S. pressure that had "radicalized" the revolution in the first place and added: "To know how much farther Cuba will go, it would be easier to ask the U.S. government how far it plans to go."[7] The United States first accused the Cubans of communist leanings, then made them rely on the Soviets for aid, and finally turned around and said, "See? We told you they were communists."

The real tragedy of our government's self-fulfilling prophecy is that it seems to have learned nothing from the Cuban experience and is bent on repeating the same course in Central America.

It is frequently charged that the Cuban revolution may have eliminated hunger but at the cost of political freedom. The most troubling dimension of this charge is that it suggests that freedom and food are mutually exclusive choices for third-world countries. This is a view we vigorously reject. The limits on political liberty in Cuba are real, and their causes can be analyzed. To tie those limits to the policies that have eliminated hunger is to perpetuate a vision of despair—food versus freedom—offering no hope for the future of the third world.

Even with the revolution consolidated, important freedoms are still circumscribed in Cuba. Social norms, while having changed radically, are still influenced by a 1950s Spanish middle-class moralism that would please Jerry Falwell. Political dissent—be it by individual citizens, opposition parties, party caucuses, or in public forums is severely curbed. Elections for Cuba's highest legislative body, People's Power, can be labeled "a battle of biographies," for the candidates post their pictures and life histories on designated bulletin boards. They make no public appearances and do not take stands on issues. While Cuban leaders have chided journalists for their self-censorship and urged them to write more critically, many important issues are untouchable. A member of the Central Committee told us that the greatest failure of the revolution is that on all levels Cubans prefer to go along with the tide rather than speak out and risk being labeled "conflictive." For those who get into serious trouble, too often the accused stands guilty until proven innocent.

We believe that the limits of political freedom in Cuba have not been part of a trade-off for the right to eat, but are in great measure a consequence of the unrelenting hostility and repeated attempts at subversion by the United States. These actions have created a permanent siege mentality in Cuba. Americans know this mentality all too well—from the years following the Japanese attack on Pearl Harbor, or from our recurrent "red scares" that some would revive today. Rather than safeguard rights and freedoms, societies under siege, real or imagined, are prone to see every dissent, every deviation from the norm, as the work of the enemy bent on subversion from within.

U.S. attacks on Cuba are hardly a figment of Cuba's imagination. The United States sponsored the Bay of Pigs invasion in 1961. According to the U.S. Senate Intelligence Committee, between 1960 and 1965 there were at least eight CIA plots to assassinate President Castro. To this day—and even more blatantly under the Reagan presidency—the U.S. government, in defiance of U.S. law, collaborates with U.S.-based terrorist organizations working to sabotage Cuba's economy and overthrow its government.[8]

Our government outlaws Cuba from the West and then decries its dependence on the Soviet Union. Our government imposes a trade embargo and then revels in Cuba's economic troubles. Our government invades the island, repeatedly tries to assassinate its leaders, sanctions terrorist attacks, and then bemoans the lack of freedom.

What have been the aims of our government's Cuba policy throughout the past twenty-five years? The initial aim was to topple the government. This policy had the opposite effect: it strengthened internal support. Each time the United States makes a threatening move, Cubans take to the streets to rally behind *their* revolution. Reports that such mobilizations are forced are simply false. In the face of U.S. threats, who cares that the meat didn't come on time or that there's no deodorant in the stores? There is no greater unifying force than a foreign bully.

If our government's aim has been to make Cuba an international pariah, that too has backfired. Cuba now has economic and diplomatic relations with most nations, including all of Western Europe and at least fifteen countries in Latin America. (The Organization of American States voted in 1975 to reverse its eleven-year economic and political "quarantine" against the island.) Cuba plays a leading role in the nonaligned movement and within the United Nations. U.S. hostility has actually served to heighten Cuba's international prestige, especially in the third world. Even nations that differ with Cuba's politics are often sympathetic towards the beleaguered David standing up to the menacing Goliath.

If our government's aim has been to make Cuba's image so tarnished that other third-world countries will not be tempted to take the same route, that too has been a resounding failure. Revolutions spring from local conditions—Cuba can neither export revolutions nor can the United States prevent them. But the United States has managed to turn Cuba into a symbol of defiance that has become far more powerful than any weapons Cuba could export to revolutionaries abroad.

If our government's aim has been to influence the Castro government, perhaps to encourage it to become less dependent on the Soviet Union, to restrain its activities abroad, or to liberalize its internal politics, its policies of all sticks and no carrots have failed dismally.

So, we should ask ourselves, what good has come from U.S. policy? As far as we can see, absolutely none.

Not only has our government's Cuba policy been bankrupt, it has also been inconsistent with the rest of U.S. foreign policy. Why do we have diplomatic relations with other socialist countries—including the Soviet Union and China, the biggest and presumably the most threatening—but refuse to deal with tiny Cuba? The Chinese president is wined and dined across the United States, while the Cuban president is treated like a criminal and confined to a twenty-five-mile radius around the United Nations in New York. While Americans are free to visit the Soviet Union and Eastern Europe and hordes of Americans are now rushing to get an inside look at China, Reagan has imposed a ban on tourism to Cuba. In 1984 the Supreme Court upheld this ban, so that any American who joins the thousands of Canadians and Western Europeans soaking up the sun on Cuba's world-renowned beaches will be subject to a $50,000 fine and up to ten years in jail. Cuba is one of four countries on the U.S. Trade with the Enemy Act list.[9] U.S. ships make regular stops at both

Chinese and Soviet ports, but no U.S. ships can stop in Cuba. Until 1977, ships from third countries stopping in Cuban ports were banned from the United States. We sell wheat to Moscow but not to Havana. If Cuba is merely a proxy of the Soviet Union, why trounce on the puppet but not the puppeteer?

Diplomat Wayne Smith, head of the State Department's Cuba desk from 1976 to 1979 and then chief of the U.S. Interests Section in Havana from 1979 to 1982, reports that on numerous occasions Cuban officials signalled their desire for improved relations and their readiness to discuss such areas of mutual concern as Central America and the return of Cuban criminals who came to the United States during the 1980 Mariel boatlift. But the Reagan administration chose to ignore these openings and to continue its policy of confrontation. "Having begun with confrontation, we have stuck with it year after year," says Smith. "With all the tremendous resources and wide options available to us, we seem not to have the wit and imagination to bring them into play. It is distressing to see a great nation limit itself to a unidimensional approach. In the Cuban context, diplomacy rather than confrontation is seen as the last resort."[10]

The Cuban revolution has mellowed somewhat with age. As Fidel's beard becomes sprinkled with gray, so his rhetoric becomes less abrasive. Unlike in the early years, today he seldom makes such inflammatory remarks as "Try invading Cuba and there'll be two hundred thousand dead Yankees." While refusing to compromise on revolutionary principles, he now admits there's plenty of room for accommodation. "Sooner or later," he says, "economic and political relations will have to develop between Cuba and the United States. This is dictated by geography, history, and the interests of both countries. First of all, we are neighbors. We cannot move, nor can the United States."[11]

The Cubans have also indicated their desire for trade with the United States. Cuba wants U.S. machinery and other manufactured goods, it wants American technology, it wants to diversify its trading partners, it wants to lessen its dependence on the Soviet Union. Cuban Trade Minister Marcelo Fernandez has said that if the U.S. embargo were lifted, trade between the two countries could amount to as much as $1 billion a year.[12] Cuba has also shown its eagerness to enter into joint ventures and buy-back arrangements with U.S. companies like those now commonplace in Eastern Europe. Such trade is obviously not only in Cuba's interests, but in the interests of U.S. businesses as well. During the Carter administration, when prospects looked good for a breakthrough in U.S.-Cuba relations, hundreds of U.S. business executives visited Cuba and urged the U.S. government to lift the blockade.

Sooner or later, the United States will have to overcome the biggest obstacle to the formulation of a realistic Cuba policy: admitting that Castro's revolution is here to stay. Perhaps it was understandable in 1960 to think that the revolution was a temporary aberration. Cuban exiles in Miami kept their bags packed and didn't bother to cash in their return tickets. But twenty-five years later, it is time to cast off illusions.

The next obstacle is accepting that Latin America is no longer "our backyard." It is no longer "our" hemisphere. Until we accept this, we will find ourselves, as in Central America, engaged in the futile task of trying to "save" countries that were never ours and "roll back" revolutions that pose no threat to the real interests of the American people.

We must accept every people's right to change, to rid themselves of systems which have brought only needless hunger and suffering for the majority. And not only accept, but *support* their right to change. While Cuba does not provide a "model"—for every country must find its own path—it does demonstrate that hunger is, in fact, needless.

CHRONOLOGY

1953 JULY 26   Fidel Castro together with 123 other men and women launched an armed attack on Cuba's second largest military barracks, the Moncada Garrison, in Santiago de Cuba.

1956 DECEMBER 2   Fidel Castro and 81 other revolutionaries sailed from Mexico to Cuba in the yacht *Granma*, marking the beginning of the guerrilla struggle in the Sierra Maestra mountains.

1958 NEW YEAR'S EVE   Cuban dictator Fulgencio Batista flees the island.

1959 JANUARY 8   Fidel Castro makes triumphal entry into Havana.
MARCH 17   Eisenhower orders CIA to begin training Cuban exiles to overthrow Castro.
MAY 17   First agrarian reform law decreed, giving land titles to one hundred thousand peasant families and eventually nationalizing 44 percent of the land.

1960 MARCH 14   Cuba and the Soviet Union sign major trade agreement.
JUNE 29   Cuba nationalizes U.S.-owned oil refineries for refusing to refine Soviet crude oil.
JULY 6   President Eisenhower cancels Cuba's sugar quota.
JULY 10   The Soviet Union agrees to buy the sugar affected by the quota cancellation.
AUGUST 7   Cuba nationalizes all U.S.-owned industrial and agrarian enterprises.
OCTOBER 14   Urban Reform Law drastically cuts rents and provides for renters to become owners.
OCTOBER 19   First U.S. embargo prohibits exports to Cuba, except for nonsubsidized foodstuffs and medicines.

1961 APRIL 17–19   Bay of Pigs invasion   The invasion of Cuba by a 1,500-man army of CIA-trained Cuban exiles ends in military disaster for the United States and the capture of 1,222 of the invaders. Castro declares the socialist nature of Cuba's revolution.

MAY   Literacy campaign begins; in four months, illiteracy is reduced from 24 percent to 7 percent.

1962 FEBRUARY 7   An embargo on U.S.-Cuban trade (except medical supplies) goes into effect.

FEBRUARY   Organization of American States votes fifteen to four to exclude Cuba from the organization and for member states to break all diplomatic ties.

MARCH 12   Cuba's food rationing program begins.

SEPTEMBER 26   U.S. Congress passes resolution giving the President the right to intervene in Cuba if the United States is threatened.

OCTOBER 22   President Kennedy announces the presence of Soviet nuclear missiles in Cuba and establishes naval blockade of the island.

OCTOBER 27   Kennedy proposes that Soviets remove weapons from Cuba in exchange for an end to the blockade and assurances that the United States will not invade Cuba.

NOVEMBER 8   U.S. Department of Defense announces that all Soviet missile bases in Cuba have been dismantled.

1963 OCTOBER   Second Agrarian Reform Law takes effect, eliminating all private farms over 1,000 acres and increasing the state sector to 63 percent.

1968 New Revolutionary Offensive—all private retail businesses nationalized.

1970 The sugar harvest is Cuba's largest ever—8.5 million tons—but falls short of 10-million-ton goal.

1973 NOVEMBER   13th Congress of Central Organization of Cuban Trade Unions (CTC) strengthens role of unions and ties wages to productivity.

1974 In the revolution's first elections, Matanzas province elects delegates to People's Power; in 1976 voting is extended throughout island.

1975 DECEMBER   Cuba's Communist Party holds its first congress; green light given to cooperative movement.

1977 New Economic Management and Planning System (SDPE) implemented throughout economy; gives enterprises greater autonomy and financial responsibility.

1979 Cuba allows Cuban-Americans to return to visit relatives.

1980 MARCH 25   Wage Reform increases the average wage by 12 percent.

APRIL 21   In response to a Cuban declaration that any Cubans wishing to leave the country can be picked up at the port of Mariel, a boatlift begins.

SPRING   Opening of Farmers' Markets.

SEPTEMBER 26   After one hundred and twenty-five thousand Cubans leave the country, the Cuban government closes the port of Mariel to U.S.-bound emigration.

DECEMBER   Cuba's Communist Party holds second congress.

1981 DECEMBER 14   Retail prices raised for the first time since 1962.

1983 MAY   ANAP Congress debates future of farmers' markets. Expansion of state retail marketing system.

RESOURCE GUIDE

Organizations

Brigada Antonio Maceo

P. O. Box 20219
Greeley Square Station
New York, NY 10116

Organization of progressive Cubans living in the United States; has eight regional offices; organizes yearly work-study contingent to Cuba; publishes quarterly bulletin *Baraguá*.

Center for Cuban Studies

124 West 23rd Street
New York, NY 10010

Publishes *Cuba Update*, a bimonthly newsletter.
Promotes educational and cultural exchanges; publishes educational materials.

Chicago Cuba Committee

P. O. Box 10607
Fort Dearborn Station
Chicago, IL 60610

Círculo de Cultura Cubana

GPO Box 2174
New York, NY 10116

Publishes quarterly bulletin and magazine *Areito*, both in Spanish. Promotes educational and cultural exchanges between Cubans in Cuba and Cubans living abroad.

Cuba Resource Group

1927 Dwight Way, Apt. 105
Berkeley, CA 94601

Information center and library.

Cuba Resource Center, Inc.

11 John Street, Room 506
New York, NY 10038

Publishes quarterly magazine *Cuba Times*.

Cuban-American Committee
1346 Connecticut Avenue, N.W., Suite 1032
Washington, DC 20036

Lobbies for closer U.S.-Cuban relations and promotes the interests of the Cuban-American community.

Cuban Studies/Estudios Cubanos
Center for Latin American Studies
Univ. of Pittsburgh
Pittsburgh, PA 15260

Publishes biannual journal *Cuban Studies/Estudios Cubanos*.

Ediciónes Vitral, Inc.
GPO Box 20043
Greeley Square Station
New York, NY 10116

Distributes Cuban records and books.

National Lawyers Guild—Cuba Subcommittee
343 S. Dearborn, Suite 918
Chicago, IL 60604

Sends yearly lawyers' delegation to Cuba; lobbies for normalization of U.S.-Cuba relations.

Venceremos Brigade, National Office
P. O. Box 673
New York, NY 10035

Sends yearly work contingent of North Americans to Cuba; publishes and distributes educational and audiovisual materials; has eleven regional offices.

Distributors of Cuban films (both documentary and feature)

Cinema Guild
1697 Broadway
New York, NY 10019

New Yorker Films
16 W. 61 Street
New York, NY 10023

For Visa and General Information

Cuban Interest Section
2630 16th Street, N.W.
Washington, DC 20009

For Cuban Periodicals

Ediciones Cubanas
Obispo #461, Apto. 605
La Habana, Cuba

(*Granma Weekly Review*, *Bohemia* and dozens more)

The Reagan administration has restricted travel to Cuba to journalists, professional researchers, guests of the Cuban government, those with special licenses (such as performers and athletes), and Cuban-Americans visiting relatives. In June 1984 the Supreme Court upheld the restrictions. For travel information, contact Marazul Tours, 250 W. 57th Street, Suite 1311, New York, NY 10107, or Moncada Tours, 1927 Dwight Way, Apt. 105, Berkeley, CA 94601.

NOTES

THE FOOD WINDOW

1. Lowry Nelson, *Rural Cuba* (Minneapolis: University of Minnesota Press, 1950), p. 47.
2. See, for example, *Granma Weekly Review*'s special edition marking the revolution's 25th anniversary, 18 December 1983.
3. Frances Moore Lappé and Joseph Collins, *Food First: Beyond the Myth of Scarcity* (New York: Ballantine, 1978), pp. 7–8.

CHAPTER 1   On the Eve of Revolution

1. *FAO Production Yearbook, 1958* (Rome: Food and Agriculture Organization of the United Nations, 1959).
2. Robin Blackburn, "Prologue to the Cuban Revolution," *New Left Review*, October 1964, p. 83.
3. Before the revolution, dollar to peso exchange rates are misleading. Currently, 1 dollar can be officially exchanged for about 0.75 pesos; on the black market, a dollar brings about 4 pesos. But in a society where medical care is free, the price of food *controlled*, rent linked to income—to cite a few examples—dollar comparisons of income levels are meaningless. Accordingly, we will use pesos throughout the book, without converting them to dollars. Agrupación Católica Universitaria, *Por qué Reforma Agraria?* (n.p., mimeographed, 1956–57), p. 191.
4. The Catholic University Association survey concluded that 91 percent of farmworkers were undernourished. But a critical look at this survey reveals methodological flaws that tend to inflate the figures on malnutrition. For example, the study claims that farmworkers consumed 1,000 calories a day less than the optimal diet. When calculating caloric intake, however, they failed to include such foods as fruit and sugar. Another example is that after calculating the average height of the agricultural worker as 5 feet 4 inches, they used "commonly accepted tables" of height for weight (no reference given) to conclude that Cubans were 16 pounds underweight. However, a check of standard height/weight tables (such as Metropolitan Life tables) shows these workers to be within the optimal range for their heights. We therefore believe that the survey's conclusion that 91 percent was undernourished is exaggerated. Our misgivings about the statistics, however, in no way detract from the validity of the survey's general statements about the poverty of the farmworkers or the inadequate and monotonous diet.
5. Lowry Nelson, *Rural Cuba* (Minneapolis: University of Minnesota Press, 1950), pp. 4f.
6. Ibid., pp. 209f.
7. Personal interview with Nitza Villapoll, January 1982.
8. Erna Fergusson, *Cuba* (New York: A.A. Knopf, 1946), p. 247.
9. Claes Brundenius, *Economic Growth, Basic Needs and Income Distribution in Revolutionary Cuba* (Lund: Research Policy Institute, 1981), p. 142.
10. *Areíto*, interview with Carlos Rafael Rodríguez, 7:25:5.
11. Jacques Chonchol, "El primer bienio de reforma agraria (1959–1961)," in *Reformas agrarias en América Latina*, Oscar Delgado, ed. (Mexico City: Fondo de Cultura Económico, 1965), p. 469.
12. International Labour Office, *The Landless Farmer in Latin America* (Geneva, 1957), pp. 66–67;

13. Carmelo Mesa-Lago, *The Economy of Socialist Cuba: A Two-Decade Appraisal* (Albuquerque: University Of New Mexico Press, 1981), p. 20.
14. Jacques Chonchol, "Memorandum Sobre el Proceso de la Reforma Agraria en Cuba," *Cuadernos Latino-Americanos de Economía Humana* 3:7 (January–April 1960):48, says 5 percent.
15. James O'Connor, *The Origins of Socialism in Cuba* (Ithaca: Cornell University Press, 1970), p. 58; *Census of Cuba*, 1946.
16. Blackburn, p. 83.
17. Wyatt MacGaffey and Clifford R. Barnett, *Cuba: Its People, Its Society, Its Culture* (New Haven: Hraf Press, 1962), p. 144.
18. Blackburn, p. 83.
19. Hugh Thomas, *Cuba: The Pursuit of Freedom* (New York: Harper and Row, 1971), p. 1119.
20. Margaret Randall, *Cuban Women Now* (Toronto: The Women's Press, 1974), p. 9.
21. Sydney Clark, *All the Best in Cuba* (New York: Dodd, Mead and Company, 1956), p. 129.
22. Nelson, p. 146.
23. Thomas, p. 1177.
24. Blackburn, p. 83.
25. Jorge Domínguez, *Cuba: Order and Revolution* (Cambridge: Harvard University Press, 1978), p. 93.
26. Thomas, p. 1110.
27. Ibid., p. 1107.
28. Fergusson, p. 283.
29. Warren Miller, *90 Miles From Home: The Face of Cuba Today* (Greenwich: Fawcett Publications, 1961), p. 32.
30. Fergusson, p.287.
31. Blackburn, p. 59.
32. Thomas, p. 1096 cites *Census of 1953*, p. xliii.
33. Arthur MacEwan, *Revolution and Economic Development* (New York: St. Martin's Press, 1981), p. 19.
34. O'Connor, p. 58.
35. Thomas, p. 1100.
36. MacGaffey, p. 45.
37. Dudley Seers, "The Economic and Social Background," in Dudley Seers, ed., *Cuba: The Economic and Social Revolution* (Chapel Hill: University of North Carolina Press, 1964), p. 18.
38. International Bank for Reconstruction and Development (herein referred to as 'World Bank'), *Report on Cuba* (Baltimore: Johns Hopkins Press, 1951), p. 408.
39. Ibid., p. 421.
40. Nelson P. Valdés, "The Radical Transformation of Cuban Education," in Rolando E. Bonachea and Nelson P. Valdés, eds., *Cuba in Revolution* (Garden City: Doubleday, 1972), p. 423.
41. Ricardo Leyva, "Health and Revolution in Cuba," in *Cuba in Revolution*, p. 474.
42. Leyva, p. 472 cites Robert Goldston, *The Cuban Revolution* (New York: Bobbs-Merrill, 1970), p. 58.
43. World Bank, p. 441.
44. Agrupación Católica Universitaria, p. 201.
45. World Bank, p. 87.
46. Personal interview with Miguel García, 11 October 1983.

47. Jan Knippers Black, et al., *Area Handbook for Cuba* (Washington, D.C.: American University, 1976), p. 18.
48. World Bank, p. 87; Census, 1946, pp. 71–72.
49. O'Connor, p. 72.
50. MacEwan, p. 17.
51. O'Connor, p. 65.
52. Andrés Bianchi, "Agriculture—The Pre-Revolutionary Background," Seers, p. 85 cites *Anuario Azucarero, 1959.*
53. Census, 1946, p. 150.
54. Bianchi in Seers, p. 82.
55. Census, 1946, pp. 143–44.
56. Edward Boorstein, *The Economic Transformation of Cuba* (New York: Modern Readers Paperbacks, 1968), p. 3; Seers, p. 19.
57. U.S. Department of Commerce, Bureau of Foreign Commerce, "Investment in Cuba," July, 1956.
58. Census, 1946, p. 291.
59. O'Connor, p. 59; Boorstein, p. 2.
60. Thomas, p. 1152.
61. The government based the quotas for the mills and growers on four factors: the sugar quotas assigned to Cuba, one by the U.S. Congress, the other by the International Sugar Agreement; the estimate of domestic demand; and amount for reserve stocks. O'Connor, p. 59.
62. Ibid., p. 64.
63. World Bank, p. 798.
64. Ibid., p. 200.
65. Nita R. Manitzas, "El Marco de la Revolución," David Barkin and Nita R. Manitzas, eds., *Cuba: Camino Abierto* (Mexico City: Siglo XXI editores sa, 1973), p. 19.
66. Boorstein, p. 12.
67. Thomas, p. 1172.
68. Eric N. Baklanoff, "Economic Development after World War II," Robert Freeman Smith, ed., *Background to Revolution* (Huntington: Robert E. Krieger Publishing Company, 1979), pp. 220–21.
69. Thomas, p. 1172.
70. Donald Villarejo, "American Investment in Cuba," *New University Thought*, 1 (1960):79–88.
71. Leo Huberman and Paul M. Sweezy, *Cuba: Anatomy of a Revolution* (New York: Monthly Review Press, 1960), p. 22 cites the U.S. Department of Commerce, 1956.
72. Thomas, p. 1163.
73. Ibid., p. 1167.
74. Villarejo, p. 84.
75. Seers, p. 15 cites Robert F. Smith, *The United States and Cuba: Business and Diplomacy, 1917–1960* (New York: Bookman Asc., 1960), p. 160.
76. World Bank, p. 739.
77. Boorstein, p. 4.
78. William A. Williams, *Cuba, Castro, and the U.S.* (New York: New Monthly Review Press, 1962), p. 15.
79. A maximum of only 22 percent of Cuba's sugar quota was allowed to enter the United States as refined sugar and even that was thanks to Washington lobbying by one of the island's few sugar refineries—which belonged to the Hershey Co.
80. MacGaffey, p. 79.

81. O'Connor, p. 25.
82. Eric R. Wolf and Edward C. Hansen, *The Human Condition in Latin America* (Oxford: Oxford University Press, 1972), p. 308.
83. World Bank, p. 442.
84. Ibid., pp. 443 and 449.

CHAPTER 2   How the Poor Got More

1. John Gerassi, ed., *Venceremos!: The Speeches and Writings of Che Guevara*, (New York: Simon and Schuster, 1968), p. 99.
2. Fidel Castro, *History Will Absolve Me* (Havana: Book Institute, 1967), p. 11.
3. Fidel Castro, 26 July 1970 speech.
4. *Obra Revolucionaria*, "Informe del primer ministro Fidel Castro sobre el abastecimiento y su regulación," 7 (Havana, 1962):17.
5. Arthur MacEwan, *Revolution and Economic Development* (New York: St. Martin's Press, 1981), pp. 53f.
6. Ibid., p. 84.
7. Gerassi, p. 99.
8. James O'Connor, *The Origins of Socialism in Cuba* (Ithaca: Cornell University Press, 1970), p. 246.
9. International Labour Organization, *The Landless Farmer in Latin America* (Geneva, 1957), pp. 66–67.
10. Brian H. Pollitt, "Agrarian Reform and the 'Agricultural Proletariat' in Cuba, 1958–66: Further Notes and Some Second Thoughts," Occasional Papers, No. 30 (Glasgow: Institute of Latin American Studies, University of Glasgow, 1980), p. 10.
11. Jorge Domínguez, *Cuba: Order and Revolution* (Cambridge: Harvard University Press, 1978), p. 182.
12. Claes Brundenius, *Economic Growth, Basic Needs and Income Distribution in Revolutionary Cuba* (Lund, Sweden: Research Policy Institute, University of Lund, 1981), p. 148.
13. Maurice Zeitlin, *Revolutionary Politics and the Cuban Working Class* (Princeton: Princeton University, 1967), p. 60.
14. Carmelo Mesa-Lago, *The Economy of Socialist Cuba: A Two-Decade Appraisal* (Albuquerque: University of New Mexico Press, 1981), p. 172.
15. Eric R. Wolf and Edward C. Hansen, *The Human Condition in Latin America* (Oxford: Oxford University Press, 1972), p. 337.
16. Edward Boorstein, *The Economic Transformation of Cuba* (New York: Modern Readers Paperbacks, 1968), p. 94.
17. Andrés Bianchi, "Agriculture: The Pre-Revolutionary Background," in Dudley Seers, ed., *Cuba: The Economic and Social Revolution* (Chapel Hill: University of North Carolina Press, 1964), p. 136.
18. Boorstein, p. 97.
19. *Obra Revolucionaria* "Primera reunión nacional de producción," 30 (Havana, August 1961), p. 9.
20. Dudley Seers, "The Economic and Social Background," in Seers, ed., p. 20.
21. Instituto Nacional de Reforma Económica, "Carta Pública Quincenal," carta no. 12 (February 15, 1956), p. 6.
22. Boorstein, p. 114.
23. Ibid., p. 70; Archibald Ritter, *The Economic Development of Revolutionary Cuba* (New York: Praeger Publishers, 1974), p. 96.
24. Edmundo Desnoes, *Inconsolable Memories* (New York: New American Library, 1967), p. 18.
25. *Obra Revolucionaria* 30, p. 9.

26. O'Connor, p. 269.
27. *Obra Revolucionaria* 30, p. 160.
28. Ritter, p. 83.
29. *Obra Revolucionaria* 30, p. 160.
30. Hugh Thomas, *Cuba: The Pursuit of Freedom* (New York: Harper and Row, 1971), p. 1333.
31. Boorstein, p. 46.
32. *Obra Revolucionaria* 30, p. 8.
33. In this book we are dealing only with the food ration book (*la libreta de comida*), which in addition to food contains detergent, soap, toilet paper, and cooking fuel. There is a separate ration card (*la libreta de ropa*) for nonfood items such as sheets, towels, shoes, toilet articles, and fabric, as well as ration coupons for gasoline. As with the food items, today many of these same goods are also available off the ration at higher prices (gasoline, for example, costs 1.03 pesos/gal. on the ration and 2.00 pesos/gal. off the ration).
34. Ibid., p. 235.
35. Ibid., p. 238.
36. Ibid., p. 247.
37. Lee Lockwood, *Castro's Cuba, Cuba's Fidel* (New York: Vintage Books, 1969), p. 350.
38. Leo Huberman and Paul M. Sweezy, *Cuba: Anatomy of a Revolution* (New York: Monthly Review Press, 1960), p. 196 cites *Memorandum sobre la planificación económica en Cuba* (Havana, 19 September 1960).

CHAPTER 3 Living on the Libreta

1. Adolfo Gilly, *Inside the Cuban Revolution* (New York: Monthly Review Press, 1964), p. 69.
2. Christopher Dickey, *Washington Post*, 31 August 1982.
3. U.S. Agency for International Development, "Consumer Food Subsidies, Study V" (Cambridge, Mass.: Oelgeschlager, Gunn and Hain, Inc., 1981), p. 24.
4 Martin Kenner and James Petras, eds., *Fidel Castro Speaks* (New York: Grove Press, Inc., 1969), p. 225.
5. Carmelo Mesa-Lago, *The Economy of Socialist Cuba: A Two-Decade Appraisal* (Albuquerque: University of New Mexico Press, 1981), p. 158.
6. Jorge Risquet, "Sobre problemas de fuerza de trabajo y productividad," *Granma*, 1 August 1970, p. 4.
7. Oscar Lewis, *Living the Revolution: Neighbors* (Urbana: University of Illinois, 1978), p. 564.

CHAPTER 4 Cuba à la Carte

1. Nelson P. Valdés, "Cuba: Social Rights and Basic Needs" (Washington, D.C.: n.p., 25 February 1983), p. 101 cites Miguel Dotres.
2. The Cuban Institute for Research on Internal Demand (ICIOIDI) reports that in 1970, 93 percent of basic food items were rationed and that by 1980, only 41 percent were rationed.
3. *Granma*, November 1983.
4. Interview with Ramón, a resident of Havana, 17 October 1980.
5. Information compiled in the mid-1970s.
6. The black market in clothes, especially U.S.-made jeans, and electrical goods, especially tape decks, is still going strong.
7. Interview with a vice minister at the Ministerio de Comercio Interior (MINCIN), 24 November 1983.

8. Interview with Carlos Rafael Rodríguez, January, 1982.
9. *Main Report to the Second Congress of the Communist Party of Cuba: Documents and Speeches* (Havana: Political Publishers, 1981), pp. 28–46.
10. Personal communication with Karen Wald, 13 January 1984, who cites the Ministry of Education's report to the National Assembly of People's Power, 1981.
11. Ibid.
12. Sydney Clark, *All the Best in Cuba* (New York: Dodd, Mead, and Co., 1956), p. 83.
13. *Main Report*, p. 275.
14. Fidel Castro, closing ANAP speech, 17 May 1982.
15. Interview with Lionel Martin, January 1982.

CHAPTER 5   The Farmers' Market: A Dash of Capitalism

1. Personal interview with Carlos Rafael Rodríguez, January 1982.
2. *Cuba Update*, June 1980 and September 1980. See especially the interview with Eugenio Balari, director of the Institute of Research on Consumer Demand.
3. *Granma*, 17 March 1982.
4. Personal interview with an ANAP official, January 1982.
5. *Granma*, 17 March 1982.
6. Fidel Castro speech to the ANAP Congress, May 1982.
7. Castro speech to the Congress of the Young Communist League (UJC), 4 April 1982.
8. After all, private farmers could not use the money for productive investments since agricultural machinery and even many simple implements and chemical inputs are sold only to state farms and producer cooperatives. As a result of policies we discuss in Chapter 13, individual farmers are allowed to purchase only old, prerevolution tractors and other farm machinery from other private farmers.
9. Castro speech to the UJC.
10. Castro speech to the ANAP Congress, May 1983.
11. Castro speech to the UJC.
12. *Granma*, 17 March 1982.
13. Castro speech to the UJC.
14. Ibid.
15. Personal interview with Rogelio Garayta, an ANAP official, 18 November 1983; Carlos Rafael Rodríguez, 22 November 1983.
16. Ibid.

CHAPTER 6   Is Rationing Socialist?

1. *Granma* 14 December 1981.
2. Claes Brundenius, *Economic Growth, Basic Needs and Income Distribution in Revolutionary Cuba* (Lund: Research Policy Institute, 1981), p. 158. While not specified, this figure presumably is not just the difference between production costs and retail prices, but also includes the cost of transportation, storage, administrative and other marketing costs.
3. *Granma*, 14 December 1981.
4. "Responde Humberto Pérez," *Bohemia*, 11 March 1983, p. 35.
5. See, for instance, José M. Norniella Rodríguez, "El Mercado Paralelo: Una Vía del Sistema de Dirección y Planificación de la Economía para Eliminar el Racionamiento," *Cuestiones de la Economía Planificada* III, p. 6ff.

6. For an in-depth discussion of economic policy changes in the 1970s see *The Cuban Economic Model, Latin American Perspectives* (Summer 1975).
7. *Bohemia*, p. 35.
8. Fidel Castro speech to the ANAP Congress, March 1983.
9. If the stumbling block for a Cuba without rationing is what would happen to low-income households, it's logical to ask, who are the poor in today's Cuba? An estimate of the number of low-income persons or households does not appear in the government's 600-page statistical yearbook. As we mentioned in the introduction, the Cuban government is not forthcoming with information on income distribution. Our own observations lead us to conclude that Cuba's poor households are mostly retired people living alone on fixed pensions (rare because most older people live with other family members); families with only one wage earner (making a low salary); and, in many cases, female-headed households. We met, for example, a woman with two children in a rural area outside Havana whose husband had abandoned her two years before to go to Florida. Her only source of income was to use sugar sent her by relatives in the eastern provinces (where the sugar ration is two pounds higher) to make candy to sell to neighbors (something technically illegal to do). Another family we met in Havana, a couple with three young children and only the husband working, was constantly short of money. A 1980 *Granma* article reported that seven hundred thousand persons were receiving social security benefits (which includes people receiving retirement and disability pensions, as well as funds for accidents, sickness, and maternity leave) or social assistance (equivalent of welfare).
10. This is calculated from Carlos Rafael Rodríguez's estimate of 25 pesos per person per month as cited in Brundenius, p. 158.

CHAPTER 7   Is There Hunger in Cuba?

1. "Castro's Sea of Troubles," *Newsweek*, 3 March 1980.
2. *Washington Report on the Hemisphere*, 25 January 1983.
3. Lawrence H. Theriot, *Cuba Faces the Economic Realities of the 80s*, East-West Trade Policy Staff Paper (U.S. Government Printing Office: March 1982), p. 5.
4. Antonio Gordon, "The Nutriture of Cubans: Historical Perspective and Nutritional Analysis," *Cuban Studies* 13 (no. 2, Summer 1983):25.
5. See Sergio Roca and Carmelo Mesa-Lago entries in Bibliography.
6. Claes Brundenius, *Economic Growth, Basic Needs and Income Distribution in Revolutionary Cuba* (Lund, Sweden: Research Policy Institute, 1967), p. 112.
7. Ibid., p. 28; Carmelo Mesa-Lago, "Availability and Reliability of Statistics in Socialist Cuba," *Latin American Research Review* 4 (1969):1:53–91; Nancy Forster, "Cuban Agricultural Productivity: A Comparison of State and Private Farm Sectors," *Cuban Studies* 11:2/12:1 (July 1981–January 1982).
8. Jacques Mayer May, *Ecology of Malnutrition in the Caribbean* (New York: Hafner Press, 1973), p. 6.
9. Frances Moore Lappé and Joseph Collins, *Food First: Beyond the Myth of Scarcity* (San Francisco: Institute for Food and Development Policy, 1982).
10. Nelson P. Valdés, "Cuba: Social Rights and Basic Needs," paper presented to the Inter-American Commission on Human Rights, Washington D.C., 25 February 1983, p. 22 cites Howard Handelman, "Cuban Food Policy and Popular Nutritional Levels," *Cuban Studies*, July 1981, p. 129.
11. *Cuba, Desarrollo económico y social durante el período 1958–1980* (Havana: Comité Estatal de Estadísticas), pp. 79 and 81; *Anuario Estadístico*

de Cuba 1982 (Havana: Comité Estatal de Estadísticas), p. 238.

12. Instituto Nacional de Reforma Económica, "Carta Pública Quincenal" carta no. 5 (30 October 1955). Their study places beef consumption at 47.8 pounds and Harry T. Oshima's 1953 estimate, in "A New Estimate of the National Income and Product of Cuba in 1953," *Food Research Institute Studies* (Stanford University) 2:3 (November 1961) is 66 pounds per year, although it is not clear whether he is including pork in this figure.

13. *Anuario*, 1982, p. 291.

14. INRE, carta no. 5.

15. In José Yglesias, *In the Fist of the Revolution: Life in a Cuban Country Town* (New York: Vintage Books, 1968), p. 142, journalist Yglesias, describing life in a small Cuban town during the 1960s, spoke to a 56-year-old mother who worked in a sugar mill from seven at night until three in the morning. Asked about the food situation since the revolution, she couldn't say it was any worse, because for her it had always been bad. "How can I tell you I do not have ham when I never had ham? You know, sir, when I had ham? One of my sons used to work for the Americans in their garden and when they had ham and had sliced all the meat from the bone, they would wrap up the bone and give it to him and say, 'Here, give it to your mother'. I would throw it in a pot with water and vegetables—and beans if there were any—and hope it would fill my children's stomachs."

16. *The State of Food and Agriculture* (Rome: Food and Agriculture Organization, 1981), p. 172.

17. One aspect of distribution which the government has little control over is distribution *within* the family. Poor distribution in the home could mean that while the family as a whole eats well, some members are not receiving their share. From our observations, food is fairly well distributed and, if anything, the most vulnerable groups—pregnant women and children—get more than their share. We did find, however, that women with young children tend to divide the family's meat ration between the husband and children, taking little or nothing for themselves. And the special rations, such as those for pregnant women or people with ulcers, usually just mean a little extra food for the whole family. (Few Cuban women, pregnant or not, could sit down to a meal of chicken while the rest of the family was eating eggs.)

18. Ricardo Leyva, "Health and Revolution in Cuba" in Rolando E. Bonachea and Nelson P. Valdés, eds., *Cuba in Revolution* (Garden City: Doubleday, 1972), p. 488.

19. Personal interview with Arnaldo Tejeiro, head of statistics, MINSAP, 25 November 1983.

20. Barnett and MacGaffey, *Twentieth Century Cuba* p. 198 cites the higher figure, WHO statistics, the lower one, and the Cubans themselves, in *Salud para todos*, p. 23 say 70.

21. Comité Estatal de Estadísticas, *Cuba en Cifra*, 1982, p. 28.

22. *Prensa Latina*, 4 March 1984.

23. *UN Demographic Yearbook*, June 1983.

24. U.S. Department of Health, "Monthly Vital Statistics Report" 31:13 (5 October 1983).

25. Ministerio de Salud Pública, "Mortalid infantil según provincia," *Informe Anual 1982*, p. 24.

26. José R. Jordán, *Desarrollo humano en Cuba* (Havana: Editorial Científico-Técnica, 1979).

27. Personal interview with José R. Jordán, Instituto de Desarrollo Humano, 24 November 1983.

28. A 1981 study of black Cuban males confirmed that the black population was also taller since the revolution. See Manuel Rivero de la Calle, "La Población Negra Masculina de Cuba: Algunas Características Antropológicas," *Anales del Caribe* vol. 1 (Havana:1981), pp. 39–98.
29. Ministerio de Salud Pública, *Salud para todos* (Havana, 9 July 1983), p. 23.
30. S. Conover, et al., "Reflections on Health Care in Cuba" *Lancet* 2 (1 November 1980), pp. 958–60.
31. A. Theriot, p. 5.
32. R. R. Puffer and C. V. Serrano, "Características de la mortalidad en la niñez." Publicación Científica 262 (Organización Panamericana de la Salud, 1973).
32. Norman Jolliffe, et al., "Nutritional Survey of the Sixth Grade School Population of Cuba," *The Journal of Nutrition* 64 (1958): 394.
33. Ministerio de Educación en Cuba, "Matrícula del Curso, 1956–57."
34. See note in Chapter 2 on this survey.
35. World Bank, *Report on Cuba* (Baltimore: Johns Hopkins University, 1951), p. 442.
36. Antonio Gordon, "Nutritional Status of Cuban Refugees: A Field Study on the Health and Nutriture of Refugees Processed at Opa Locka, Florida," *The American Journal of Clinical Nutrition* 35 (March 1982):582–90.
37. Interview with Jordán.
38. Interview with Tejeiro; *Anuario* 1980.
39. C. Santos Hernández and E. Gómez Cabale, "Encuesta de egresados de hogares de recuperación nutricional," *Revista Cubana de Pediatría* 49 (July 1977):391–410.
40. Interview with Tejeiro.

CHAPTER 8   Split Peas Again?

1. See Instituto Nacional de Reforma Económica, *Carta Pública Quincenal* carta no. 27 (30 September 1956), for a discussion of the history of wheat consumption and cultivation in Cuba.
2. Juan Aguilar Derpich, "The Island that Discovered the Sea," *Ceres* (July/August 1979), p. 36.
3. Ibid.
4. Personal interview with Nitza Villapoll, November 1983.
5. Juice and fruit are primarily distributed through schools and to infants and old people. The government would like to use export rejects to make juice for the local market, but has only one small processing plant. Problems in securing the right technology are said to have delayed the construction of two additional plants. By the early 1980s, the better Havana restaurants were offering orange or grapefruit juice, something unseen even in the best restaurants in the early 1970s. Since the resort hotels specializing in tourist groups from Canada and Europe offer buffet-style trays of citrus fruit and juices, we can only wonder how much of domestic consumption goes to foreigners.
6. Lowry Nelson, *Rural Cuba* (Minneapolis: University of Minnesota Press, 1950), p. 209.
7. *Main Report to the Second Congress of the Communist Party of Cuba: Documents and Speeches (Havana: Political Publishers, 1981)*, p. 46.
8. Personal correspondence with Eugenio Balari, Instituto de la Demanda Interna, 11 July 1983.
9. The U.S. National Academy of Science recommends 56 grams of protein for the "reference man." Protein requirements for different nations must be adjusted according to the quality of the protein in the diet. Animal proteins are

usually more useable than vegetable proteins, so that for a nation like Cuba, where a large portion of the protein is vegetable protein (two-thirds as compared with one-third in the United States), the protein requirement would theoretically be higher. But the quality of Cuban vegetable protein is very good, since it is usually eaten in some type of complementary combination such as beans and rice. Furthermore, the animal sources of protein in the Cuban diet come largely from dairy products, which are of even higher quality than meat. On balance, we think that the protein requirements for Cuba are comparable to those of the United States. (For a discussion of protein quality, see *Diet for a Small Planet*.)

10. Second Congress, p. 46.
11. MINSAP, Cuba: *La salud en la revolución* (Havana, 1975), p. 142.
12. Edmundo Desnoes, *Inconsolable Memories* (New York: New American Library, 1967), p. 39.
13. Ada Dritsas Roca, "Living with the Libreta," *Cuba Review 6* (no. 2, December 1976):12.
14. Adolfo Gilly, *Inside the Cuban Revolution* (New York: Monthly Review Press, 1964), p. 69.
15. "A Cuba, A Cuba, A Cuba Iré," a song which Carlos Puebla made famous internationally and became a symbol of Cuban national pride.
16. Antonio Núñez Jiménez, *En marcha con Fidel* (Havana: Editorial Letras, 1982), p. 243.
17. Fidel Castro's March 1968 speech, in Martin Kenner and James Petras, eds., *Fidel Castro Speaks* (New York: Grove Press, 1969), pp. 266–67.
18. Fredelle Maynard, "Cuba: The Revolutionary Life," *The Atlantic* (October 1979).
19. Fidel Castro speech, "Rally in Havana," 13 December 1972.
20. Kenner and Petras, p. 243.
21. Personal interview with Anita Suárez, November 1983.
22. MINSAP, *Para tu salad, corre o camina, Educación para la salud* (Havana: Editorial Científico-Técnica, 1983), p. 14.
23. Personal interview with Carlos Rafael Rodríguez, November 1980.
24. Ibid.

CHAPTER 9   Sugar vs. *Viandas*

1. A. Antonio Núñez Jiménez, *En marcha con Fidel* (Havana: Editorial Letras, 1982), p. 125.
2. Food and Agriculture Organization (FAO), *Food Balance Sheets 1979–81*; Comité Estatal de Estadísticas (CEE), *Anuario Estadístico de Cuba 1982*.
3. FAO, *Production Yearbook 1958*; CEE, *Anuario Estadístico de Cuba 1958*.
4. *Anuario*, 1982.
5. Cited in Archibald R.M. Ritter, *The Economic Development of Revolutionary Cuba* (New York: Praeger Publishers, 1974), p. 134.
6. Ibid., Note 10, p. 160.
7. John Gerassi, ed., *Venceremos!: The Speeches and Writings of Che Guevara* (New York: Simon and Schuster, 1968), p. 353.
8. Edward Boorstein, *The Economic Transformation of Cuba* (New York: Monthly Review Press, 1968), p.182.
9. World Bank, *Report on Cuba* (Baltimore: Johns Hopkins University, 1951), pp. 3–13.
10. Andrés Bianchi, "Agriculture—Post-Revolutionary Development," in Dudley Seers, ed., *Cuba: The Economic and Social Revolution* (Chapel Hill, N.C.: University of North Carolina Press, 1964), p. 130.
11. Gerassi, p. 173

12. O'Connor, p. 216.
13. Ibid.
14. 1961 Conferencia Nacional de Producción printed in *Obra Revolucionaria* (Havana).
15. O'Connor, p. 105.
16. O'Connor, p. 223; Hugh Thomas, *Cuba: The Pursuit of Freedom* (New York: Harper and Row, 1971), p. 1324.
17. Ritter, p. 109.
18. Claes Brundenius, *Economic Growth, Basic Needs and Income Distribution in Revolutionary Cuba* (Lund, Sweden: Research Policy Institute, 1981), pp. 65–66.
19. Ritter, p. 137 cites J. Noyola, "La Revolución Cubana y Sus Efectos en el Desarrollo Económico," *El Trimestre Económico* 28 (no. 3, July–September 1961):418.
20. *Obra Revolucionaria*
21. Jacques Chonchol, "El primer bienio de reforma agraria (1959–1961)," in *Reformas agrarias en América Latina* (Mexico City: Fondo de Cultura Económico, 1965), p. 512.; Ritter, p. 112.
22. Gerassi, p. 173.
23. Ritter, pp. 109–13.
24. Bianchi, p. 144 cites Santos Ríos, "Informe," *Obra Revolucionaria* 30, p. 32.
25. Below the historical average by 28 percent. Arthur MacEwan, *Revolution and Economic Development in Cuba* (New York: St. Martin's Press, 1981), p. 35.
26. Fidel Castro speech to ANAP Congress in *Speeches at Three Congresses* (Havana: Editora Política, 1982), p. 150.
27. Personal interview with Carlos Rafael Rodríguez, November 1980.
28. O'Connor, p. 226.
29. Ritter, p. 148 cites O. Duyos, "Los Problemas Actuales del Acopio y Los Precios de Compra de los Productos Agrícolas," *Cuba Socialista* (no. 33 May 1964):76.
30. Chonchol, p. 121.
31. MacEwan, p. 64.
32. Bianchi, p. 137.
33. Ibid., p. 138, note 125 cites Carlos Rafael Rodríguez, "Entrevista," in *F. Castro, O. Dorticós, Guevara, Rodríguez Hablan*, p. 15.
34. See, for instance, Bianchi, p. 138.
35. Ibid., p. 139; Ritter, p. 104.
36. O'Connor, p. 224.
37. Thomas, p. 1324.
38. Brian H. Pollitt, "Agrarian Reform and the 'Agricultural Proletariat' in Cuba, 1958–66: Some Notes," Occasional Paper No. 27 (Glasgow: Institute of Latin American Studies, 1979).
39. Sergio Aranda, *La revolución agraria en Cuba* (Mexico City: Siglo XXI, 1968), p. 22.
40. O'Connor, p. 220 cites "El partido y la tercera zafra del pueblo en Camaguey," *Cuba Socialista* 3 (no. 27, January 1963):131.
41. Bianchi, p. 147.
42. Gerassi, pp. 353–54
43. Boorstein, pp. 201–2
44. *Granma* (English Edition) 3 January 1966. Note that Castro is using a price for sugar of about five cents a pound. In 1965 China and the Soviet Union were reportedly paying the equivalent of 6.11 cents a pound.
45. Boorstein, p. 200.

46. Ritter, p. 166.
47. Ibid. Ironically, Cuba's abysmally low sugar output in 1963 was a principal reason for the spectacular price rise. One can't help but wonder if anyone in Cuba realized that if Cuba recovered its previous production levels the world price would be likely to plummet.
48. It is difficult to calculate the real value of prices paid by the socialist countries since they are generally tied to the import of goods from these countries. For a discussion of Cuba-Soviet trade relations, see Susan Eckstein, "Capitalist Constraints on Cuban Socialist Developments," *Comparative Politics*, April 1980; and Carmelo Mesa-Lago, *The Economy of Socialist Cuba: A Two-Decade Appraisal* (Albuquerque: University of New Mexico Press, 1981), pp. 87–92.
49. Boorstein, pp. 203–04.
50. Bianchi, p. 147 cites Carlos Rafael Rodríguez' speech to the Congress in *Hoy* 18 August 1962.
51. Ritter, p. 187 cites Castro speech of 4 November 1969.
52. Ibid., p. 181.
53. Ibid., pp. 188–189.
54. Ibid.
55. MacEwan, p. 118.
56. Ibid.; Ritter, pp. 188–89.
57. Castro speech of 26 July 1970.
58. Castro speech at the First Party Congress, December 1975.

CHAPTER 10 A Shaky Balance

1. Address in Peoria, Ill., 25 September 1956.
2. Personal interview with Gálvez Taupier, vice minister of sugar, November 1983.
3. Archibald R.M. Ritter, *The Economic Development of Revolutionary Cuba* (New York: Praeger Publishers, 1974), p. 174.
4. Personal interview with Rafael Garcell, official with Ministry of Agriculture, November 1983.
5. Instituto Nacional de Reforma Económica (INRE), *Carta Pública Quincenal* carta no. 14, 15 March 1956.
6. Comité Estatal de Estadísticas, *Anuario Estadístico de Cuba 1982*, p. 333; personal interview with Manuel Anderez Velázquez, vice president of Cuba's Academy of Science, 18 November 1983. Anderez Velazquéz says 5 percent.
7. *Anuario*, p. 333.
8. Ibid., p. 369.
9. United States Department of Agriculture, *Foreign Agriculture Circular: Fresh and Processed Fruits*, January 1982.
10. *Census of Cuba*, 1946; *Anuario*, 1980.
11. Jacques Chonchol, "El primer bienio de reforma agraria (1959–1961)," in *Reformas agrarias en América Latina* (Mexico City: Fondo de Cultura Económico, 1965), p. 47; INRE, no. 14, 15 March 1956. The INRE document gives a complete history of U.S.-Cuba "rice relations," and quotes Congressman T.H. Thompson of Louisiana in 1956 as threatening to cut Cuba's sugar quota if it refuses to increase rice imports from the United States.
12. FAO, *Production Yearbook 1982*. The expansion of rice cultivation to the current 372,229 acres represents a reversal of the policies of the mid-1960s when rice production plummeted and imports rose dramatically on the theory that Cuba could buy rice more cheaply, especially from the Chinese, than it could produce it. This comparative advantage rationale seemed fine

until promised deliveries of Chinese rice went undelivered in 1966, in an apparent attempt to pressure Cuba to break with the Soviet Union.

13. Personal interview with Carlos Rafael Rodríguez, November 1983.
14. Personal interview with official from JUCEPLAN (Junta Central de Planificación), 1982.
15. Ibid.
16. Anderez Velázquez interview.
17. FAO, *Production Yearbook*, 1958 and 1982.
18. Whereas Cuba's corn yields stood at a moderate 1234 kilograms per hectare in 1980, the Dominican Republic yields reached 2042, El Salvador maintained a yield of 1953, Trinidad 4167, and St. Vincent 3125. However Puerto Rico hovered around an abysmal production yield of 920 kilograms per hectares, far below the Caribbean average.
19. *Anuario*, 1980; Rodríguez interview, 1983; Anderez Velázquez interview, 1983.
20. INRE, no. 30, p. 2 cites CEPAL, 1953.
21. Personal interview with FAO official, November 1983.
22. Census, 1946; *Anuario*, 1982: 412,000 compared with 212,000 acres.
23. Comité Estatal de Estadísticas (CEE), *Cuba: Desarrollo económico y social durante el período 1958–1980*, p. 62.
24. Ritter, p. 188ff.
25. FAO, *Production Yearbook*, 1958 and 1980.
26. Anuario, 1982 gives production figures for the state sector only.
27. FAO, *Food Balance Sheet*, 1979–81.
28. *Reuters*, 17 January 1982.
29. Foreign dairy experts doubt the validity of these figures, saying that it is biologically impossible. Top North American Holstein record holders produce 150 to 160 pounds a day during their peak lactation. Correspondence with Dr. Eugene Donefer, Department of Animal Science, Macdonald College, Canada.
30. CEE, p. 62.
31. Cuba has been buffered from the full foreign exchange costs of such large imports by the U.N. World Food Program which supplied food aid until 1982, when behind-the-scenes pressures from the Reagan Administration halted the donations. Ironically, the Reagan Administration argued that the aid should be halted because there are no needy people in Cuba.
32. Personal interview with Gálvez Taupier, vice minister of sugar, 23 November 1983.
33. *International Sugar Journal* 84 (1982):255.
34. Ibid.
35. Charles Burck, "Tempest in the Sugar Pot," *Fortune* (February 1977), p.109.
36. Latin American Commodities Report (LACR), 4 June 1982.
37. Ibid.
38. *Verde Olivo*, 1983: 53–81.
39. LACR, 4 June 1982.
40. Personal interview with Rafael Garcell, official with Ministry of Agriculture, November 1983.
41. Rodríguez interview, November 1983.

CHAPTER 11 The Agrarian Revolution

1. Laurette Sejourne, *La Mujer Cubana*, (Mexico City: Siglo XXI, 1980), p. 99.
2. Leo Huberman and Paul Sweezy, *Cuba: Anatomy of a Revolution* (New York: Monthly Review Press, 1960), p. 78.

3. David Barkin, "La redistribución del consumo," in David Barkin and Nita R. Manitzas, eds., *Cuba: Camino abierto* (Mexico City: Siglo XXI, 1973), p. 193.
4. Fidel Castro speech in Santa Clara, 26 July 1959, as cited in Antonio Nuñez Jimenez, *En marcha con Fidel* (Havana: Editorial Letras, 1982), p. 201.
5. Personal communication, Solon Barraclough, March 3, 1984.
6. Jacques Chonchol, "El primer bienio de reforma agraria (1959–1961), in *Reformas agrarias en America Latina* (Mexico City: Fondo de Cultura Economica, 1965), pp. 483 and 509. Chonchol cites the legal department of INRA. We advisedly use the word *control* since the government turned over part (the estimates range as high as 60 percent) of the expropriated land to land-poor peasants.
7. Michel Gutelman, "The Socialization of the Means of Production in Cuba," in Rolando E. Bonachea and Nelson P. Valdés, eds., *Cuba in Revolution* (New York: Doubleday, 1972), p. 255.
8. Carlos Rafael Rodríguez, *Cuba en el tránsito al socialismo: 1959–1963* (Mexico City: Siglo XXI, 1978), p. 143.
9. Lee Lockwood, *Castro's Cuba, Cuba's Fidel* (New York: Vintage Books, 1969), p. 96.
10. Ibid., p. 97.
11. Arthur MacEwan, *Revolution and Economic Development in Cuba* (New York: St. Martin's Press, 1981), pp. 50 f.
12. Gutelman, p. 242.
13. James O'Connor, *The Origins of Socialism in Cuba* (Ithaca: Cornell University, 1970), p. 99.
14. Lockwood, p. 97.
15. See, for example, Fidel's speech of 17 May 1974, marking the fifteenth anniversary of the reform.
16. For a comprehensive breakdown, see Gutelman in *Cuba in Revolution*.
17. Jacques Chonchol, "El primer bienio de reforma agraria (1959–1961)," in Oscar Delgado, ed., *Reformas agrarias en América Latina* (Mexico City: Fondo de Cultura Económico, 1965), p. 483.
18. Gutelman, p. 247.
19. O'Connor, p.109.
20. "Conversión de las cooperativas en granjas del pueblo cañeras," *Trimestre* (April–June 1962), p. 111, cited in O'Connor, p.110.
21. Andrew Pearse, *The Latin American Peasant* (London: Frank Cass, 1975), pp. 249–50.
22. Lockwood, p. 98.
23. Sergio Aranda, *La revolución agraria en Cuba* (Mexico City: Siglo XXI, 1968), p. 184.
24. MacEwan, p. 56.
25. Figures calculated from table on p.137 of Carlos Rafael Rodríguez, *Cuba en el tránsito al socialismo (1959–1963)*.
26. Aranda, p. 32.
27. Pearse, p. 245.
28. Aranda, p. 144.
29. Andrés Bianchi, "Agriculture—The Post-Revolutionary Development," in Dudley Seers, ed., *Cuba: The Economic and Social Revolution* (Chapel Hill: University of North Carolina Press, 1964), p. 140.
30. Archibald R.M. Ritter, *The Economic Development of Revolutionary Cuba* (New York: Praeger Publishers, 1974), pp. 102–3.
31. Fidel's speech, 10 April 1962.
32. O'Connor, p. 130.

33. MacEwan, p. 73.
34. Fidel's closing speech at the Fifth ANAP Congress, 1971.
35. Fidel Castro, *Speeches at Three Congresses* (Havana: Editora Politica, 1982).
36. Personal interview with Rogelio Garayta, an official at ANAP, 22 January 1982.
37. Ibid.
38. The decline in the private sector is largely due to the retirement or death of small farmer-owners without heirs willing to farm and from the sales of farmland to the government. The reduced percentage of land in private hands may also reflect an increase in the total amount of land under cultivation. In 1983 an ANAP official told us that the farmers' market experience led them to believe that official figures underestimate the amount of private farm land. A new survey is now being undertaken to ensure that all land is accounted for. Personal interview with Rogelio Garayta, November, 1983.
39. Castro, p. 187.
40. Ibid., p. 34.
41. Garayta interview, November 1983.

CHAPTER 12   A Superior Form of Production?

1. Personal interview with Rogelio Garayta, chief legal counsel of ANAP, October 1980.
2. Credit and service cooperatives are considered the first step in cooperative farming. CCS members do not work the land together, but pool from 2 to 4 percent of their sales into a general fund used to buy equipment and build storage facilities, irrigation systems, and the like. In 1983, there were 2,034 such cooperatives, with over 100,000 members (farmers and their families). "Estructura orgánica de ANAP," n.p., 1983.
3. Fidel Castro's speech to the ANAP Congress, 1982; Comite Estatal de Estadisticas, *Anuario Estadístico de Cuba, 1982*, p. 210.
4. "Análisis del movimiento cooperativo hasta el 31 de agosto de 1983," ANAP, n.d.
5. Personal interview with Guy Chapond, head of the FAO Mission, 23 October 1980.
6. ANAP, Análisis.
7. Ibid. An average of 43 percent of their land is devoted to the principal crop, the rest used mainly for mixed food crops and livestock. By comparison, state farms are highly specialized, concentrating on a single crop to a much greater extent.
8. This change in policy has led to striking differences in the quality of housing and other amenities since the government decided to no longer foot the bill. Not only are newer houses simpler, but in some cooperatives many of the members still live in the traditional thatched-roof shacks. In contrast, take the case of "República de Chile," an older tobacco cooperative in the Pinar del Rio province. A 1982 visit to this idyllic cooperative, nestled in one of the most breathtaking valleys, gives a bird's-eye view of the Cuban leadership's vision of what rural Cuba should look like. The cooperative has a beautiful road leading up to it, schools and a health center nearby, lots of new trucks and tractors, and a small village for the co-op members complete with stores, ice cream parlor (Coppelita), and, believe it or not, a beauty parlor for the women. The houses are lovely duplex apartments that would make any city dweller envious. And to top it off, each apartment came equipped with furniture, refrigerator (previously an unknown luxury for peasants), stove, television, and even a brand new Soviet-made radio! The

rent for each apartment was a mere 6 percent of members' income and they were supposed to be charged another 4 percent for the furnishings. But one farmer who had been living in an apartment for two years told us that as yet, nobody had asked him to start paying for them.

9. ANAP, Análisis.

10. Ibid.

11. Orlando Gómez, "Garantiza el estado socialista seguridad para los cooperativistas en su vejez, invalidez, maternidad y fallecimiento," *Granma*, 5 April 1983.

12. Orlando Gómez, "Contribuirán los campesinos a los gastos del pais para su desarrollo económico, social y la defensa de la Patria," *Granma*, 6 July 1983.13. *Anuario*, 1982, p. 208, Table VIII.4.

13. Ibid., p. 210.

14. Ibid.

15. *Granma*, 17 May 1979, interview with José Ramírez Cruz.

16. Personal interview with Carlos Rafael Rodríguez, November 1983.

17. Personal interview with Manuel Anderez Velázquez, vice president of the Cuban Academy of Science, 18 November 1983.

18. James O'Connor, *The Origins of Socialism in Cuba* (Ithaca: Cornell University, 1970), p. 113.

19. See James Wessel, *Trading the Future* (San Francisco: Institute for Food and Development Policy, 1983), especially chapter three.

20. *Anuario*, 1982, p. 213, Table VIII.12.

21. In the case of food crops, one study of Cuba's agricultural productivity in the 1970s divided production by land cultivated and found private sector yields for food crops to be consistently higher than those of state farms—on the order of 50 to 100 percent and in some cases as much as 600 percent higher. Nancy Forster, "Cuban Agricultural Productivity: A Comparison of State and Private Farm Sectors," *Cuban Studies* 11/12 (no. 2, July 1981–January 1982, no. 1):116.

22. Personal interview with Rafael Pozo, administrator of state farm Miguel Soneira Rios (35 miles southeast of Havana) November 1983.

23. Rodríguez interview, November 1983.

24. The controversy of material vs. moral incentives has been thoroughly discussed in much of the literature on Cuba. See, for example, Bertram Silverman, *Man and Socialism in Cuba: The Great Debate* (New York: Atheneum, 1971); Robert M. Bernard, *The Theory of Moral Incentives in Cuba* (University, Alabama: The University of Alabama Press, 1971); Carmelo Mesa-Lago, "Ideological, Political and Economic Factors in the Cuban Controversy on Material Versus Moral Incentives," *Journal of Interamerican Studies and World Affairs* 14 (February 1972):49–111, and "Revolutionary Morality?," *Society* 9 (July–August 1972):70–76; Arthur MacEwan, *Revolution and Economic Development in Cuba* (New York: St. Martin's Press, 1981), especially, pp. 132–38; PCC, *Main Report to the First Congress of the Communist Party of Cuba* (Moscow: Progress Publishers, 1976); *Granma Weekly Review*, 25 November 1973; López Coll and Amando Santiago, "Notas sobre el proceso de planificación en Cuba," *Economía y Desarrollo* no. 29 (May–June 1975).

25. Archibald R.M. Ritter, *The Economic Development of Revolutionary Cuba* (New York: Praeger Publishers, 1974), p. 181 cites Delagación de Cuba a la XI Conferencia Regional de la FAO, Venezuela, October 1970, "Dos Años de Desarrollo Agropecuario Cubano, 1968–1970," *Economía y Desarrollo*, no. 4 (October–December 1970), p. 35; See, also, Partido Comunista de Cuba, *Main Report to First Party Congress* (Moscow; Progress Publishers,

1976) pp. 125–28 for a frank discussion of the mistakes during this period.

26. Rodríguez interview, November 1983.

27. Visit to the state farm Miguel Soneira Rios, 19 January 1982.

28. *Anuario*, 1982, p. 210, Table VIII.7.

29. Personal interview with Luis O. Gálvez Taupier, vice minister of sugar, 21 January 1982.

30. Personal interview with Rogelio Garayta, ANAP official, November 1983.

31. Miguel Soneira Rios state farm visit, 19 January 1982.

32. Pozo interview, January 1982.

33. Carmelo Mesa-Lago, *Cuba in the 1970s: Pragmatism and Institutionalization* (Albuquerque: University of New Mexico Press, 1974), p. 90.

34. Personal interview with Rafael Garcell, Ministry of Agriculture official, November 1983.

CHAPTER 13   Our Menu in Havana

1. Overseas Development Council, *U.S. Foreign Policy and the Third World* (Washington, D.C., 1983). The Physical Quality of Life Index (PQLI) compares the countries of the world on the basis of infant mortality, life expectancy at age one, and literacy. At 94 on a scale of 1 to 100, Cuba is only 2 points behind the United States and 5 points ahead of Costa Rica. Neighboring Haiti's rating is a shocking 41. Such international comparisons, however, are not without intrinsic flaws, and their findings are not as valid as the preciseness of the statistics would suggest. On this point, see Donald McGranahan, *International Comparability of Statistics on Income Distribution*, and *Methodological Problems in Selection and Analysis of Socioeconomic Development Indicators*, both from the United Nations Research Institute for Social Development, Geneva, 1979.

2. Lawrence H. Theriot, *Cuba Faces the Economic Realities of the 1980s*, an East-West Trade Policy Staff Paper, U.S. Government Printing Office, March 1982, p. 5.

3. Ibid., p. 6.

4. While there is much speculation about the size of Soviet subsidy to the Cubans a recent study claims that it is surely far less than the $3 billion figure cited in congressional and CIA documents. See Andrew Zimbalist, "Soviet Aid, U.S. Blockade, and the Cuban Economy," in Andrew Zimbalist and Howard Sherman, *Comparative Economic Systems: A Political Economic Approach*, Academic Press, forthcoming 1986.

5. Nicolas Guillén, *Man-making Words*, translated by Robert Márquez and David McMurray, (Amherst: University of Massachusetts Press, 1972), p. 21.

6. Howard Bray, "The New Wave of Puerto Rican Immigrants," *New York Times Magazine*, 3 July 1983.

7. Che Guevara in an interview with Laura Berggvist in *Look*, 8 November 1960.

8. For thorough documentation, see Warren Hinckle and Willam Turner, *The Fish is Red: The Story of the Secret War Against Castro* (New York: Harper and Row, 1981).

9. See Joel Charney, *Obstacles of Recovery in Vietnam and Kampuchea: U.S. Embargo of Humanitarian Aid* (Boston: Oxfam America, forthcoming 1984).

10. Carla Anne Robbins, *The Cuban Threat* (New York: McGraw-Hill, 1983), p. xii.

11. "U.S. Blockade: A Documentary History," Center for Cuban Studies, December 1979 cites the January 1975 interview in *Oui* magazine.

12. Ibid., p. 67.

GLOSSARY

***Asociación Nacional de Agricultores Pequeños*/ANAP** *(National Association of Small Farmers)* Organization of about two hundred thousand private farmers (including members of production cooperatives) or about 90 percent of all private farmers. Founded in 1961.

bodega Store where rationed goods are sold; nonrationed items also available.

carnicería Butcher shop.

comedor obrero Workers' cafeteria where subsidized meals are offered to employees.

***Comité de Defensa de la Revolución*/CDR** *(Committee for the Defense of the Revolution)* Neighborhood committees originally established to guard against sabotage; now they organize crime watch patrols, collect recyclables, vaccinate children, organize community cleanups, etc. The overwhelming majority of Cubans over 14 are members.

congrí Name for the traditional Cuban dish of rice mixed with black beans. Also known as *moros y cristianos* (Moors and Christians).

***Cooperativa de Crédito y Servicio*/CCS** *(Credit and Service Cooperative)* Loose association of private farmers who seek credit as a group and share heavy equipment, but do work the land collectively. Officially considered the first step in the formation of production cooperatives. In 1980 there were 2,180 CCSs.

***Cooperativa de Producción Agropecuaria*/CPA** *(Agricultural Production Cooperative)* Organization of private farmers who pool their resources, work collectively, and divide the profits among themselves. Since the 1975 Communist Party decision to foster cooperatives, they have rapidly grown in number—reaching 1,480 in 1983.

dieta *(diet)* Extra ration provided for those with special health needs.

empresa estatal State-owned and operated enterprise em-

220

ploying salaried workers. In the countryside used interchangably with *granja estatal* to refer to a state farm.

feria del agro State-operated produce market for nonrationed goods.

Federación de Mujeres Cubanas/FMC *(Federation of Cuban Women)* Organization created in 1960 to increase the participation of women in the revolution. In 1980, 80 percent of Cuban women belonged to the Federation.

Instituto Nacional de Reforma Agraria/INRA *(National Institute of Agrarian Reform)* Institute created in 1959 to carry out the revolution's agrarian policies and supervise production on state enterprises. In 1961 it merged with the Ministry of Agriculture.

Junta Central de Planificación/JUCEPLAN Central Planning Board.

lechería Store where dairy products are sold.

libreta Ration book.

malanga *(taro)* An edible starchy root that is used in Cuba as a basic food, especially for weaning children.

mercados libres campesinos *(farmers' free markets)* Instituted in 1980 to allow farmers to sell their produce directly to consumers.

merienda Morning or afternoon snack usually consisting of something sweet.

OFICODA State agency in charge of distributing ration books.

Partido Comunista de Cuba/PCC *(Cuban Communist Party)* Formed in 1965, it is Cuba's sole party. It is not a mass organization; in 1980 it had about four hundred and thirty-four thousand members (less than 5 percent of the Cuban population).

Poder Popular *(People's Power)* Created in the mid-1970s, it is Cuba's elected government apparatus, having largely administrative duties. Functions at municipal, provincial, and national levels.

puesto Vegetable stand for rationed goods; nonrationed goods also available.

Venta Libre por la libre/*(free sale)* Goods sold on a non-rationed basis.

viandas (no English equivalent) A general term referring to any sort of tuber, such as taro, cassava, and yucca, as well as plantains. Traditionally a popular mainstay of the Cuban diet, supplies have diminished since the early 1960s.

zafra The annual sugar cane harvest occurring between late December and early May.

BIBLIOGRAPHY

Agrupación Católica Universitaria. *Por qué Reforma Agraria?*. N.p., mimeo, 1956–57.

Albert, Michael and Hahnel, Robin. *Socialism Today and Tomorrow*. Boston: South End Press, 1981.

ANAP. "Resúmen de tres congresos: selección de fragmentos de los discursos del Comandante F. Castro en los congresos de la ANAP." N.d.

————. "V Congreso Campesino." 5 May 1977.

Aranda, Sergio. *La revolución agraria en Cuba*. Mexico City: Siglo XXI, 1968.

Aykroyd, W.R. *The Story of Sugar*. Chicago: Quadrangle Books, 1967.

Banco Nacional de Cuba. *Economic Report*. Havana, August 1982.

Barkin, David and Manitzas, Nita R., eds. *Cuba: Camino Abierto*. Mexico City: Siglo XXI, 1973.

Bergmann, Theodor. *Farm Policies in Socialist Countries*. Lexington, Mass.: Lexington Books, 1975.

Black, Jan Knippers. *Area Handbook for Cuba*. Washington, D.C.: American University, 1976.

Blackburn, Robin. "Prologue to the Cuban Revolution." *New Left Review*, October 1963.

Blasier, Cole and Mesa-Lago, Carmelo, eds. *Cuba in the World*. Pittsburgh: University of Pittsburgh Press, 1979.

Bonachea, Rolando E. and Valdés, Nelson P. *Cuba in Revolution*. Garden City: Anchor Books, 1972.

Boorstein, Edward. *The Economic Transformation of Cuba*. New York: Monthly Review Press, 1968.

Brundenius, Claes. *Economic Growth, Basic Needs and Income Distribution in Revolutionary Cuba*. Lund, Sweden: University of Lund, Research Policy Institute, 1981.

————. "Measuring Income Distribution in Pre- and Post-Revolutionary Cuba." *Cuban Studies* 9:2 (July 1979).

————. "Measuring Economic Growth and Income Distribution in Revolutionary Cuba." Lund, Sweden: Research Policy Institute, Discussion Paper Series 130, July 1979.

Brunner, Heinrich. *Cuban Sugar Policy From 1963–1970*. Pittsburgh: University of Pittsburgh Press, 1977.

Burck, Charles. "Tempest in the Sugar Pot," *Fortune* (February 1977).

Cajanus: The Caribbean Food and Nutrition Institute Quarterly 15 (1982):2.

Cannon, Terence. *Revolutionary Cuba*. New York: Thomas Y. Crowell, 1981.

Cardenal, Ernesto. *In Cuba*. New York: New Directions, 1974.

Castro, Fidel. *Current Problems of Underdeveloped Countries: Selection of Speeches*. Havana: Oficina de Publicaciones del Consejo de Estado, 1979.

————. *History Will Absolve Me*. Havana: Guairas Book Institute, 1967.

————. *Opening Address: 2nd Congress of the Association of Third World Economists*. Havana, 26 April 1981.

————. *Speeches At Three Congresses*. Havana: Editora Politica, 1982.

————. "World Economic and Social Crisis: Its Impact on the Underdeveloped Countries, Its Somber Prospects and the Needs to Struggle If We Are To Survive." Report to the Seventh Summit Conference of Non-Aligned Countries. Havana: Publishing Office of the Council of State, 1983.

Central Intelligence Agency. *The Cuban Economy: A Statistical Review.* National Foreign Assessment Center, March 1981.

CEPAL. *Estilo de desarrollo y políticas sociales.* Mexico City: Siglo XXI, 1980.

Chadwick, Lee. *Cuba Today.* Westport, Conn.: Lawrence Hill and Co., 1975.

Chonchol, Jacques. "El primer bienio de reforma agraria (1959–1961)." In *Reformas agrarias en América Latina.* Oscar Delgado, ed. Mexico City: Fondo de Cultura Económica, 1965.

————. "Memorandum sobre el Proceso de la Reforma Agraria en Cuba." *Cuadernos Latino-Americanos de Economía Humana* 3 (January–April 1960):7.

————. "La reforma agraria cubana: reaciones y perspectivas." *Trimestre Económico,* 1965.

Clark, Sydney. *All the Best in Cuba.* New York: Dodd, Mead and Co., 1956.

Conover, S., Donovan S., and Susser, E. "Reflections on Health Care in Cuba." *Lancet* 2 (1 November 1980).

Council of Ministers. *Cuban Family Code.* New York: Center for Cuban Studies, 8 March 1975.

Corteguera, Raúl Riverón, et. al. "Mortalidad preescolar (1–4 años) en Cuba, 1961–1975." *Boletín Médico del Hospital Infantil de Mexico,* 1978.

————. "Mortalidad infantil en Cuba 1962–1973." *Revista Cubana de Pediatría* 47 (1975):321–28.

————. "Enfermedades diarréicas agudas en Cuba." *Revista Cubana de Pediatría* 51 (1979):181–93.

Cuba, Republic of:
Comité Estatal de Estadísticas. *Anuario Estadístico de Cuba,* 1975, 1977, 1978, 1979, 1980, 1981, 1982.

————. *Cuba en Cifras,* 1979, 1982.

————. *Cuba, Desarrollo económico y social durante el período 1958–1980.*

————. *Guía Estadística,* 1979 and 1980.

————. *Informe de consumidores y movimientos de altos y bajos, 3rd semestre, 1980.*

————. *Principales características laborales de la población de Cuba— Encuesta demográfica nacional de 1979.*

————. *Unidades organizativas asociadas,* 22 January 1982.

Comité Estatal de Trabajo y Seguridad Social. *Resolución No. 476.*

————. *Reforma general de salários.*

Ministerio de Agricultura. *Memoria de censo agrícola nacional, 1946.*

————. *Censo agricola nacional, 1946.*

Ministerio de Educación de Cuba. "Matrícula del Curso 1956–57."

Ministerio de Salud Pública de Cuba. *Informe Anual 1978,* 1980, 1981 and 1982.

————. *Balance Anual 1981.*

————. *Programas Básicas de area de salud y su evaluación 1982.*

————. *Salud para todos.* 9 July 1983.

————. *Sistema nacional de vigilancia nutricional en el sector salud,* 1977–1980.

Departamento de Censos y Encuestas. *Investigación sobre el uso de la tierra en el sector privado.* Havana: Dirección Estadística de Población y Censos, May 1975.

Derpich, Juan Aguilar. "The Island that Discovered the Sea." *Ceres* July/August 1979.

Desnoes, Edmundo. *Inconsolable Memories.* New York: New American Library, 1967.

Díaz-Briquets, Sergio and Pérez, Lisandro. "Cuba: The Demography of a Revolution." *Population Bulletin* 36:1. Washington, D.C.: Population Reference Bureau, 1981.

DiPerna, Paula. *The Complete Travel Guide to Cuba.* New York: St. Martin's Press, 1979.

"Discurso del Ministro de la Industria Azucarera de Cuba en la Inauguración del XVIII Congreso de la ISSCT en la Habana." Havana, n.d.

Domínguez, Jorge. *Cuba: Order and Revolution.* Cambridge: Harvard University Press, 1978.

————. *Cuba: Internal and International Affairs.* Beverly Hlls: Sage Publications, 1982.

Dorschner, John and Fabricio, Roberto. *The Winds of December.* New York: Coward, McCann and Geoghegan, 1980.

Draper, Theodore. *Castroism in Theory and Practice.* New York: Praeger, 1965.

Dumont, René. *Cuba: Socialism and Development.* New York: Grove Press, 1970.

————. *Is Cuba Socialist?* New York: The Viking Press, 1974.

Durán, Marco Antonio. "La reforma agraria en Cuba." *Trimestre Económico,* July–September 1960.

Eckstein, Susan. "Capitalist Constraints on Cuban Socialist Developments." *Comparative Politics,* April 1980.

————. "Income Distribution and Consumption in Postrevolutionary Cuba: An Addendum to Brundenius." *Cuban Studies* 10 (January 1980):1.

Economía y Desarrollo. No. 12 July/August 1972; no. 12 May/June 1973; no. 67 March/April 1982; no. 68 May/June 1982; no. 63 July/August 1981; no. 69 July/August 1982. Bimonthly publication of the Economics Faculty, University of Havana.

Editora Política. *Lineamientos económicos y sociales para el quinquenio, 1981–1985.* Havana, 1981.

"Encuesta de los trabajadores rurales 1956–57." Documentos. Havana, Cuba. N.d.

Enders, Thomas O. "Radio Broadcasting to Cuba." Statement before the Senate Committee on Foreign Relations, 1 July 1982. ·

Fagen, Richard. *The Transformation of Political Culture in Cuba.* Stanford: Stanford University Press, 1969.

Fergusson, Erna. *Cuba.* New York: Alfred A. Knopf, 1946.

Flora, Jan L. "Agriculture: Leading Sector or Bottleneck in Cuban Development?"

Annual Meeting of the Rural Sociology Association, San Francisco, September 1982. [Also published in Spanish in *Estudios Rurales Laninoamericanos*, n.d. pp. 25–50.]

Food and Agriculture Organization (FAO). *FAO Yearbook*. Production Yearbook through 1980 ('81 Yearbook) and Trade Yearbook through 1979 ('80 Yearbook).

———. *Provisional Food Balance Sheets*, 1972–1974 averages and 1978–1980 averages.

———. *Food Balance Sheet* 1972–1974, 1975–1977.

Forster, Nancy. "Cuban Agricultural Productivity: A Comparison of State and Private Farm Sectors." *Cuban Studies* 11:2/12:1 July 1981–January 1982.

Forster, Nancy and Handelman, Howard. "Peasant Smallholders and State Farms: The Role of the Private Agricultural Sector in Cuba's Socialist Economy." San Francisco: September 1982, Annual Meeting Rural Sociology Association.

Fraginals, Manuel Moreno. *The Sugar Mill: The Socioeconomic Complex of Sugar in Cuba 1760–1860*. New York: Monthly Review Press, 1976.

Gerassi, John, ed. *Venceremos!: The Speeches and Writings of Che Guevara*. New York: Simon and Schuster, 1968.

Gilly, Adolfo. *Inside the Cuban Revolution*. New York: Monthly Review Press, 1964.

"General Wage Reform." *Granma* supplement, 6 April 1980.

Goldenberg, Boris. *The Cuban Revolution and Latin America*. New York: Praeger, 1965.

González, Edward. *Cuba Under Castro: The Limits of Charisma*. Boston: Houghton Mifflin Co., 1974.

Gómez, Enzo Dueñas and Corteguera, Raúl Riverón. "La neonatología en Cuba." *Boletín de la Oficina Santitaria Pan Americana* 86:5:406–19.

Gordon, Antonio. "The Nutriture of Cubans: Historical Perspective and Nutritional Analysis." *Cuban Studies* 13 (no. 2, Summer 1983):1–40.

———. "Nutritional Status of Cuban Refugees: A Field Study on the Health and Nutriture of Refugees Processed at Opa Locka, Florida." *The American Journal of Clinical Nutrition*. 35 (March 1982):582–90.

Green, Gil. *Cuba at 25: The Continuing Revolution*. New York: International Publishers, 1983.

Griffiths, John and Peter, eds. *Cuba: The Second Decade*. London: Writers and Readers Publishing Cooperative, 1979.

Guerra y Sánchez, Ramiro. *Sugar and Society in the Caribbean: An Economic History of Cuban Agriculture*. New Haven: Yale University Press, 1964.

Guevara, Ernesto Che. *El socialismo y el hombre en Cuba*. Mexico: Editorial Grijalbo, 1971.

Gutelman, Michel. *La agricultura socializada en Cuba*. Mexico City: Era, 1970.

———. "The Socialization of the Means of Production in Cuba." *Agrarian Problems and Peasant Movements in Latin America*. Rodolfo Stavenhagen, ed. New York: Anchor Books, 1970.

Hagelberg, Gerald B. *The Caribbean Sugar Industry*. New Haven: Yale University, 1974.

Halperin, Maurice. *The Taming of Fidel Castro*. Berkeley: University of California Press, 1981.

Handelman, Howard. "Cuban Food Policy and Popular Nutritional Levels." *Cuban Studies*, 11/12 (no. 2, July 1981–January 1982, no. 1).

Handelman, Howard and Handelman, Nancy. "Cuba Today: Impressions of the Revolution in its Twentieth Year." American Universities Field Staff Reports, No.8, 1979.

Harnecker, Marta. *Cuba: Dictatorship or Democracy?*. Westport, Conn.: Lawrence Hill and Co., 1980.

Health Care in Cuba. New York: The Venceremos Brigade, 1975.

Hernández, C. Santos and Cabale, E. Gómez. "Encuesta de egresados de hogares de recuperación nutricional," *Revista Cubana de Pediatría* 49 (July 1977):394–410.

Hinckle, Warren and Turner, William. *The Fish is Red: The Story of the Secret War Against Castro*. New York: Harper and Row, 1981.

Hoeffel, Paul and Levinson, Sandra. "The U.S. Blockade: A Documentary History." *Cuba in Focus*. New York: Center for Cuban Studies, December 1979.

Holt-Seeland, Inger. *Women of Cuba*. Westport, Conn.: Lawrence Hill and Co., 1982.

Horowitz, Irving Lewis, ed. *Cuban Communism*. Fourth edition. New Brunswick: Transaction Books, 1981

Huberman, Leo and Sweezy, Paul. *Cuba: Anatomy of a Revolution*. New York: Monthly Review Press, 1960.

———. *Socialism in Cuba*. New York: Monthly Review Press, 1969.

"Informe del primer ministro Fidel Castro sobre el abastecimiento y su regulación." *Obra Revolucionaria* no. 7, 1962.

Instituto Cubano de Geodesia y Cartografía. *Atlas de Cuba*. Havana: Consejo de Redacción del Atlas de Cuba, 1978.

Instituto Nacional de Reforma Económica. *Carta Pública Quincenal*. Havana, nos. 1–98, 1955–1959.

International Bank for Reconstruction and Development (World Bank). *Report on Cuba*. Baltimore: Johns Hopkins Press, 1951.

———. *Cuba: Economic Change and Educational Reform 1955–1974*. Washington, D.C.: Staff Working Paper, no. 317. Martin Carnoy, et. al. (authors).

"Investigaciones científicas de la demanda en Cuba." *Obra Revolucionaria*. Havana, 1979.

Jacobs, Richard. "People's Power: A Study of the State System in Cuba." *Transition* 2 (no. 2, 1979):75–100.

Joint Economic Committee, Congress of the United States. "Cuba Faces the Economic Realities of the 1980's." Washington, D.C.: Government Printing Office, 1982.

Jolliffe, Norman, et al. "Nutrition Status Survey of the Sixth Grade School Population of Cuba." *The Journal of Nutrition* 64 (1958):355–98.

Jordán, José R. *Desarrollo humano en Cuba*. Havana: Editorial Científico-Técnica, 1979.

Jordán, José R., et al. "Investigación nacional, crecimiento y desarrollo, Cuba 1972–1974. II. Técnica de las mediciones y controles de calidad." *Revista Cubana de Pediatría* 49 (1977):513–30.

Karol, J.S. *Guerrillas in Power: the Course of the Cuban Revolution*. New York: Hill and Wang, 1970.

Kenner, Martin and Petras, James, eds. *Fidel Castro Speaks.* New York: Grove Press, 1969.

Lappé, Frances Moore. *Diet for a Small Planet.* New York: Ballantine Books, 1982.

Lappé, Frances Moore and Collins, Joseph. *Food First: Beyond the Myth of Scarcity.* San Francisco: Institute for Food and Development Policy, 1982.

————. *World Hunger: Ten Myths.* San Francisco: Institute for Food and Development Policy, 1982.

Latin American Documentation. *Cuba* 9:17. Washington, D.C.: The LADOC Keyhole Series.

Le Grande, William M. "Cuban Dependency: A Comparison of Pre-Revolutionary and Post-Revolutionary International Economic Relations." *Cuban Studies* 9 (no. 2, July 1979):1–28.

Lewis, Oscar, Lewis, Ruth M. and Rigdon, Susan M. *Living the Revolution: Four Men.* Vol. 1. Urbana: University of Illinois Press, 1977.

————. *Living the Revolution: Four Women.* Vol. 2. Urbana: University of Illinois Press, 1977.

————. *Living the Revolution: Neighbors.* Vol. 3. Urbana: University of Illinois Press, 1978.

Lockwood, Lee. *Castro's Cuba, Cuba's Fidel.* New York: Vintage Books, 1969.

López Segrera, Francisco. *Cuba: capitalismo dependiente y subdesarrollo (1510–1959).* Havana: Editorial de Ciencias Sociales, 1981.

MacEwan, Arthur. *Revolution and Economic Development in Cuba.* New York: St. Martin's Press, 1981.

McGaffey, Wyatt and Barnett, Clifford. *Cuba: Its People, Its Society, Its Culture.* Westport, CT: Greenwood Publishing Co., 1962.

Mallin, Jay, ed. *"Che" Guevara on Revolution.* New York: Delta Publishing Co., 1969.

Martínez-Alier, J. "The Cuban Sugar Cane Planters, 1934–1960." *Oxford Agrarian Studies* 2 (1973):3–31.

Matthews, Hebert L. *Fidel Castro.* New York: Simon and Schuster, 1969.

May, Jacques Mayer. *Ecology of Malnutrition in the Caribbean.* New York: Hafner Press, 1973.

Maynard, Fredelle. "Cuba: The Revolutionary Life." *The Atlantic,* October 1979.

Mears, Leon G. "The Food Situtation in Cuba—Where Shortages Plague the Castro Government." *Foreign Agriculture,* May 1962.

Mesa-Lago, Carmelo. "Availability and Reliability of Statistics in Socialist Cuba." *Latin American Research Review* 4 (1969):1:53–91; 4:2:47–81.

————. *Cuba in the 1970s: Pragmatism and Institutionalization.* Albuquerque: University of New Mexico Press, 1974.

————. *The Economy of Socialist Cuba: A Two-Decade Appraisal.* Albuquerque: University of New Mexico Press, 1981.

Miller, Warren. *90 Miles from Home: the Face of Cuba Today.* Greenwich: Fawcett Publications, 1961.

Mills, C. Wright. *Listen Yankee: The Revolution in Cuba.* New York: Ballantine, 1960.

Mottin, Marie-France. *Cuba quand même: Vies quotidiennes dans la révolution.* Paris: Éditions du Seuil, 1980.

Navarro, Vicente. "Health, Health Services and Health Planning in Cuba." *Inter-

national Journal of Health Services 2 (no. 3, August 1972):397–432.

Nelson, Lowry. *Cuba: The Measure of a Revolution*. Minneapolis: University of Minnesota Press, 1972.

————. *Rural Cuba*. Minneapolis: University of Minnesota Press, 1950.

Núñez Jiménez, Antonio. *En marcha con Fidel*. Havana: Editorial Letras, 1982. [English edition forthcoming].

O'Connor, James. *The Origins of Socialism in Cuba*. Ithaca: Cornell University Press, 1970.

Ortíz, Fernando. *Cuban Counterpoint: Tobacco and Sugar*. New York: Vintage Books, 1970.

Oshima, Harry T. "A New Estimate of the National Income and Product of Cuba in 1953." *Food Research Institute Studies* (Stanford University) 2 (no. 3, November 1961).

Partido Comunista de Cuba (PCC). *Constitución de la república de Cuba*. Departamento de Orientación Revolucionaria, ed. Havana, 1976.

————. *Main Report to the First Congress of the Communist Party of Cuba*. Moscow: Progress Publishers, 1976.

————. *Los campesinos cubanos y la revolución*. Departamento de Orientación Revolucionaria, ed. Havana, 1973.

————. *Main Report to the Second Congress of the Communist Party of Cuba*. Havana: Political Publishers, 1981.

————. *Sobre la cuestión agraria y las relaciones con el compesinado: tésis y resolución*. Essay, Departmento de Orientación Revolucionaria del Comité Central de PCC, Havana, 1976.

Pearse, Andrew. *The Latin American Peasant*. London: Frank Cass, 1975.

Pérez, Humberto. "Lo que el pueblo debe saber." Interview by Marta Harnecker in *Bohemia*, 16 February 1979; "Responde Humberto Pérez," *Bohemia* 11 March 1983.

Pollitt, Brian H. "Agrarian Reform and the 'Agricultural Proletariat' in Cuba, 1958–1966: Further Notes and Some Second Thoughts." Institute of Latin American Studies, University of Glasgow, Occasional Papers, no. 30, 1980.

————. "Some Problems in Enumerating the 'Peasantry' in Pre-Revolutionary Cuba." *The Journal of Peasant Studies* 4 (no. 2, 1977):162–80.

Puffer, R.R. and Serrano, C.V. "Características de la mortalidad en la niñez." Publicación Científica 262. Organización Panamericana de la Salud, 1973.

"Primera reunión nacional de producción." *Obra Revolucionaria* 30 (August 1961).

Randall, Margaret. *Breaking the Silences: An Anthology of Twentieth Century Poetry by Cuban Women*. Vancouver, B.C.: Pulp Press Book Publishers, 1982.

————. *Cuban Women Now: Interviews With Cuban Women*. Toronto: The Women's Press, 1974.

————. *Women in Cuba: Twenty Years Later*. New York: Smyrna Press, 1981.

Reckord, Barry. *Does Fidel Castro Eat More Than Your Father?* London: Andre Deutsch, 1971.

Regalado, Anterno. *Las luchas campesinas en Cuba*. Havana: Editorial Orbe, 1979.

"La revolución agraria en Cuba y el desarrollo económico. *Economía y Desarrollo*, May/June 1979.

"The Right to Eat." *Cuba Review* 6 (no. 4, December 1976).

Ritter, Archibald. *The Economic Development of Revolutionary Cuba.* New York: Praeger Publishers, 1974.

Rizo, Julián. "The New System of Economic Management and Planning." N.p., 2 June, 1976.

———. "La zafra 1980–1981: nueva calidad en el proceso cañero azucarero." *Cuba Socialista.* No. 1 (Havana) 1981.

Robbins, Carla Anne. *The Cuban Threat.* New York: McGraw-Hill, 1983.

Roca, Sergio. "Cuba Confronts the 1980's." *Current History* 82:481 (February 1983):74–79.

———. "Cuban Economic Policy and Ideology: The Ten Million Ton Sugar Harvest." International Studies Series, 4:02–044. Beverly Hills: Sage Publications, 1976.

———. "Distibutional Effects of the Cuban Revolution." Presented at the 88th Annual Meeting of the American Economic Association, Dallas, Texas, December 1975.

———. "Methodological Approaches and Evaluation of Two Decades of Redistribution in Cuba." Paper presented at the Meetings of the Allied Social Science Associations, Association for Comparative Economic Studies Session, Atlanta, Georgia, December 1979.

Rodríguez, Carlos Rafael. *Cuba en el tránsito al socialismo: 1959–1963.* Mexico City: Siglo XXI, 1978.

———. "The Cuban Revolution and the Peasantry." Ministry of Foreign Affairs, Information Department, Cuba. Originally published in *Cuba Socialista,* n.d.

———. "La segunda reforma agraria cubana: causas y derivaciones." *Reformas agrarias en América Latina* Delgado, Oscar, ed. Mexico City: Fondo de Cultura Económico, n.d.

Santamaría, Haydée. *Moncada.* Secaucus, N.J.: Lyle Stuart Inc., 1980.

Seers, Dudley, et al. *Cuba: The Economic and Social Revolution.* Chapel Hill: University of North Carolina, 1964.

Sejourne, Laurette. *La mujer cubana en el quehacer de la historia.* Mexico City: Siglo XXI, 1980.

Silverman, Bertram, ed. *Man and Socialism in Cuba: The Great Debate.* New York: Atheneum, 1971.

"Sobre la reforma de precios minoristas, y las gratuidades indebidas." *Granma,* 14 December 1981.

Suárez, Andrés. *Cuba: Castroism and Communism, 1959–1966.* Cambridge, Mass.: M.I.T. Press, 1967.

Sugar World: A Newsletter on issues of concern to sugar workers 5:5 (Toronto, December 1982).

Smith, Robert F., ed. *Background to Revolution.* Huntington, New York: Robert E. Krieger Publishing Co., 1979.

Smith, Wayne. "Dateline Havana: Myopic Diplomacy." *Foreign Policy* 48 (Fall 1982):157–74.

Steele, Jonathan. "Cuban regime's popularity is not just a front," *The Guardian,* 14 August 1983.

Theriot, Lawrence H. *Cuba Faces the Economic Realities of the 80s.* East-West Trade Policy Staff Paper, U.S. Government Printing Office, March 1982.

Thomas, Hugh. *Cuba: The Pursuit of Freedom*. New York: Harper and Row, 1971.

"U.S. Blockade: A Documentary History." Center for Cuban Studies, December 1979.

United Nations Demographic Yearbook. June 1983.

Valdés, Nelson P. "Cuba: Social Rights and Basic Needs." Paper presented to the Inter-American Commission on Human Rights, Washington, D.C., 25 February 1983.

————. "The Cuban Revolution: Economic Organization and Bureaucracy." *Latin American Perspectives* 6:1 (no. 20, Winter 1979).

————. "Revolution and Institutionalization in Cuba." *Cuban Studies* 6 (1976): 1–37.

Villapoll, Nitza. *Cocina al minuto*. Havana: Orbe, 1981.

————. "Hábitos alimentarios africanos en América Latina." In *Africa en América Latina*. Manuel Moreno Fraginals, ed., pp. 325–36. Mexico City: Siglo XXI, 1977.

Villarejo, Donald. "American Investment in Cuba." *New University Thought*. 1 (1960):79–88.

Ward, Fred. *Inside Cuba Today*. New York: Crown Publishers, 1978.

Weinstein, Martin, ed. *Revolutionary Cuba in the World Arena*. Philadelphia: Institute for the Study of Human Issues, 1979.

Wessel, James. *Trading the Future*. San Francisco: Institute for Food and Development Policy, 1983.

Williams, William A. *Cuba, Castro, and the U.S.*. New York: Monthly Review Press, 1962.

Wolf, Eric R. and Hansen, Edward C. *The Human Condition in Latin America*. Oxford: Oxford University Press, 1972.

————. *Peasant Wars of the Twentieth Century*. New York: Harper and Row, 1969. January 1979.

Yglesias, Jose. *In the Fist of the Revolution: Life in a Cuban Country Town*. New York: Vintage Books, 1968.

Zeitlin, Maurice. *Revolutionary Politics and the Cuban Working Class*. Princeton: Princeton University, 1967.

OTHER MATERIALS:

Cuban Magazines and Newspapers

ANAP (Asociación Nacional de Agricultores Pequenos)

AREITO (New York)

Bohemia (Havana)

Cuba Internacional (Havana)

Cuba Times (New York)

Cuban Studies/Estudios Cubanos (University of Pittsburgh)

Cuba Update (Center for Cuban Studies, New York)

Granma Weekly Review (Havana)

Granma Spanish daily paper (Havana)

Latin American Newsletters

Latin American Perspectives (Riverside, CA)

INDEX

ABOUT THE AUTHORS

Medea Benjamin is coordinator of the Central America Program of the Institute for Food and Development Policy, an international public education campaign focusing on the role hunger plays in the struggles in Central America. Benjamin worked for ten years as an economist and nutritionist in Africa, Europe and Latin America for such agencies as the Food and Agriculture Organization of the United Nations, the Swedish International Development Agency, the National Nutrition Institute of Mexico. In addition, Benjamin lived and worked in Cuba from 1979 to 1982. She holds an M.A. in Economics from the New School for Social Research and an M.A. in Nutrition from Columbia University.

Dr. Joseph Collins is an author and cofounder of the Institute for Food and Development Policy, an internationally renowned not-for-profit public education and documentation center based in San Francisco. He is a leading spokesperson on world hunger and third world development issues. Collins is the author of *Food First: Beyond the Myth of Scarcity* (Ballantine), *What Difference Could a Revolution Make? Food and Farming in the New Nicaragua, World Hunger: Ten Myths, Aid as Obstacle: Twenty Questions about our Foreign Aid and the Hungry* and several other publications. His articles have appeared in numerous publications, including *The New York Times, Los Angeles Times, Christian Science Monitor, Le Monde Diplomatique, In These Times, Ceres,* and *Mother Jones.* His research and consultation have taken him throughout the world—to Africa, Asia, Latin America and Europe.

Dr. Michael Scott is Director of Overseas Programs for Oxfam America, a Boston-based development and relief organization working in 33 countries around the world. Scott has been instrumental in shaping the vision and direction of Oxfam America, stressing self-reliance and grassroots involvement as essential components of all projects. His work frequently takes him to many African, Asian and Latin American countries. Before joining Oxfam America in 1977, he worked as a consultant to the Mexican government and for the United Nations Food and Agriculture Organization. He has written several articles and spoken in many forums about hunger and development issues. He received his doctorate at the University of California at Santa Barbara.

GROVE PRESS BOOKS ON LATIN AMERICA

Barnes, John / EVITA—FIRST LADY: A Biography of Eva Peron / The first major biography of the beautiful and strong-willed leader of the impoverished Argentina of the 1940's. / $1.95 / 17087-3

Barry, Tom, Wood, Beth, and Preusch, Deb / DOLLARS AND DICTATORS: A Guide to Central America / "A thorough and comprehensive study of the effect the ubiquitous corporate presence in the region has had on its politics and on American foreign policy."—*The Progressive* / $6.95 / 62485-8

Borges, Jorge Luis / FICCIONES (ed. and intro. by Anthony Kerrigan) / A collection of short fictional pieces from the man whom *Time* has called "the greatest living writer in the Spanish language today." / $6.95 / 17244-2

Borges, Jorge Luis / A PERSONAL ANTHOLOGY (ed. and frwd. by Anthony Kerrigan) / Borges' personal selections of his work, including "The Circular Ruins," "Death and the Compass," and "A New Refutation of Time." / $6.95 / 17270-1

Fried, Jonathan, et al., eds. / GUATEMALA IN REBELLION: Unfinished History / A sourcebook on the history of Guatemala and its current crisis. / $8.95 / 62455-6

Gettleman, Marvin, et al., eds. / EL SALVADOR: Central America in the New Cold War / A collection of essays, articles, and eye-witness reports on the conflict in El Salvador. "Highly recommended for students, scholars, and policy-makers."—*Library Journal* / $9.95 / 17956-0

Neruda, Pablo / FIVE DECADES: POEMS, 1925-1970 (Bilingual ed. tr. by Ben Belitt) / A collection of more than 200 poems by the Nobel Prize-winning Chilean poet. / $12.50 / 17869-6

Neruda, Pablo / NEW POEMS (1968-1970) (Bilingual ed. tr. and intro. by Ben Belitt) / $8.95 / 17793-2

Neruda, Pablo / SELECTED POEMS (Bilingual ed. tr. by Ben Belitt) / A selection of Neruda's finest work. Intro. by Luis Monguio. / $5.95 / 17243-4

Paz, Octavio / THE LABYRINTH OF SOLITUDE, THE OTHER MEXICO, AND OTHER ESSAYS (New preface by the author. Tr. by Lysander Kemp, Yara Milos and Rachel Phillips Belach) / A collection of Paz's best-known works and six new essays, one especially written for this volume. / $9.95 / 17992-7

Paz, Octavio / THE OTHER MEXICO: Critique of the Pyramid (tr. by Lysander Kemp) / Paz defined the character and culture of Mexico in what has now become a modern classic of critical interpretation. / $2.45 / 17773-8

Rosset, Peter and Vandermeer, John / THE NICARAGUA READER: Documents of a Revolution Under Fire / A sourcebook of articles on the Nicaraguan revolution and U.S. intervention / $8.95 / 62498-X

Rulfo, Juan / PEDRO PARAMO: A Novel of Mexico (tr. by Lysander Kemp) By the Mexican author whom the *New York Times* says will "rank among the immortals." / $3.95 / 17446-1

Thelwell, Michael / THE HARDER THEY COME / The "masterly achieved novel" (Harold Bloom) by Jamaica's finest novelist. Inspired by the now-classic film by Perry Henzell, starring Jimmy Cliff, it tells the story of a legendary gunman and folk hero who lived in Kingston in the late 1950's. / $7.95 / 17599-9

Books may be ordered directly from Grove Press. Add $1.00 per book postage and handling and send check or money order to: Order Dept., Grove Press, Inc., 196 West Houston Street, New York, N.Y. 10014

Selected Grove Press Paperbacks

62480-7   ACKER, KATHY / Great Expectations: A Novel / $6.95
17458-5   ALLEN, DONALD & BUTTERICK, GEORGE F., eds. / The Postmoderns: The New American Poetry Revised / $9.95
17397-X   ANONYMOUS / My Secret Life / $4.95
62433-5   BARASH, D. and LIPTON, J. / Stop Nuclear War! A Handbook / $7.95
17087-3   BARNES, JOHN / Evita—First Lady: A Biography of Eva Peron / $4.95
17208-6   BECKETT, SAMUEL / Endgame / $3.50
17299-X   BECKETT, SAMUEL / Three Novels: Molloy, Malone Dies and The Unnamable / $6.95
17204-3   BECKETT, SAMUEL / Waiting for Godot / $3.50
62064-X   BECKETT, SAMUEL / Worstward Ho / $5.95
17244-2   BORGES, JORGE LUIS / Ficciones / $6.95
17112-8   BRECHT, BERTOLT / Galileo / $2.95
17106-3   BRECHT, BERTOLT / Mother Courage and Her Children / $2.45
17393-7   BRETON ANDRE / Nadja / $5.95
17439-9   BULGAKOV, MIKHAIL / The Master and Margarita / $4.95
17108-X   BURROUGHS, WILLIAM S. / Naked Lunch / $4.95
17749-5   BURROUGHS, WILLIAM S. / The Soft Machine, Nova Express, The Wild Boys: Three Novels / $5.95
62488-2   CLARK, AL, ed. / The Film Year Book 1984 / $12.95
17535-2   COWARD, NOEL / Three Plays (Private Lives, Hay Fever, Blithe Spirit) / $7.95
17219-1   CUMMINGS, E.E. / 100 Selected Poems / $2.95
17327-9   FANON, FRANZ / The Wretched of the Earth / $4.95
17483-6   FROMM, ERICH / The Forgotten Language / $6.95
17390-2   GENET, JEAN / The Maids and Deathwatch: Two Plays / $6.95
17838-6   GENET, JEAN / Querelle / $4.95
17662-6   GERVASI, TOM / Arsenal of Democracy II / $12.95
17956-0   GETTLEMAN, MARVIN, et.al. eds. / El Salvador: Central America in the New Cold War / $9.95
17648-0   GIRODIAS, MAURICE, ed. / The Olympia Reader / $5.95
62490-4   GUITAR PLAYER MAGAZINE / The Guitar Player Book (Revised and Updated Edition) $11.95
62003-8   HITLER, ADOLF / Hitler's Secret Book / $7.95
17125-X   HOCHHUTH, ROLF / The Deputy / $7.95
62115-8   HOLMES, BURTON / The Olympian Games in Athens, 1896 / $6.95

17209-4	IONESCO, EUGENE / Four Plays (The Bald Soprano, The Lesson, The Chairs, and Jack or The Submission) / $6.95
17226-4	IONESCO, EUGENE / Rhinocerous / $5.95
62123-9	JOHNSON, CHARLES / Oxherding Tale / $6.95
17254-X	KEENE, DONALD, ed. / Modern Japanese Literature / $12.50
17952-8	KEROUAC, JACK / The Subterraneans / $3.50
62424-6	LAWRENCE, D.H. / Lady Chatterley's Lover / $3.95
17016-4	MAMET, DAVID / American Buffalo / $4.95
17760-6	MILLER, HENRY / Tropic of Cancer / $4.95
17295-7	MILLER, HENRY / Tropic of Capricorn / $3.95
17869-6	NERUDA, PABLO / Five Decades: Poems 1925-1970. Bilingual ed. / $12.50
17092-X	ODETS, CLIFFORD / Six Plays (Waiting for Lefty, Awake and Sing, Golden Boy, Rocket to the Moon, Till the Day I Die, Paradise Lost) / $7.95
17650-2	OE, KENZABURO / A Personal Matter / $6.95
17232-9	PINTER, HAROLD / The Birthday Party & The Room / $6.95
17251-5	PINTER, HAROLD / The Homecoming / $5.95
17539-5	POMERANCE, BERNARD / The Elephant Man / $4.25
17827-0	RAHULA, WALPOLA / What the Buddha Taught / $6.95
17658-8	REAGE, PAULINE / The Story of O, Part II; Return to the Chateau / $3.95
62169-7	RECHY, JOHN / City of Night / $4.50
62001-1	ROSSET, BARNEY and JORDAN, FRED, eds. / Evergreen Review No. 98 / $5.95
62498-X	ROSSET, PETER and VANDERMEER, JOHN / The Nicaragua Reader / $8.95
17119-5	SADE, MARQUIS DE / The 120 Days of Sodom and Other Writings / $12.50
62009-7	SEGALL, J. PETER / Deduct This Book: How Not to Pay Taxes While Ronald Reagan is President / $6.95
17467-4	SELBY, HUBERT / Last Exit to Brooklyn / $2.95
17948-X	SHAWN, WALLACE, and GREGORY, ANDRE / My Dinner with Andre / $5.95
17797-5	SNOW, EDGAR / Red Star Over China / $9.95
17260-4	STOPPARD, TOM / Rosencrantz and Guildenstern Are Dead / $3.95
17474-7	SUZUKI, D.T. / Introduction to Zen Buddhism / $3.95
17599-9	THELWELL, MICHAEL / The Harder They Come: A Novel about Jamaica / $7.95
17969-2	TOOLE, JOHN KENNEDY / A Confederacy of Dunces / $4.50
17418-6	WATTS, ALAN W. / The Spirit of Zen / $3.95

GROVE PRESS, INC., 196 West Houston St., New York, N.Y. 10014